DEVOLUTION IN PRACTICE
PUBLIC POLICY DIFFERENCES WITHIN THE UK

edited by

John Adams and Peter Robinson

E·S·R·C
ECONOMIC
& SOCIAL
RESEARCH
COUNCIL

30-32 Southampton Street, London WC2E 7RA
Tel: 020 7470 6100 Fax: 020 7470 6111
info@ippr.org.uk
www.ippr.org
Registered charity 800065

The Institute for Public Policy Research (ippr), established in 1988, is Britain's leading independent think tank on the centre left. The values that drive our work include delivering social justice, deepening democracy, increasing environmental sustainability and enhancing human rights. Through our well-researched and clearly argued policy analysis, our publications, our media events, our strong networks in government, academia and the corporate and voluntary sector, we play a vital role in maintaining the momentum of progressive thought.

ippr's aim is to bridge the political divide between the social democratic liberal and liberal traditions, the intellectual divide between the academics and the policy makers and the cultural divide between the policy-making establishment and the citizen. As an independent institute, we have the freedom to determine our research agenda. ippr has charitable status and is funded by a mixture of corporate, charitable, trade union and individual donations.

Research is ongoing, and new projects are being developed, in a wide range of policy areas including sustainability, health and social care, social policy, citizenship and governance, education, economics, democracy and community, media and digital society and public private partnerships. We will shortly embark on major new projects in the fields of social justice, overseas development and democratic renewal. In 2003 we will be moving to new premises where we aim to grow into a permanent centre for contemporary progressive thought, recognised both at home and globally.

For further information you can contact ippr's external affairs department on info@ippr.org.uk, you can view our website at www.ippr.org and you can buy our books from central books on 0845 458 9911 or email ippr@centralbooks.com.

Production & design by **emphasis-publishing.co.uk**
ISBN 1 86030 199 1
© IPPR 2002

Contents

Preface

This publication is the result of a joint project undertaken by ippr and the ESRC Devolution and Constitutional Change Programme between August 2001 and July 2002. It is the first project ippr have run jointly with an ESRC Programme.

Devolution and Constitutional Change is one of the Research Programmes funded by the UK's Economic and Social Research Council. It is a major £4.7 million investment in social science research set up by the ESRC in 2000 to explore the impact of the devolution dynamic and to feed the research into policy debates.

More information on the activities of the ESRC Devolution Programme is available from:

Professor Charles Jeffery
Programme Director
ESRC Devolution Programme
University of Birmingham
Birmingham B15 2TT
Tel: +44 (0) 121 414 2991
Fax: +44 (0) 121 414 2992
Email: devolution@bham.ac.uk
Web: www.devolution.ac.uk

Acknowledgements

The editors would like to thank all those who have contributed to the ideas contained in this book, through seminars and informal discussions. In particular we would like to thank all the authors.

We would also like to thank Prof John Tomaney (University of Newcastle upon Tyne), Robin Wilson (Democratic Dialogue), Jim McCormick (Scottish Council Foundation), Jane Thomas (Campaign for Yorkshire) and Brionie Huish (British Council).

We would further thank the following staff and volunteers at ippr for their contribution to this publication: Paul Greenhill, Lisa Harker, James McGowan, Joy Millward, Helena Scott, Will Somerville, Sarah Spencer, Beatrice Stern, Matthew Taylor and Philip Taylor. Many officials in Whitehall and devolved institutions provided significant help, but prefer to remain anonymous. Our apologies go to those we have failed to mention. It must be pointed out that while we have benefited from much advice and assistance from many quarters, responsibility for the final version rests with the editors alone.

IPPR and the ESRC Devolution Programme gratefully acknowledge financial support for this research project from Yorkshire Forward, the English Regions Network, UNISON and the Scottish Executive. Without their willingness to invest in and contribute to the original and independent research this project could not have been undertaken. The findings of our research, however, do not necessarily represent the views of our funding partners.

About the authors

John Adams is a Senior Research Fellow at IPPR. He helped draw up the Labour Party's proposals for devolution prior to 1997, and was a Special Advisor at the Welsh Office from 1997-1998. He has worked for the Campaign for the English Regions, where he is currently a Board member.

Paul Benneworth is a Research Associate at the Centre for Urban and Regional Development Studies (CURDS), at the University of Newcastle.

James Cornford was the founder Director of IPPR. He is a former Special Advisor at the Cabinet Office, and is currently Chair of both the School for Social Entrepreneurs and the Campaign for Freedom of Information.

Andrew Gillespie is the Executive Director of CURDS and Professor of Communications Geography at the University of Newcastle. He is also the Chair of the Regional Policy Forum.

Ian Gordon is Professor of Human Geography at the London School of Economics. He is also Director of LSE London.

David Heald is Professor of Accountancy at the University of Aberdeen, and Director of its Centre for Regional Public Finance. He has also served as a specialist advisor to the House of Commons Treasury Select Committee.

Charles Jeffery is Director of the ESRC Research Programme on Devolution and Constitutional Change and Deputy Director of the Institute for German Studies at the University of Birmingham.

Michael Keating is Professor of Regional Studies at the European University Institute and Professor of Scottish Politics at the University of Aberdeen. He previously taught at the universities of Strathclyde and Western Ontario.

Phillip Lowe is the Duke of Northumberland Professor of Rural Economy at the University of Newcastle, and Director of its Centre for Rural Economy.

Alasdair McLeod is a Research Assistant at the Centre for Regional Public Finance at the University of Aberdeen. He formerly worked in the Scottish Executive Finance Group.

Kevin Morgan is Professor of European Regional Development, at the Department of City and Regional Planning at Cardiff University. In 1997 he was Chair of the cross-party referendum campaign *Yes for Wales*.

Gareth Rees is Professor of Education and Deputy Director of the Cardiff University School of Social Sciences.

David Reynolds is Professor of Education at the University of Exeter. He is also an Advisor to the Standards and Effectiveness Unit/City Academies Support Service in the Department for Education and Skills.

Peter Robinson is Senior Economist at IPPR and editor of *New Economy*. He has been involved in work on employment, education, pensions and long-term care. He was a co-author of *Building Better Partnerships*, from the Commission on Public Private Partnerships and of *A New Contract for Retirement*. He is also a Research Associate at the Centre for Economic Performance, and teaches at the London School of Economics.

Michael Sullivan is Director of the National Centre for Public Policy and Professor of Social Policy at the University of Wales, Swansea.

Neil Ward is Professor of Human Geography at Leeds University. He was a member of the Government's Rural Task Force and the Prime Minister's Performance and Innovation Unit Rural Economies Team.

Kevin Woods is William R Lindsay Professor of Health Policy and Economic Evaluation in the University of Glasgow. He has been Director of Strategy and Performance Management in the Scottish Executive Department of Health and has held a number of management positions in the NHS in England.

Foreword

The constitutional debates on devolution took place in the shadow of two dominant political realities: the disproportionate weight of England in the United Kingdom and the disproportionate effects of the electoral system. Scotland, Wales and parts of England were ruled by governments for which the majority of their electors had not voted, but there was not (and still is not) a majority either for the break up of the UK or for electoral reform. The point of leverage has been the changing balance of Scottish opinion from union to nation. Devolution or lopsided quasi-federalism has come into being on the basis of Scottish sentiment and its critical importance to the fortunes of the Labour Party.

Behind it lay the largely unexamined assumption that devolved governments would follow policies more in tune with the views of their electorates, be more responsive to 'local' needs and aspirations and be more effective at implementing those policies, than were congested Westminster and distant Whitehall. Allied uneasily to national sentiment was an intellectual argument about overloaded government at the centre. Against this alliance were ranged the ancien regime itself, the interest of the UK governing classes, political and official, in preserving their powers, and, possibly more important in the long run, the belief, both widespread and deep seated, in Equity: that every citizen from Land's End to John O'Groats should enjoy the same entitlements and levels of public service as every other. The fact that this was far from being the case under our centralised majoritarian system was a reproach and cause for complaint, not a matter of choice or congratulation. As Mr Callaghan once put it, everybody should be brought up to the average.

The new constitutional settlement, flawed, incomplete and unstable though it is, provides the opportunity for legitimate difference. In its youth ippr played some part in the debate on the nuts and bolts of constitutional reform. I welcome the fact that it has now turned its attention to the practical consequences of devolution: what difference is devolution making in those areas of public policy where the devolved administrations share powers and influence. I welcome also ippr's skill in persuading academic specialists to share the early fruits of their researches, and salute the ESRC for finding the resources to support their work.

It is early days yet. The contributors remind us of the inertia in the system, of the difficulty of making rapid changes to the practices of long established agencies or to inherited patterns of public expenditure. The room for manoeuvre may be small, but the changes cumulative. And these include changes in institutional arrangements, practices and procedures as well as in policy as such. As Michael Keating rightly reminds us, the base line is not uniformity, either of outcome or process. He sets out lucidly in his introduction both the likely reasons for increasing variation in policy and practice and the powerful constraints which commitment to common security, a common market and a common welfare state place upon it. If there is cause for concern, it is with the failure of central government to appreciate or adapt to the scale of the change it has initiated. Concurrent parliamentary majorities have greatly eased the early stages of devolution. They won't last forever. The most prominent decisions for difference (university fees and care of the elderly in Scotland) have depended on resources derived from a perverse and inequitable fiscal formula. In a time of general prosperity and rising public expenditure, nobody wants to rock the boat. But they will. The argument for Equity will switch from outcomes to resources. As far as one can tell, central government is ill prepared to handle the fall out, let alone anticipate it.

Many years ago I set the following question in a first year Politics examination at Edinburgh University: 'England is the worst governed part of the United Kingdom'. No candidate answered it. It was then perhaps an impossible question. This book should make it less so.

James Cornford
Founder Director of ippr and Chair of the School for Social Entrepreneurs

Executive summary

The establishment of devolved governments in Scotland, Wales, Northern Ireland and London has arguably been this Government's most radical reform. However, devolution is not just a constitutional reform. It has profound implications for public services and there has been, as yet, comparatively little attention paid to the consequences of differentiated policy making.

This book is the result of a research project jointly co-ordinated by ippr and the ESRC Devolution Programme. It examines how public policy is evolving across the United Kingdom by focussing on a range of areas such as health and long-term care, education, industrial and regional policy. It takes each of these areas in turn and examines how policy is diverging, what pressures have led to this divergence, when does divergence become problematic and how can 'good practice' be spread across the UK.

It also examines broader questions. Do variations in policy between different parts of the UK matter? How are relations evolving between governments in different parts of the UK? Do the perceived inequities in public spending, highlighted by devolution, create pressure for a new fiscal settlement? Has the policy variation of the devolved institutions created a dynamic for further devolution in England, and if so what should a new devolution settlement look like?

Devolution and public policy in the United Kingdom: divergence or convergence?

In the first chapter Michael Keating sets the scene for the rest of the publication, and discusses the general principles surrounding policy divergence. He examines the implications of the formal structures for devolution, and notes that modern government does not operate on the basis of watertight divisions of functions.

A serious constraint on policy divergence in practice may be the limited policy capacity of the devolved administrations. Interest groups might be a force for divergence (and Scotland has more of these than Wales) but even under the 'new form of politics' these interest groups must now confront each other in a open political system, vying for attention and competing for limited resources. Many have found the transition from lobbyist to participant in a policy process difficult.

Keating notes that the UK is a common security area, a common market and a single welfare state: each of these impose constraints upon divergence in practice. There is genuine concern to maintain co-operation in criminal law matters, and concern to maintain a common market may lead to some limitations on the devolved bodies. However, perhaps most important is the single welfare state, in which we have shared assumptions of the post-war welfare settlement (that is, broadly equivalent services free at the point of use). 'Social citizenship' in the UK has been linked to a British identity, and many credit the welfare state in forging a sense of British, if not UK, identity.

The devolution settlement is at an early stage, and since the administrations, in Britain at least, are broadly in line politically there have been no causes for major policy divergence. We can nevertheless frame some typologies of policy divergence.

- *Non-comparable* policies exist when an issue exists in only one territory, the Welsh language for example.

- *Policy autonomy* exists where policy can be made according to local needs and preferences, for example education, social services or the structure of local government.

- *Concurrent policies* exist when similar policies are somewhat independently pursued, this may apply to health, where demands are similar and interest groups operate on a UK basis.

- *Policy uniformity* occurs when practical considerations or external pressures make for a single line, the International Criminal Court for example.

- Finally, *policy competition* is a form of policy autonomy but which is worth highlighting separately. In this case, policy is made to demonstrate innovation and imagination, encouraging experimentation and learning from best practice.

Health policy and the NHS in the UK: 1997-2002

This chapter, written by Kevin Woods, notes that devolution means that health policy, and the funding and organisation of healthcare services, could develop differently in the four countries of the UK. Very few health-related matters remain within the competence of the UK government.

As Woods notes, the biggest health related differences between the countries of the UK are the health status of their populations and the level of funding for the NHS. Age adjusted mortality rates per 1000 people in 1997 vary between 10.3 for women in England and 12.1 in Scotland. Per capita health and personal social services spending in 1999/2000 was highest in Scotland at £1271 compared with a UK average of £1072, and England of £1041. There are more available hospital beds in Scotland, Wales and Northern Ireland than in England; there are also more GPs per capita, and their level of prescribing is higher. The exception to this pattern is the private health care sector, which is much smaller outside England.

Despite devolution the historic pressure on the UK Exchequer to find additional resources for health means that it will remain difficult for any UK administration to avoid an interest in health and the NHS throughout the UK. Indeed the Chancellor's review of the long-term funding needs of the NHS (the Wanless report) was a UK review. Health policies and the modernisation of the NHS have been the subject of more Joint Ministerial Committee meetings than any other domestic policy subject.

The prominence of health and NHS policy amongst the responsibilities of the devolved administrations means that making a success of them could be an important determinant of public views on the overall achievements of devolution, and making a success of health policy is commonly understood to require distinctive policies suited to the circumstances of each country.

No other health issue has demonstrated the power and consequences of political devolution than the issue of free personal care for the elderly, one of the recommendations of the Royal Commission on Long Term Care. Once the decision was made by the Scottish Executive to back free personal care, the money had to be found from within the Scottish block. Whatever the rights or wrongs of this policy, it was what the Scottish Parliament wanted. In bowing to Parliamentary pressure the Scottish Executive brought the meaning of political devolution to life for the wider public, not only in Scotland but throughout the UK.

Woods concludes that, in general, after three years of devolved government it appears that the forces of continuity – inherited policy, party political allegiance, the Barnett formula, a UK identity for the NHS and a rapidly expanding health budget – remain dominant for all that some differences have emerged. Nevertheless, it is still early days post-devolution and increasingly new politicians and new political institutions are making their mark on health and health care. As the devolution process evolves, it seems increasingly necessary to speak of the UK's national health services rather than of its NHS.

Industrial and regional policy in a devolved United Kingdom

This chapter, written by Andrew Gillespie and Paul Benneworth, starts by reminding us of the difficulties in distinguishing between industrial and regional policy. Industrial policy need not be blind to regional differences, and even spatially blind policies such as technology or sectoral policies will often have differential regional impacts. However, these are effectively unintended consequences as they are *national* industrial policies. However, the same type of policies can be framed with regional differentiation, and if they are framed specifically to reduce the degree of regional variation in industrial performance they become synonymous with regional policies.

The advent of devolution in 1999 was clearly likely to lead to divergence in industrial policies, as Scotland and Wales would pursue policies which were likely to reflect their different needs. Furthermore, UK industrial policies were likely to become more territorially sensitive, leading to an increasingly spatially differentiated set of industrial policies emerging. Effectively, therefore the distinctions between industrial and regional policies will further blur.

The Scottish Development Agency (from 1989 Scottish Enterprise) and the Welsh Development Agency (WDA) have been strong advocates for their countries, and even pre-devolution were able to gain sanction to deviate from the official prescriptions of the centre. In contrast neither England nor the English regions had at this time a development agency, nor state bodies that could effectively 'campaign' for more regionally sensitive policies. This permitted Scotland and Wales to compete more aggressively with the English regions to attract inward investment. Gillespie and Benneworth also note that Scottish Enterprise quite early began to address issues of endogenous capacity, helped by the fact it had more powers than the WDA.

Post-devolution we might have expected more spatially sensitive policies in the UK's industrial policy, but evidence would suggest that the DTI has continued to be spatially insensitive and apply industrial policy activities to all parts of England equally. Despite rhetoric of 'widening the winner's circle' the current supply side approach reinforces the existing contours of the English knowledge economy.

One of the first outcomes from devolution has been the shift in the devolved territories to use policy tools to promote the interests of the territory rather than addressing local market failures to improve UK competitiveness. There are signs that there might be some convergence towards this position in the English regions. This new convergence is a shift of the centre of gravity of industrial policy towards greater regional sensitivity. Gillespie and Benneworth end by concluding that it is ironic that perhaps the greatest responsibility for the maturing of industrial policy in the English regions can be lain at the door of the devolved institutions of Scotland and Wales.

Developing differently: educational policy in England, Wales, Scotland and Northern Ireland

This chapter, written by David Reynolds, suggests that perhaps Labour's educational policies were developed to reflect the perceived needs of the English educational system, which have less salience in the other three countries of the UK. The three countries were also historically higher spenders on education per pupil than England, and Scotland and Wales exhibited customarily higher levels of achievement at the 'top end' of the ability range.

Reynolds argues that the exercise of the 'market-based' solution to the historical British problem of poorer educational standards is not necessarily appropriate for the non-English countries. First, a much higher proportion of the population lives in rural areas or small towns in which there is effectively no choice of school. Secondly, the absence of published performance data in Scotland and Wales on the achievements of primary schools made 'consumer information' less persuasive. Wales indeed has ceased to publish national performance tables for secondary schools.

Thirdly, the three devolved territories have also seen an absence of the harsh rhetoric that has characterised England, where the period of office of Chris Woodhead was marked by attacks on the quality of education being offered. And the final distinctive feature of education in the three nations has been much less central prescription of methods, which has been a central plank of the 'standards agenda' in England. Local education authorities also retain a more central role than that envisaged in England, where 90 per cent of funding is to be devolved to schools by 2004.

Reynolds concludes that while there has been advantage in not adhering to English policies in terms of deciding what *not* to do there must be further work on and understanding of what *to* do, in terms of distinctive policies. A challenge made more difficult by concerns over the educational research communities' capacity in both Wales and Scotland. In conclusion, it seems as if the three nations are moving towards a new 'producer-driven' set of arrangements to replace the 'consumer-driven' policies that predominate in England.

Devolution and the restructuring of post-16 education and training in the UK

This chapter, written by Gareth Rees, notes that the difficulties of analysing the impact of devolution on the post-16 education and training sector are exacerbated by the heterogeneous nature of post-16 provision. Furthermore, the different elements of the post-16 sector have radically divergent relationships with the devolved institutions. For example, higher education occupies an ambiguous position in relation to the devolved institutions, not least because of its continued dependence on UK-wide systems of resource allocation such as the Research Assessment Exercise (RAE).

The well-known inequalities in power between the devolution settlements in Scotland, Wales and Northern Ireland have already resulted in quite significant contrasts between policies. Most notably perhaps, the restructuring of arrangements for student fees in Scotland have been significantly different from what has happened in Wales where the National Assembly simply does not have the power to abolish tuition fees.

One of the major policy initiatives in Wales in education has been the restructuring of the organisational framework for the Learning and Skills Sector through the establishment of the National Council-ELWa. The Education and Training Action Group, whose Plan presaged much of the reorganisation, was established before the creation of the National Assembly in the immediate aftermath of the 1997 General Election. Rees notes that the Plan changed as it was debated in the National Assembly: in particular, the role of business interests was significantly constrained at the expense of local education authorities and other educational groupings. In part this reflects fundamental features of civil society in Wales where the role of the public sector (and especially local authorities) has historically been extremely powerful.

There are important pressures which continue to exert an influence in the direction of convergence of policy outcomes (it has been claimed, for example, that the Welsh proposals for the Learning and Skills Sector provided the blueprint for the development of the Learning and Skills Councils in England). Policy divergence is also restricted by the continuing influence of a 'British system', including employment and social security policy and most crucially spending. Furthermore, the Sector Skills Councils are currently being established as UK-wide organisations.

Whatever changes in the policy-making process and the policies which emanate from it, there is currently little evidence to suggest that there are significant changes in the ways that post-16 education and training actually operate on the ground. Still less can it be argued that the advent of democratic devolution has brought about differential progress towards wider policy aims, such as greater social inclusion or more rapid economic growth. This is partly explicable by the modest nature of policy divergence so far, but Rees concludes with a salutary reminder that the impacts of policies on educational outcomes are generally rather modest.

Devolution and the governance of rural affairs in the UK

This chapter, written by Neil Ward and Phillip Lowe, starts by noting that the UK is a relatively urbanised country in European terms, but one with wide disparities in population density. The north and west of the UK contains peripheral rural areas still facing economic stagnation and low incomes. However, around most cities and much of southern and central England we see accessible rural areas experiencing population and employment growth with development pressures.

Recent years have seen a rising sense of crisis surrounding rural affairs across the UK, and rural areas have been subject to a profound set of restructuring processes. Two key new policy challenges have emerged: first the re-territorialisation of food production, and secondly the redefinition of the role of the rural in the regional, which concerns the distinctive value of rural places in an urbanised society.

Pre-devolution structures of governance allowed some leeway for different emphases, reflecting the distinct rural and regional geographies at work. The results of devolution to date have been a heightened public and political profile for rural affairs in the devolved territories. While the opportunity has been taken to re-label departments (for example, the 'Environment and Rural Affairs Department' in Scotland), the bulk of spending and activity goes on agriculture (although the scope for divergence lies more in other areas of rural policy). We also see the beginnings of a consciousness about the role of agriculture and the rural environment in regional development in England.

However, there is no real acceleration in policy divergence as common European frameworks have acted as a brake on divergent trends in important areas such as agriculture, and have raised particular problems in devolving crucial spending and resourcing decisions. The financing of CAP reform illustrates the difference that devolution has made to the governance of rural affairs. While MAFF (as then was) decided to apply modulation to 'green' the CAP and switch farm spending from production aids to support for the broader rural economy, there was much less enthusiasm in Scotland, Wales and Northern Ireland. It was only sold to the Scots and the Welsh by the Treasury conceding that it would provide the match-funding element rather than it coming from the devolved budgets. Ward and Lowe warn that ratcheting up modulation could prove a real test for devolution, and for the management of a single co-ordinated line on CAP reform.

Ward and Lowe also conclude that the handling of the outbreak of the Foot and Mouth Disease illustrates the comparative efficiency of the devolved administrations and illustrates the scope for competition between devolved structures. Scotland, as a smaller country with a smaller administrative establishment, could work more effectively and co-operatively across departments and with partners.

Beyond Barnett? Financing devolution

As David Heald and Alisdair McLeod note, although there are now devolved administrations outside England, the United Kingdom is still essentially a unitary state. Moreover, in comparison with other unitary states, there is highly centralised and unified control over public expenditure and taxation, exercised directly by, or on behalf of, the Treasury.

The Barnett system is best viewed as first a political accommodation and secondly as a means of containing political conflict. Much of the political attention currently paid to the Barnett formula hinges on the contradictory assertions that it is extravagantly generous to the devolved administrations, or that it is imposing destructive financial pressures upon them.

Applied systematically, the Barnett formula would result, over time, in equal expenditure per capita on devolved services in aggregate across the UK. A formula such as Barnett, which distributes equal per capita increments to each country, automatically delivers smaller percentage spending increases to those territories with the highest starting values of the index. The inter-country comparisons show England on an index of 96, Scotland on 118, Wales on 113 and Northern Ireland on 133 (on the base UK=100).

Heald and McLeod argue that the devolved administrations have to resist pressures to replicate the changes in English comparable programmes. Suggestions that, for example, health in Scotland should therefore take its share of the formula consequences have to be firmly resisted. Quite apart from denying policy choice, the base positions of the programmes are different.

Should evidence of convergence appear, a needs assessment would be much more likely. If a needs assessment had been completed for all four countries, we would still have to address the issue of how to manage changes, upwards or downward, from the actual expenditure indexes to the needs indexes. Consequently, Heald and McLeod argue, something looking rather like the Barnett formula, operating on increments, would be quite likely to follow a needs assessment. Machinery, such as a Territorial Exchequer Board, to undertake the data collection and statistical analysis will be required if there is to be a needs assessment, the technical and political difficulties of which should not be underestimated.

The 'official' Treasury has long been suspicious that the territories are over-generously funded, and also too far out of reach. However, the 'ministerial' Treasury has been hesitant about opening up territorial political issues, especially as the achievable public expenditure savings are likely to be limited. Paradoxically, this makes the Treasury an unlikely ally of the devolved administrations in attempting to build on the Barnett system, rather than attempt anything radical. Above all, the Treasury would resist attempts to breach its highly centralised control of revenue. The approach of the 2003 elections will bring more attention, particularly in Scotland, to the issue of 'fiscal autonomy'. Whatever the precise powers of the devolved administrations we must remember their vulnerable position on revenue raising when control over the definition of tax bases and bands remains with the Treasury.

Uniformity and diversity in policy provision: insights from the US, Germany and Canada

As Charles Jeffery argues, a theoretically powerful agreement in favour of territorial variation is that of regions as 'laboratories of democracy'. A traditional argument in the US, those suspicious of federal government tend to support the laboratory idea as one unleashing the creativity necessary to compete in a rapidly changing economic environment; others concerned more strongly with social equity favour minimum levels of federally determined standards, fearing that 'laboratory' federalism in practice equates to a 'race to the bottom' with states competitively cutting back policy standards to maintain competitive advantages.

The argument for regional 'laboratories of democracy' has not been widely mobilised in European contexts, in part because of the whiff of 'race to the bottom' that adheres to them and because there has been a stronger notion of social equity in European states. But arguments for a more uniform policy provision now seem to be weakening, and strikingly no member state in the EU became more centralised since 1980, while half have decentralised authority to a regional tier of government.

Jeffery draws a distinction between economic and social policy laboratories. The revival of 'laboratories of democracy' in the US has had a primarily economic rationale, with a normative shift in the uniformity-diversity balance and an earlier confidence in the capacity of federal government eroded. The reunification of Germany, and the economic disparities between east and west, has also led to a renewed debate about the right balance to strike, and some *Länder* (led by Bavaria) feel that the status quo restricts their capacity to maintain their competitiveness in a global market and are propagating an alternative normative vision of 'competitive' rather than co-operative federalism. Canada is different. Historically one of the more decentralised federations political debate is highly territorialised. There is a different kind of collective normative judgement at play here: it is an expression of pan-Canadianism, which overarches a vast and diverse society.

More than economic policy, differentiation in social policy would seem to strike at the heart of the idea of 'social citizenship'. This is where the fear of a 'race to the bottom' comes in: some of the decentralist reforms in the US over the last two decades have widened the discretion states may apply in social policy questions.

In welfare, only in the US is there an acceptance that state-to-state differences in policy standards are appropriate. In Germany common nation-wide standards have been maintained despite calls to loosen the federal policy framework. And in Canada considerable efforts have been made to renew the idea of a pan-Canadian social union in the recast form of a more collaborative federalism, less subject to the power of the federal purse.

Jeffery argues that a higher level of commitment to norms of social citizenship is reflected in healthcare. In Germany and Canada the delivery of healthcare is clearly constrained by a normative consensus on the need to maintain a 'solidarity community' (Germany) or 'social union' (Canada). In the US, healthcare is subject to a significant level of regional variation, but there is also an underlying federal regulation providing for a minimum level of uniformity of provision across the US (Medicare and Medicaid).

What happens in the US, Germany and Canada suggests that senses of what is appropriate and what is not may vary over time. Within the UK a meaningful debate about 'items in common' and 'items to vary' has barely started, so it is doubtful that the norms underlying the current balance of uniformity and diversity in post-devolution UK are widely understood. Jeffery concludes that this is largely because the UK government has not done so.

Divergence and the centre

In this chapter John Adams and Peter Robinson note that in the debate surrounding divergence within post-devolution UK, different forms of divergence seem to treated similarly, and they try to separate out the different forms of divergence. The five forms suggested are: whether different values exist in the different nations; how the structures of the administrations are changing; how the process of decision-making is changing;

what new differences in policy are emerging; and if devolution is leading to different outcomes in key areas of public policy.

Adams and Robinson then address the role of the centre in a post-devolution era. At a time when the Treasury has been providing a sustained period of increased funding for public services, it is crucial that Whitehall and the devolved administrations work together to try and meet the expectations of the UK public for service improvements. If citizens feel that those services fail to deliver, there could be a major political backlash that might damage both the devolution process and the case for public services.

The centre also has a role in achieving social and economic justice between the various nations and regions of the UK. Clearly this must be achieved in a way compatible with the principle of devolution. Whitehall must come to terms with devolution and have a clearer concept of its territorial functions, and recognise when it operates on an English basis, when it performs UK-wide functions and it is performing a quasi-federal responsibility.

Whitehall must start to promote territorial justice in both social and economic policy, and take a strategic approach to addressing those inequalities in policy outcomes that could undermine the unity of the UK. There is real irony in the fact that it is in those policy areas where the desire for solidarity appears to be strongest (most notably health) that the scope for the centre to help deal with inequalities in outcomes appears to be weakest.

In practice, devolution seems to have strengthened the role of the Treasury. It both determines public expenditure decisions, and is one of the few UK departments dealing with the whole sweep of domestic public policy. Only the Treasury appears in a position to think through the implications of the concept of territorial justice.

Devolution is a process not an event, and the publication of the regional devolution White Paper – *Your Region, Your Choice* – is welcomed. It may also have the effect of spurring the DTI to sort out its role post-devolution. Despite the talk of a Barnett squeeze there is as yet little evidence of convergence in public spending across the territories of the UK, and we can expect a North East Assembly to make the issue one of its first and top priorities. It is very hard to see why the 'prudential' system for capital spending, signalled in Northern Ireland and for forthcoming English regional assemblies, should not also be extended to the devolved Scottish and Welsh administrations. Furthermore, in the medium term the complexities of the Welsh devolution settlement must be addressed. The halfway house of executive devolution makes significant but needless demands upon both Whitehall and Westminster and it is in the interests of all sides to foster a cleaner division of powers.

I:
Introduction

1 Devolution and public policy in the United Kingdom: divergence or convergence?

Michael Keating

That devolution should generate substantive differences in public policy across the component parts of the United Kingdom may seem obvious, since that is precisely what it is meant to do. Yet in the protracted debates over more than thirty years, relatively little systematic attention has been given to this or to its implications, while, since 1999 the media have got into the habit of describing every distinct measure taken for Scotland or Wales as an 'anomaly'.

Comparative experience shows that decentralisation and federalism do provide scope for policy differentiation, but that there are also powerful pressures for convergence. This chapter looks at the scope for policy divergence under the UK devolution settlement. It is organised in six sections. This introduction sets the scene. Then I examine structural factors, notably the formal devolution settlement and intergovernmental relations; political factors including the party balance and the emergence of territorial policy communities; the context of the single market and welfare state; and European influences. Finally I look at the dynamics of policy making in complex systems and the prospects for change.

The first point to make in this discussion is that policy making in modern government is typically an incremental process in which the weight of existing commitments limits the scope for innovation. The difficulties of the present British government in actually spending the money it has committed to enhance public services is a recent testament to this. Devolution in the United Kingdom, in contrast for example to the Spanish experience, builds on an existing and well established system of administrative devolution in which each of the component territories had a distinct way of making or adapting policy and delivering services. Against some of my colleagues, I never believed that the Scottish Office and its associated agencies had a substantial policy autonomy, but there were matters on which it was allowed to go its own way within the limits of overall UK policy. The Welsh Office, on the other hand, was more closely tied into Whitehall networks, sponsored very little legislation and took fewer initiatives. Government in Northern Ireland was an inheritance from the Stormont regime, which had extensive devolved powers although tended to shadow British welfare state provision. How much policy divergence occurs under devolution must therefore be measured not against some abstract model of uniformity, but against the pattern of convergence and divergence existing in the past.

Structural factors

An obvious point to start the analysis is the formal division of powers under the respective devolution Acts. Both the Scottish Parliament and the Northern Ireland Assembly have a general competence over all matters not specifically kept at Westminster, although these are expressed rather differently. Scotland faces just a single list of reserved matters, while in Northern Ireland there is a distinction between reserved matters, which may be devolved in the future, and excepted matters, which are kept permanently for Westminster. Both bodies have primary legislative competence over non-reserved matters, but also have some executive responsibility in matters where the primary responsibility remains with the centre, notably in economic development matters.

An examination of the two Acts shows some common elements but also the traces of past provisions such as the Stormont system, or the Scots law tradition. There is also a tendency for the centre to be concerned in Scotland with keeping matters related to the common UK market, while in Northern Ireland the prime concern is with security. The National Assembly for Wales, on the other hand, has only secondary legislative and executive responsibility for a list of powers devolved from Westminster and must get parliamentary approval for any changes in primary laws. Reserved and devolved powers are listed in Appendix 1.

Modern government does not work on the basis of watertight divisions of competences and there is a high degree of functional dependence between devolved and reserved questions. This is particularly noticeable in welfare state matters where, generally speaking, Westminster has reserved cash payments while personal social services, training and housing are devolved. This has already caused some problems in the treatment of housing benefit, and in the Scottish proposals for financing long-term care for the elderly when the Scottish Executive has tried to claim back funds from the Department of Work and Pensions that would be saved by its new scheme.

There are large interdependencies between the unemployment benefits scheme (reserved) and labour market policy (partly devolved) which have been highlighted by the New Deal programme. These might produce policy distortions or perverse incentives – a cynic might argue that there is no incentive for the devolved governments to spend money getting people into work since that would serve to reduce total welfare payments into their territories. There are also functional overlaps in energy matters, with Whitehall responsible for policy but the Scottish Executive retaining power to approve the construction of new power stations on planning and environmental grounds. Given the present UK government's apparent intention to resume the construction of nuclear power stations, there will be pressures within the Scottish Parliament, if not the Executive, to resist this. Overlaps have also arisen in the treatment of asylum seekers. While the division of powers intended by the Acts is reasonably clear, there is also scope for devolved administrations to expand the application of their competences by invoking the aims of policy rather than the means. Already the Scottish Executive has launched a strategy on broadband telecommunications although telecommunications is clearly a reserved matter.

Before devolution, the territorial offices were tied into the Whitehall policy network through a dense network of ministerial and official committees and regular working contacts among ministers and civil servants. Papers were exchanged, each level knew what the other was doing and there was care not to get too far out of line. Yet while the Whitehall departments generally took the lead in joint policy making there was no formal hierarchy and indeed no UK department at all in large areas of policy including education, housing, local government and social services. The devolution settlement builds on this administrative heritage with the effect that, over large areas of public policy, there is now no 'centre' at all.

This contrasts with Germany, where the division of powers (legislation to the *Bund*, execution to the *Länder*) means that both levels have parallel ministries, or Spain, where the central ministries have shown little inclination to retreat in face of the autonomous administrations. There was an attempt in Italy to solve the problem by abolishing ministries but they managed to pop up again in new forms. Even Canada and the United States have federal departments for health and the US (but not Canada) has one for education. This, combined with the end of the old interministerial committees and contacts, could have powerful centrifugal effects. It is partly to combat this tendency that the Joint Ministerial Committees have been set up but, while these appear to be a means of exchanging ideas and innovations, they are a far cry from the interdepartmental committees that prepared policies in the pre-devolution age and there would obviously be great political sensitivity about their being seen as a top-down measure to impose policy from the centre.

Another mechanism for co-ordination are the Concordats, non-statutory frameworks for agreement on areas of functional interdependence (listed in Appendix 2). These provide for policy variation to be limited and for a negotiation of differences, but it is clear that London will have the last word in the event of disagreement. It is by no means clear how they would fare were different political parties in control at the two levels. There are also legal mechanisms for pulling devolved administrations and assemblies into line should they exceed their powers but these, too, are untested given the consonance of political alignments between London and Edinburgh and Cardiff. This makes a big contrast with Spain, where political antagonisms produced a spate of court references in the 1980s, which served to set the bounds for devolved government.

A more serious constraint in practice may be the limited policy capacity of the devolved administrations. This reflects their historic inheritance so that Scotland has quite a large capacity for research and development in education and housing. It also has a disproportionate share of UK agricultural research, previously seen as contributing to a common effort and which may now come into question. On health policy, on the other hand, the devolved administrations may have to select areas for attention and then look to experience elsewhere. While this could involve a certain amount of horizontal learning among the devolved bodies, or from Europe, Whitehall is likely to be the main reference here.

There have been some changes in policy capacity since devolution, with the appointment of many more ministers with their own ideas and the recruitment of specialist advisors. Innovative groupings of functions, such as the combination of industry with further and higher education in Scotland, or the replacement of ministries of agriculture with departments of rural affairs, are another force for innovation. Under the Labour government, many policy initiatives have come out of the Prime Minister's office and the Treasury rather than functional departments, and devolved administrations have sometimes been involved in these. The Treasury's scheme for evidence-based policy, for example, provides funding for research and innovation and draws in both Whitehall and devolved departments. Adams and Robinson in Chapter 12 draw attention to the way in which the Treasury has grown under Labour into a lead department for policy across a wide range of matters, and in this it seems to have drawn in the devolved administrations.

Devolution was intended not only to transfer powers downwards territorially but to foster a new type of politics, with more participation on the part of backbenchers and civil society generally. Experience of the Scottish Parliament shows that the committees, while they could never function like their counterparts in the US Congress, are more important than those at Westminster. The Parliament is certainly more important than most of its counterparts in other federal or devolved systems, no doubt reflecting the salience (if not the power) of Parliament in British public life. It sustains a debate about public policy that was scarcely possible before devolution, and draws in many more actors to the policy process. In areas outside party contention, like the future of the enterprise support network, committee input has been mentioned as a significant contribution to policy. The Scottish Executive's review of Higher Education has been timed to link into the equivalent inquiry from the relevant Scottish Parliament committee. This reinforces a distinct pattern of political life in Scotland and encourages new policy communities.

Politics and policy communities

Party politics is obviously a factor in determining the degree of convergence or divergence of policy but so far we have limited evidence from which to judge the practical importance of this. Scotland and Wales are controlled by Labour-Liberal Democrat coalitions not far removed politically from the Government in Whitehall, although coalition politics has already produced two highly salient shifts in Scotland, on student fees and long-term care for the elderly. Coalition politics is also responsible for the emphasis on, and the distinct approach to, rural policy in Scotland and Wales; in England the impetus seems to have come from interest group mobilisation and the presence of Labour MPs in rural seats. In the event of differences in control at the two levels of government, there would obviously be more pressure for divergence, which might put strain on the system of accommodation put in place at a time of consistent political alignments. I believe that the system is perfectly capable of accommodating this, but new rules of the game would have to be learned and the courts would certainly enter into the policy process.

A radical difference in ideological stance between London and the territories on basis welfare state and common market issues, however, would be difficult to sustain, for reasons discussed below (p11-13). Even in the absence of partisan divisions, however, there could be differences, as we see from the hints that the Scottish Executive might not be as keen on private provision of public services as the government in London. The two main British parties have traditionally been highly centralist and have found it very difficult to adapt to the political realities of devolution, as Labour's troubles in London and Wales have shown. Scottish Conservatives are torn in a battle between those who want to rebuild themselves as a more authentically Scottish expression of centre-right opinion and those who want to cleave to the anti-European and right-wing views prevailing down south. These intra-party differences could be important in the case of diverging pressures coming from territorial policy communities, that is the constellation of interest groups forming around the devolved institutions.

Scotland has always had its own interest groups, which fall into three types. There are purely Scottish groups, Scottish groups affiliated to British or UK federations, and Scottish branches of British groups. The balance among these owes a lot to historic factors, for example the refusal of the British Trades Union Congress to accept affiliations from trades councils, which led to the establishment of the Scottish Trades Union Congress. Scottish groups in the fields of law and education have never been part of wider UK bodies, since these areas have been treated separately since the union of 1707.

In other cases, the growth of Scottish groups is a response to administrative devolution and the need for an interlocutor with the Scottish Office. Wales has many fewer distinctive interest groups, although there has been some growth since the 1970s. Northern Ireland is more complex again, with some groups operating on a Northern Ireland basis, some on a UK basis and some on an all-Ireland basis. In Scotland, devolution has led to a more formal division of responsibilities between Scottish groups and their UK counterparts. The Confederation of British Industry, for example, has given autonomy to its Scottish branch in devolved matters and increased its research capacity. Some bodies that operated mainly at the local level have established an all-Scotland presence. Many groups have sought to strengthen their policy capacity by hiring researchers, policy consultants and parliamentary liaison officers. They have also had to reorient their networks and lobbying to take account of the new three-level politics.

There are emerging patterns, which we can analyse by reference to three sets of institutional factors. First is the location of the group and its members, whether within Scotland, at the UK level or international. In the case of business firms and sectors, this would refer to the ownership of the firms and the location of their production. In the case of trades unions or social organisations, this would refer to the location of their members. Second is the field of operation of the group or, in the case of firms, the market. Third is the level at which the activity is regulated. So the main teachers' union is based in Scotland, organises only Scottish teachers and the sector is regulated entirely at the Scottish level. The main focus for policy attention is therefore the Scottish Executive and Parliament. Big firms doing business in Scotland are mostly externally owned, are regulated mainly at UK and European levels and trade in UK and global markets. We find, accordingly, that the main focus of attention for their representative groups are UK government departments. They do, however, need to pay more attention to the Scottish level than in the past, because some matters affecting them, such as transport or planning policy, are devolved. As a result, they do have to play in the Scottish arena to sustain legitimacy in the face of increased political exposure.

Small firms tend to be locally owned, trade locally and are more dependent on the public goods produced by devolved governments, including enterprise support services and infrastructure. They are also less well integrated into the UK-wide networks of influence and so are more strongly oriented to the Scottish level. Other groups are subject to conflicting pressures. The Scotch Whisky industry operates locally, but is externally owned, depends heavily on export markets and is regulated at UK and, to some extent, European levels. It therefore tends to look still to London, although there is a Scottish dimension.

Agriculture, an industry owned and operating locally, is almost entirely devolved but at the same time highly Europeanised. This has led to the maintenance of strong links to the UK level at the nexus of European and Scottish networks. Important financial and banking interests are headquartered in Scotland, in some cases Scottish owned, but operate in global markets and are regulated at UK and European levels. This leads them, too, to tie into UK policy networks, but without neglecting the Scottish dimension. Business groups are fairly unanimous in opposing anything that could be seen as erecting economic barriers within the United Kingdom, although they have become more supportive of local and regional business development initiatives. This makes them a force for policy convergence.

Individual trade unions are, with a few exceptions, organised on a UK basis.

Labour regulation is a largely reserved matter and there is a tendency now to leave this to the TUC and UK-level of the unions. Training policy and responsibility for local development and responses to industrial closures, however, is devolved, so the unions are drawn into the Scottish networks. Trade unions, while generally supportive of devolution up to the 1920s and since the 1970s, oppose any divergence in labour regulation across the United Kingdom, although they are very supportive of local development initiatives. They are also concerned with a range of social issues that draw them into Scottish networks. Public sector trade unions and associations are sometimes organised on an UK basis, like UNISON or the British Medical Association, while others, like the Educational Institute of Scotland, are purely Scottish.

One might expect greater pressures for uniformity in public sector pay and conditions where the negotiators are UK-based, as with doctors, since members would be unlikely to accept radically different conditions on either side of the border, and there is already some evidence of this happening. In April 2002 a proposal that Scottish general practitioners seek their own contract was voted down by their association, but the option may reappear in the future. Of course, even where negotiators and negotiations are quite separate, as in teaching, people will make comparisons. There is also a broader political spillover, as occurred also in April 2002, when the Scottish Police Federation voted to demand the right to strike, in protest against the attitudes of Home Secretary David Blunkett, who is not responsible for police in Scotland. This seemed to reflect an assumption that policy leadership in this field was still coming from the centre.

Social lobby groups and voluntary service organisations tend to be less well resourced than the others and operate usually at the Scottish level, respecting the division between reserved and devolved powers. This means that they can enter into policy networks in matters like housing, which are almost entirely devolved. They tend to be strong supporters of devolution since it has increased the points of access into the political system and given them more sympathetic interlocutors in the Parliament and its committees, and they might well prove an important agent of policy innovation.

While Scotland has long had its own interest groups and policy communities, there has been an important change in style and operation since devolution. The main role for the community before 1999 was to lobby, whether for more resources or for some bending of UK programmes to take account of Scottish interests. This allowed Scots to sustain the idea of being in a common cause, bound by shared values and a broad social consensus. Indeed this experience probably underlay some of the more naïve ideas floating around before 1999 that the Scottish Parliament could operate on the basis of consensus, banishing partisanship, conflict and lobbying.

Now the various groups must confront each other in an open political system, where they are vying for attention and competing for limited resources. They are gradually adapting to the new balance of consensus, conflict and compromise, although the failure to appreciate that disagreement is an essential part of a live democracy may be partly responsible for the tendency of sections of the media to describe every political conflict as a crisis of the system. Many groups have found the transition from lobbyist to participant in a policy process difficult. Several of them have commented that while in the past they would just complain, secure in the knowledge that nobody would respond, now they are asked what they would do instead. The mass of consultation conducted by the Scottish Executive and Parliament is welcome in itself but has put massive pressure on groups, many of which lack the resources to respond. There has been some growth of think tanks, almost all based in Edinburgh, but there is still a shortage of policy making capacity in Scottish civil society.

The devolution settlement provides for block grants for the devolved assemblies, calculated on a share of increases or decreases in corresponding English programmes (the Barnett formula). While these sums are freely disposable in Scotland, Wales and Northern Ireland, groups are likely to look at the corresponding totals to see if they have got their 'share'. UK-wide interest groups may be most aware of the implications of English spending decisions and able to make comparisons, providing another pressure for convergence. This is particularly true in matters of high political salience.

Additional health resources made available by the Chancellor of the Exchequer in 2001 and 2002 were allocated to health in Scotland in exact correspondence with the 'Barnett equivalent'. Indeed following the 2002 Budget the Scottish Cabinet announced immediately that the new resources would go, as in England, to health. This tendency to match may depend on the amount of competition for resources and on the transparency of the public accounts. In the first phase of devolution there was plenty of money to go around following the public expenditure review, the main difficulty being in spending it all; and the government presented the accounts in such a way as to make comparisons of increases in individual functions very difficult. Health, where the Scottish Executive has taken care to ring-fence Barnett increases, is an area where comparisons with English expenditure plans are relatively straightforward. In other areas, non-comparable functional headings and other technical problems make direct comparisons impossible. So pressures based on comparability are likely to be sporadic and limited to individual items of expenditure and prominent announcements, rather than systematic and across the board. Since the opposition parties in Scotland and Wales have tended to focus on the effects of the overall 'Barnett squeeze' and on individual items, there has so far been little impetus for political debate on spending priorities.

Provisions for capital spending might also be a force for uniformity. Technically it is for the devolved administrations to determine whether they will use Public Private Partnerships (PPP). Yet they do not have borrowing powers like other sub-state administrations and should they wish to finance projects publicly they would presumably have to do so from current revenue. So even if public financing were to be cheaper in the long run, as many people believe it is, devolved administrations might be steered into private finance in order to get projects going quickly. The detailed rules for PPPs in turn are controlled by the Treasury.

Context

The context for UK devolution is a modern, integrated welfare state and there are questions about how much divergence is possible in practice in these conditions. Three important sets of constraints arise from the existence of a UK common security area, a common market and the welfare state. While criminal justice is largely devolved, the lack of barriers among the parts of the UK and the need for common standards leads to a lot of co-operation and concern not to create conditions that could be exploited by wrongdoers. Hence there is a great deal of co-ordination in matters of criminal law.

Concern to maintain the common market is responsible for many of the limitations on devolved bodies, especially in Scotland and Wales. There are no powers to tax business except through the Unified Business Rate and development grants are kept in line through the concordats to prevent market distortions or bidding wars. Competition among the territories for mobile investment will also be a pressure for uniformity, since all will want to maintain a friendly business environment. Of course, this does not imply uniform policies, since there are many different models of local and regional development, but it will impose limits on the range of policies adopted and may produce convergence in regulatory, planning and environmental policies. The common labour market similarly imposes limits on the ability of devolved administrations to establish their own model of industrial relations, even within the limits of their competences. While there is a lot of support for devolving active labour market policies, neither side of industry has ever shown support for devolving labour law or regulation. The common market and travel area also influences responses to issues like Foot and Mouth Disease or the meat exports, where a separate Scottish line was not taken even where it was legally possible.

The common welfare state also poses practical and political limitations. Fears that differences in welfare provision will trigger migration have found only limited support in the experiences of other countries, since other factors such as employment and family networks have proved more powerful, but there may be some distortions. More important perhaps are the shared assumptions of the post-war welfare settlement for broadly equivalent basic services free at the point of use. 'Social citizenship' in the United Kingdom has been linked to a British identity and indeed many have credited the welfare state in forging a sense of British, if not UK, unity during the 20th century. Scotland's decisions on student fees ('Cubie') and long-term care for the elderly

('Sutherland') have tested these limits, provoking politicians and the media into discovering all manner of 'anomalies'.

It is here that the financial settlement and the Barnett formula come into play. The block grants to the devolved administrations are freely disposable, that much is clear. The devolved powers in the area of social and welfare policies are also reasonably clear, so that there is no doubt about Scotland's right to proceed with Cubie and Sutherland. Yet if finance raised on a common tax base is used to fund substantively different entitlements in the various parts of the United Kingdom, this is going to cause major political opposition. This is not to say that convergence will always be to the English line; it may that pressure within England will lead to the adoption of Scottish or Welsh innovations there. Even more problems could arise were innovations pioneered in England, since resources are immediately adjusted to take account of this, with the knock-on effects for the devolved territories merely a consequence. So if a future government were extensively to privatise the welfare state, promoting private schools and medicine and charging for services, the devolved administrations would automatically lose their corresponding public funding and have to respond. Alternatively, they would seek to reopen the settlement and gain their own powers of taxation. So marginal differences in welfare state provision are likely under devolution as we have already seen, but radical changes would destabilise the whole settlement.

Europe

Many devolved functions are subject to European Union law, notably in agriculture, fisheries, environment and industrial policy. This has become a major issue of contention in Germany and Belgium, where regions complain that it entails a loss of power not only to Europe but to central government, since it is the state as a whole that determines European policy. The response in Germany and Belgium has been to use the clause in the Treaty on European Union allowing the *Länder*, regions and communities to participate in the Council of Ministers and even to represent the member state where regional matters are involved.

Yet while this may enhance regional influence, it does not permit policy divergence, since they must represent the state as a whole and agree a common line. There is provision in the United Kingdom for devolved governments to participate in the Council of Ministers but again they must support a common line and the relevant concordats make it clear that Whitehall will have the last word on the line to be followed. The UK government is also responsible for the implementation of EU policies and has over-ride powers in case devolved administrations do not fulfil their obligations. The Structural Funds, often regarded as a means of regional emancipation, in fact have the opposite effect. Since the UK does not recognise additionality at the territorial level, the effect of structural fund designation is to earmark a part of the block grant deemed to represent the European contribution and oblige the devolved administrations to allocate another tranche as 'matching funds'. These monies are then ring-fenced and unavailable for allocation to other priorities.

So far, devolved administrations have preferred to take a common line in European matters, seeing a common UK position as the best way of maintaining their influence. This has been so even on agricultural matters in which a distinct line might have been possible, such as some of the agri-environmental regulations or the critical issue of modulation by which direct payments to farmers can be reduced in favour of measures to promote rural development.

Relations with Europe may change as a result of the debate on a European constitution, the White Paper on Governance, and the initiatives of the 'constitutional regions'. It has been suggested that regions with broad competences could contract more directly with the Commission for the implementation of EU policy, allowing for a more differentiated application and combinations of instruments. There has also been pressure to allow regions to appeal to the European Court of Justice invoking the principle of subsidiarity where they feel that their competences have been invaded, but all this is for the future.

The dynamics of devolution

The devolution settlement in the United Kingdom is at an early stage and the actors are still learning the new rules of the game. Since the administrations in Scotland and Wales are broadly in line politically with that in Whitehall and the power-sharing executive in Northern Ireland has only just begun, precariously, to function, there have been no causes for major policy divergence. Nor, in contrast to countries like Spain or Canada, has the division of powers been tested in the courts to produce a body of case law. In fact there has not to date been a single challenge by central government to the competences of the devolved bodies. We are therefore limited in our ability to speculate about the future, but we can frame some general typologies of policy, on the basis of the history of administrative devolution before 1999, of developments since then, and of experience overseas.

Five types of policy might be distinguished. First, there are non-comparable policies, where an issue exists only in certain parts of the United Kingdom. So one of the earliest initiatives of the Scottish Parliament was to address the historic issue of land reform, which has no counterpart in the other three countries. Welsh language policy and many issues in community relations are similarly unique to Wales and Northern Ireland respectively.

Second, there is policy autonomy, where Whitehall and the devolved bodies make their own policy according to local needs and preferences. This is likely to occur in wide areas of education and social services, and in organisational matters including the structure of local government in Scotland. Third, there are concurrent policies, where the territorial administrations pursue the same broad policies because of pressure from UK groups, similarity of conditions, European regulation or whatever. This may well be the case across much of health policy, where the demands are similar, interest groups operate across borders and make comparisons, and technology is an important factor in policy innovation. It is also likely to be case in higher education, where universities have historically been suspicious of devolution as something that might narrow their horizons; hence the organisation of the Research Assessment Exercise and the Quality Assurance Agency on a UK basis, sponsored jointly by the four countries.

Fourth there is policy uniformity, where practical considerations or external pressures make for a single line. Legislation on establishing the International Criminal Court, for example, has been brought forward separately in Scotland, although the effect is identical to that in England. Sometimes such matters have been handled by 'Sewel resolutions' in which the Scottish Parliament votes to agree to Westminster legislating in devolved matters. This, however, is politically sensitive and it is likely that, parliamentary time permitting, the Scottish Parliament will choose to make its own laws. Fifth, there is policy competition, a form of policy autonomy but which is worth highlighting separately. In this case, the four countries make policy for themselves in a way to demonstrate their credentials in innovation and imagination. Such initiatives make the news and are taken up by interest groups in the other jurisdictions and the effect is a diffusion of innovation and perhaps a reconvergence around the new practice. This type of convergence might be considered one of greatest contributions of devolution, in encouraging experimentation and learning from best practice but it could also produce a focus on what the Canadians have called 'boutique policies', highly visible initiatives to gain political impact in competition with other levels of government, but not necessarily making the best use of resources.

Before 1999 the territories were distinctive more in how they did things than in what they did. Some of the divergences we have seen post-devolution are also about style and approach. For example, the Scottish Executive and Welsh Assembly have been notably less keen than Whitehall on setting quantitative targets for services (with all the distortions that these cause) or on the competitive ethos by which spending agents such as local government have to compete for funding or symbolic rewards. Now there is greater scope for substantive divergence, but they continue to work within the parameters of the same welfare settlement. Devolution is a learning process and, as they learn, we are likely to see ever more policy innovation.

Acknowledgement

This paper draws on research under way in collaboration with Sean Loughlin under two programmes, the Leverhulme-funded programme on Regions and Nations in the United Kingdom directed at UCL; and the ESRC programme on devolution. The emphasis in the paper on Scotland reflects my own work there, with the assistance of Linda Stevenson.

Appendix 1
Devolved and reserved matters

Scotland

Reserved matters

- The Crown, the Union of the Kingdoms of Scotland and England, the Parliament of the United Kingdom.
- International relations, including foreign trade except for observing and implementing EU and European Convention on Human Rights matters.
- Defence and national security; treason; provisions for dealing with terrorism.
- Fiscal and monetary policy, currency, coinage and legal tender.
- Immigration and nationality, extradition.
- The criminal law in relation to drugs and firearms, and the regulation of drugs of misuse.
- Elections, except local elections.
- Official Secrets, national security.
- Law on companies and business associations, insurance, corporate insolvency and intellectual property; regulation of financial institutions and financial services.
- Competition, monopolies and mergers.
- Employment legislation including industrial relations, equal opportunities, health and safety.
- Most consumer protection; data protection.
- Post Office, postal and telegraphy services.
- Most energy matters.
- Railways and air transport; road safety.
- Social security.
- Regulation of certain professions, including medical, dental, nursing and other health professions, veterinary surgeons, architects, auditors, estate agents, insolvency practitioners and insurance intermediaries.
- Transport safety and regulation.
- Research Councils.
- Designation of assisted areas.
- Nuclear safety, control and safety of medicines, reciprocal health agreements.
- Broadcasting and film classification, licensing of theatres and cinemas, gambling.
- Weights and measures; time zones.

- Abortion, human fertilisation and embryology, genetics, xenotransplantation.
- Equality legislation.
- Regulation of activities in outer space.

Principal devolved matters

- Health.
- Education and training.
- Local government, social work, housing and planning.
- Economic development and transport; the administration of the European Structural Funds.
- The law and home affairs including most civil and criminal law and the criminal justice and prosecution system; police and prisons.
- The environment.
- Agriculture, fisheries and forestry.
- Sport and the arts.
- Research and statistics in relation to devolved matters.

Northern Ireland

Excepted matters

- The Crown, the Parliament of the United Kingdom.
- International relations, but not the surrender of fugitive offenders between Northern Ireland and Republic of Ireland.
- Participation in the all-Irish institutions.
- Observing and implementing European Union and European Convention on Human Rights matters.
- Defence and national security; treason; provisions for dealing with terrorism or subversion.
- Dignities and titles of honour.
- Immigration and nationality.
- Taxes under UK laws or existing stamp duties in Northern Ireland.
- Social Security.
- The appointment and removal of judges and director of Public Prosecutions for Northern Ireland.
- Elections, including local elections.
- Coinage, legal tender and bank notes.
- The National Savings Bank.
- National security.
- Any matter for which provision is made by this Act or the Northern Ireland Consitution Act 1973.

Reserved matters

- Navigation, but not harbours or inland waters.
- Civil aviation but not aerodromes.
- The foreshore and the sea bed and subsoil and their natural resources.
- Domicile.
- Postal services.
- Qualifications and immunities of the Assembly and its members.
- Criminal law; the surrender of fugitive offenders between Northern Ireland and Republic of Ireland.
- Public order, police, firearms and explosives, civil defence.
- The Emergency Powers Act (Northern Ireland) 1926 or any similar enactment.
- Court procedure and evidence.
- Foreign trade.
- Regulation of building societies; banking; friendly societies; the investment and securities business.
- Competition, monopolies and mergers.
- Some consumer protection matters.
- Trade marks, copyright, patent and topography rights, weights and measures.
- Telecommunications and wireless telegraphy.
- Xenotransplantation; human fertilisation and embryology; surrogacy; human genetics.
- Consumer safety, some environmental matters, data protection.
- Nuclear installations.
- Designation of assisted areas.
- Research Councils.
- Regulation of activities in outer space.

Principal devolved matters

- Health.
- Education and training.
- Social work, housing and planning.
- Economic development and transport; the administration of the European Structural Funds.
- The environment.
- Agriculture, fisheries and forestry.
- Sport and the arts.

Wales

Devolved matters

- Economic development.
- Agriculture, forestry, fisheries and food.
- Industry and training.
- Education; local government.
- Health and personal social services.
- Housing.
- Environment.
- Planning.
- Transport and roads.
- Arts, culture, the Welsh language.
- The built heritage.
- Sport and recreation.

Appendix 2
Concordats in Scotland and Wales

Memorandum of Understanding and supplementary agreements between Scottish
ministers, UK government and the Cabinet of the National Assembly of Wales
   Agreement on the Joint Ministerial Committee
   Concordat on co-ordination of European Union policy issues
   Concordat on financial assistance to industry
   Concordat on international relations
   Concordat on statistics

Scotland

1.   Concordat between Scottish ministers and the Secretary of State for Defence
2.   Subject specific concordat between the Ministry of Agriculture, Fisheries and
     Food and the Scottish Executive on Fisheries
3.   Concordat between the Department of the Environment, Transport and the
     Regions and the Scottish Executive
4.   Concordat between the Scottish Executive and the Lord Chancellor's
     Department
5.   Concordat on health and social care
6.   Concordat between the Scottish Executive and the Home Office
7.   Concordat between the Department of Social Security and the Scottish
     Executive
8.   Concordat on European Structural Funds
9.   Concordat between HM Treasury and the Scottish Executive
10. Concordat on co-ordination of the EU, international and policy issues on pub-
     lic procurement
11. Concordat between the Health and Safety Executive and the Scottish Executive
12. Concordat between the Department for Culture, Media and Sport and the
     Scottish Executive
13. Concordat between the Cabinet Office and the Scottish Executive
14. Concordat between the Department for Education and Employment and the
     Scottish Executive
15. Concordat between the General Registry Office and the Scottish Executive
16. Concordat between the Ministry of Agriculture, Fisheries and Food and the
     Scottish Executive and specific agreements on State Veterinary Services and
     Animal Disease Compensation Service, and the British Cattle Movement Service

17. Concordat between the Department of Trade and Industry and the Scottish Executive

Wales

1. Concordat with the Cabinet Office
2. Concordat with HM Treasury
3. Concordat with the Department of Health
4. Concordat with the Department of Social Security
5. Concordat with the Lord Chancellor's Department
6. Concordat with the Ministry of Defence
7. Concordat with the Department of Trade and Industry
8. Concordat with the Department of the Environment, Transport and the Regions
9. Concordat with the Department for Culture, Media and Sport
10. Concordat with the Health and Safety Executive
11. Concordat with the Ministry of Agriculture, Fisheries and Food
12. Concordat with the Wales Office, Office of the Secretary of State for Wales
13. Concordat with the Home Office

Source: Peter Lynch *Scottish Government and Politics* Edinburgh, 2001; Websites of Scottish Executive and National Assembly for Wales.

II:
Health

2. Health policy and the NHS in the UK 1997-2002
Kevin J Woods

Summary

The election of the Labour government in May 1997 and the subsequent devolution of political power to the countries of the UK in 1999 have created the possibility of health policy, and the funding and organization of healthcare services, developing differently in each place. Very few health related matters remain within the competence of the UK government and the UK Parliament. Health policies between 1997 and the establishment of the new political institutions in 1999 are reviewed as they formed an important legacy for new political actors. Six health policy themes are identified: public health; partnership; integration; equity; responsiveness; and quality.

This chapter considers the extent to which political devolution is beginning to have an impact on the content of this legacy by exploring the effects of the politics of 'partnership', parliamentary scrutiny, and inter-government relations. The degree to which health policy is diverging across the UK is discussed by reference to three examples: long-term care of the elderly; NHS governance; and public-private partnerships. The relative effects of party political alignment, policy making capacity, European Union health policy, the identity of the National Health Service (NHS), and the mechanisms for funding public services are assessed as factors that may determine if it is more appropriate to speak of the UK's national health services rather than the NHS.

Introduction

This chapter attempts to chart the impact that political devolution has had on health policy and the NHS in the countries of the UK. The election of the Labour Government in 1997 is its starting point, although formal powers were not devolved from Westminster to Wales and Scotland until July 1999; in Northern Ireland the Belfast Agreement was signed on Good Friday 1998, but power transferred in December 1999.

There are two related reasons for doing so. First, the process of constitutional reform anticipated after the 1997 general election could also be expected to encourage some variation in the content of health policy in each of the countries of the UK. Secondly, the significant changes in direction for health and health services policy promised by Labour manifestos throughout the UK, and pursued in the period 1997-1999, created a policy inheritance for the new administrations, which they could not easily abandon. April 2002 is the end point for this analysis. In the intervening period so much has happened that the chapter is necessarily selective, and since its author has been observing health policy change from a Scottish vantage point there is more on events in Scotland than in the other devolved administrations. There are some advantages in this regard. The asymmetry of the devolution settlement has transferred more political power to Scotland than Wales. The struggle for peace in Northern Ireland has inevitably affected the extent to which new institutions have been able to operate in that part of the UK and on occasion political control has reverted to Whitehall. The chapter addresses neither the question of regional government in England, nor the impact of the Greater London Authority. A final section explores a number of factors which may be expected to play a part in determining the extent to which health policy and the NHS are likely to develop differently in each part of the UK in the future.

Three broader points deserve some comment before examining experience in the health sector in detail. First, there have always been some differences in the organisation and administration of health policy in each part of the UK. For instance, circumstances in each country led to in variations in the structure of the NHS and have been described elsewhere (Ham 1999). In Scotland the existence of a separate legal system required separate legislation though this seldom amounted to more than the 'tartanisation' of proposals, differences in policy during this era of 'administrative devolution' being only marginal (Hazell and Jervis 1998). Despite this the NHS in each part of the UK has had a distinctive identity beyond labels such as NHS Wales, and the NHS in Scotland (now NHSScotland). The responsibilities of territorial Secretaries of State, and the existence of separate health departments with their own Ministers in each country are part of the explanation, especially given their role in the distribution of increased resources allocated to each country under the Barnett system. In some countries the clinical professions have also had a long-standing identity of their own, notably in Scotland, where there are three medical royal colleges of equivalent standing to their London based counterparts.

The biggest health related differences between the countries of the UK however, are the health status of their populations and the level of funding for the NHS. There are many good sources of information on the former (ONS 1999) which typically expand on headline data revealing that age adjusted mortality rates per 1000 in 1997 vary between 10.3 for women in England and 12.1 in Scotland. Recent data shows per capita health and personal social services spending in 1999-2000 was highest in Scotland at £1271 compared with a UK average of £1072, and England of £1041 (Bell and Christie 2001). These spending differences have enabled substantial differences in the level of clinical services to emerge. There are more available hospital beds in Scotland, Wales, and Northern Ireland than in England; there are also more GPs per capita, and their level of prescribing is higher (Wanless 2001). The exception to this pattern is the private health care sector, which is much smaller outside England.

In the light of decisions in the 2001 and (especially) 2002 Budgets to increase health spending in England at an unprecedented rate (see below) two related points are of importance. Assuming that each of the devolved administrations devotes to health the consequential funding they receive in accordance with the Barnett formula, the rate of increase in health spending in each country will be highest in England, and lower elsewhere; a simple reflection of the higher funding baselines in the latter. This is the 'Barnett Squeeze' that in theory should over time result in the convergence of public spending across the UK, the rate of convergence being greatest at times, as now, of expanding public spending. Current increases in health funding are intended to enable the fulfilment of the Prime Minister's commitment to increase total expenditure on health as a share of GDP to the European average. In fact, public expenditure on health in Scotland is already at the EU average. In July 2000 the Scottish Health Minister told the Parliament that in 1997 public expenditure on health in Scotland amounted to 6.4 per cent of its GDP, compared with a EU average of 6.5 per cent and a UK average of 5.8 per cent (Deacon 2000a).

A second general point to make at the outset is that health and health care policy in the devolved countries will remain of interest to Westminster even though its responsibilities in health are now primarily concerned with England. Health policies and the modernisation of the NHS have been the subject of more Joint Ministerial Committee meetings (see below) conducted under the Chairmanship of the Prime Minister than any other domestic policy subject since 1999. A number of reasons explain why this should be so. It is obviously part of the policy co-ordination process amongst administrations dominated by Labour, but there are other factors. The significance of health and the NHS as matters of public interest is only rivalled in domestic politics by concerns about education; but school education remains an important responsibility of elected local authorities whereas health expenditure and the health services are under the direct control of the 'central' administrations in Whitehall, Edinburgh, Cardiff, and Belfast.

Unlike some other aspects of policy (for example agriculture, and regional development) there is a limited (though increasing) role for the institutions of the European Union. Political and operational responsibility for the NHS rests squarely with these administrations; there are no other political institutions to share the credit or take the blame. Whilst they all face common pressures and have policy discretion the devolved administrations remain, however, largely dependent on inter-government resource transfers to fund the costs of rising public expectations of the health service. Only Scotland has the discretion to use its (marginal) tax varying powers to raise additional revenue, though all administrations can choose to reallocate resources towards health if they wish and can cope with the opportunity (and political) cost of doing so. The resultant and historically recurring pressure on the UK exchequer to find additional resources for health mean that it will remain difficult for any UK administration to avoid an interest in health and the NHS throughout the UK. Indeed, the Chancellor's review of the long-term funding needs of the NHS was a UK review (Wanless 2001).

There is another factor to consider as well, especially for the government that has established the devolved administrations. The prominence of health and NHS policy amongst the responsibilities of the devolved administrations means that making a success of them could be an important determinant of public views on the overall achievements of devolution; and making a success of health policy is commonly understood to require distinctive policies suited to the circumstances of each country, reflected for instance in slogans like 'Made in Wales' and 'Scottish solutions for Scottish problems'. Consequently, a UK government wishing to see political devolution succeed, has to accept that it may unleash demands for greater diversity in the level and organisation of health services that are all funded from a UK tax system. At what point does such diversity become reinterpreted as inequality? Is there a time in prospect when it becomes more accurate to speak of the UK's national health services rather than its NHS?

In other countries with a longer tradition of decentralised, federal government such as Canada and Australia these factors have tended to bring administrations into conflict at various times, and test the effectiveness of instruments for the conduct of inter-government relations. Canada is an especially interesting parallel for the UK given the similarities of its culture and health care system. In that country the tensions between provincial and federal government over health care have on occasion come to be the dominant domestic policy issue (Armstrong and Armstrong 1999). In a European context, recent events in Sweden are pertinent. Health care is the responsibility of local authorities with only a limited role for national government. However, the decisions of the Stockholm County Council (of Christian Democrats and Conservatives) to privatise the operation of St Goran's Hospital led the national government (of Social Democrats, Greens and former Communists) to enact legislation forbidding similar actions, and thus provoked a debate about the competence of each jurisdiction (Woods 2001).

Tensions between administrations are inevitably greatest where there are shared, overlapping or uncertain responsibilities, where there are complex arrangements for resource transfers between governments and where the process of conflict resolution is unclear. On the face of it the UK has less of these difficulties than some other countries for the approach to devolution reserved few issues to Westminster and thus reduced the potential for inter-government disputes. There are though arenas where conflict can be predicted. Prime is the issue of resource distribution and any review of the Barnett formula, which could have particular consequences for health spending given its size as a proportion of devolved government expenditure. Not so obvious but potent nonetheless is the question of inter-government policy competition, whereby the decisions of one administration force (unwelcome) issues on to the agenda of others. The debate about long-term care for the elderly (see below) is an important illustration of this dynamic. With these points in mind the chapter now examines health and related policy either side of the creation of devolved government.

Labour health policy 1997-1999

A number of preliminary points can be made about policy in this period. First is simply the amount of new policy produced and the scale of organisational change that reached into many parts of the health services. One constant however was the level of NHS funding, constrained by the new government's decision to work within its predecessors framework for the public finances. The only exception was a special allocation to tackle the high profile political objective of reducing waiting lists, which contrary to pre-election commitments rose dramatically in the months after May 1997. In contrast to this stability there was a marked shift from a view that economic incentives should drive change within a publicly funded health care system (the 'internal market') to a new emphasis on re-establishing the health services as a coherent system of care. This change, together with an explicit acknowledgement that health inequalities were the consequence of poverty requiring action through wider policy concerned with social exclusion are the defining characteristics of Labour health policy in this period.

Many of the policy changes affecting the NHS were achieved through the issue of guidance but primary legislation was needed for others in the form of the Health Act 1999, which became the last legislation affecting subsequently devolved health services policy to be considered by Westminster MPs. With devolution in prospect, the scope for developing policies distinctive from those in England undoubtedly expanded from May 1997. The diversity of the various health related Green and White Papers in each part of the UK that preceded this legislation is testament. Whilst some of this diversity was presentational and akin to the practice of 'administrative devolution' some of the proposals marked substantive differences of policy, requiring in the case of Scotland specific clauses to enact the decisions of Scottish Office Ministers, notably those relating to NHS governance and approaches to quality improvement.

The policies themselves represent a substantial programme carried through at a time of constitutional change and formed an important inheritance for the post-devolution administrations. It is important therefore to summarise some of the main points of policy in this period. Six themes are used for this purpose. They are: public health, partnership, integration, equity, responsiveness, and quality. Describing policy in this way is to some extent a matter of analytical convenience for in reality there are important links between each category. Thus, partnership working is fundamental to the policy on public health that was targeted on the reduction of health inequalities; and greater integration of health services was pursued to improve service quality.

Inevitably, some policies cut across these themes, in particular the clinical priorities of the NHS such as mental health, coronary heart disease (CHD) and stroke, and cancer. In all of these priority areas it is possible to associate policy developments with each of the six themes adopted in this paper. By way of example, CHD prevention was one of the cornerstones of the public health endeavour in all parts of the UK. Action to promote the early detection of cancer through screening programmes, and to improve service responsiveness by creating 'one-stop' diagnostic clinics featured in all countries. If these examples show the inter-related nature of policy and the difficulty of constructing a comprehensive typology, the themes do, though, provide a useful guide through a wide range of policy and the extent to which the prospect of political devolution encouraged diversity in them across the UK.

Public health

Compared with other countries in the EU the UK has an unfavourable health record, notably in regard to coronary heart disease and cancer, and there are also significant inequalities in health status associated with location, socio-economic group, gender, and ethnic origin (McLaren and Bain 1998). Addressing these problems was one of Labour's pre-election manifesto pledges and in office Labour policy sought a higher profile for disease prevention and health improvement making the reduction of health inequalities an overarching priority.

The Government's health gain strategy recognised that the determinants of health lie beyond the health services and was therefore part of wider social policy including proposals to reduce unemployment (Welfare to Work and the New Deal); to promote social inclusion (social inclusion partnerships); extend educational opportunity (the New Community Schools Programme and Sure Start) and alleviate child poverty. A promised ban on tobacco advertising failed to materialise taking some of the shine off Labour's overall public health policies, which sought changes in lifestyles and life circumstances. In England Health Action Zones (HAZ) were established to promote co-ordinated working amongst relevant agencies in defined communities. In Scotland four national demonstration projects were established – for CHD, cancer, teenage sexual health, and child health – to test and evaluate new approaches to health improvement. In Northern Ireland the nearest equivalent to these papers was the publication of 'Health and Well-Being: Into the Next Millennium' its fourth regional strategy that carried forward the theme of 'targeting health and social need (THSN)' a policy goal originating in 1992. In Wales the publication of 'Better Wales, Better Health' in July 1998 emphasised the importance of health alliances and partnerships between health authorities and local government to achieve public health targets.

Partnership

The concept of partnership also formed a central feature of policy for the health services. It figured prominently in all of the White Papers published in Great Britain at the end of 1997 and the beginning of 1998 (Department of Health 1997a; Scottish Office, Department of Health 1998a; Welsh Office 1998). In Northern Ireland shortly after the Belfast Agreement of Good Friday 1998 offered the prospect of devolved government, a consultation paper (Northern Ireland Office, Department of Health and Social Services 1998) was published in similar vein but deliberately left much for decision by an Assembly in prospect. Partnership was one of six 'Key Principles' in the English document's (Department of Health 1997a) proposals to replace the internal market. Similarly the Scottish paper promoted the idea of 'a partnership between different parts of the NHSiS to promote the integration of care and provide patients with a 'seamless service' (Scottish Office Department of Health 1998a, 2). Of particular interest to this chapter is the way the concept was given structural form in each part of the UK, the biggest difference being between the proposals in England and Scotland.

Prior to the general election Labour had been clear about its intention to abolish the competitive model built up from 1989 but the Labour manifesto (The Labour Party 1997) was less specific on what would replace it. Rejecting a return to the 'command and control' model of the NHS between 1948-1989, the White Papers sought to retain distinctive roles for organisations concerned with health strategy and planning, and NHS Trusts concerned with the operational delivery of services. Common to both was a requirement that both types of organisation would work together to deliver a Health Improvement Programme (HIP) for their area. The White Papers also announced the end of the GP Fundholding scheme that had been a centre-piece of the Conservative's 1989 reforms. Regarded by Labour as a cause of inequality in access to care and the cause of a wasteful bureaucracy, very different approaches to its replacement emerged in Scotland from those in England. In the case of Scotland, the White Paper brought a complete end to the holding of budgets by general practitioners for the purchase of secondary care services. In England the holding of secondary care budgets by some GPs for secondary care services was essentially extended to all GPs by the creation of Primary Care Groups (PCGs) as, initially, sub-committees of health authorities with responsibility for the 'commissioning' of health care.

The intention was for these PCGs to develop in time to become autonomous Primary Care Trusts (PCT). These should not be confused with similarly named bodies in Scotland (see below) as they had different roles and responsibilities. In Scotland PCTs had no 'commissioning' role, the flow of funds to secondary care being part of the remit for Health Boards. In Northern Ireland the replacement of fundholding was one of the issues left for the Assembly, and remains an outstanding item of business. In Wales 'Putting Patients First' (Welsh Office 1998) proposed the establishment of Local Health Groups (LHGs) intended to bring GPs, other health care professionals, voluntary organisations and social services staff together in support of Health Authorities which retained responsibility for the planning of services delivered by Trusts.

As subsequent developments in the governance of the NHS post devolution revealed (see below), the divergence in organisational structures based on the common idea of partnership, were far more than a 'tartanisation' of Whitehall policy. They are an expression of policy differences amongst Labour ministers in the UK government about the respective role of Health Authorities (Boards), NHS Trusts and General Practitioners in the management of the NHS. To regard these differences in the partnership model as pragmatic and only of marginal importance, driven by local circumstance and the differential uptake of fundholding (for this scheme had become much more widespread in England than in Scotland) would fail to recognise deeper antagonism in Scotland to the Conservative's policies, and to what Hazell and Jervis described as Scotland's 'communitarian' values (Hazell and Jervis 1998).

Integration

Strongly related to the partnership theme was the pursuit of greater integration in health care delivery. Health Improvement Programmes (HIPs) were a key feature of proposals to end the internal market, their title signaling the shift in emphasis to health improvement described earlier. Their principal purpose was to be a single overall strategy for each health area; for that strategy to be the product of collaborative working amongst NHS Trusts and Health Boards; and subject to consultation with the public and partner organisations such as local authorities. In short, their goal was to integrate the planning of health and service improvement for defined populations, a process that can be described as 'horizontal integration'.

In Scotland, 'Designed to Care' developed this idea of horizontal service integration further through its proposals for service provision, which envisaged the creation of two types of NHS Trust. Primary Care Trusts (PCT) brought together primary, community health, and specialist services for the mentally ill, learning disabled and elderly; and Acute Hospital Trusts, (AHT) which typically merged general hospital services into larger units of management. With the exception of the major cities of Glasgow and Edinburgh, it was envisaged that each health board area would contain one PCT and one AHT. Linking primary and secondary levels of services (vertical integration) provided by these two types of Trust was to be achieved by means of a proposed Joint Investment Fund (JIF), something of a misnomer for no specific fund was created. Instead, the JIF was intended to enable service redesign and was proposed as a non-budgetary alternative to the commissioning task placed on PCGs in England.

The merger of acute hospital trusts into new larger organisations was a distinctive feature of the proposals in Scotland and had been promised by the Labour Shadow Secretary of State for Scotland (George Robertson) immediately prior to the election. The idea was to repair the damage to clinical relationships in this sector caused by the internal market. The number of Trusts in Wales was also dramatically reduced from 25 to 16 by April 1999, part of an attack on the bureaucracy of the internal market, and concern about the size of the unelected 'quango state'. A distinctive feature of the Welsh re-organisation was the combination of acute care trusts and community health service trusts to serve defined geographical areas and promote continuity of service delivery.

The idea of integrated care was taken further by Scotland's Acute Services Review published in May 1998 (Scottish Office Department of Health 1998b). Its principal recommendation was the building of 'Managed Clinical Networks' an idea that subsequently found application in all other parts of the UK. Within the newly created Primary Care Trusts there was considerable scope for clinical networking as well. In establishing the PCTs 'Designed to Care' deliberately brought together the worlds of primary health care and specialist services for the mentally ill, learning disabled and the elderly. Within the organisational structure of the PCT it was proposed to establish Local Health Care Co-operatives (LHCCs), as voluntary organisations of GPs brought together to strengthen and support practices in delivering care to local communities. LHCCs were given various freedoms to manage resources in their area, but significantly, were not given budgets for secondary care services. By the end of 1999 95 per cent of Scotland's GPs were participating in LHCCs.

Significantly, none of the White Papers proposed any new arrangements to pursue further integration between health and social work services, an interface which has proved particularly difficult to manage throughout the UK (Scottish Office Home Department 1997). No country opted to implement the long-standing model operating in Northern Ireland of joint health and social services authorities, though in all parts there were exhortations to encourage joint working. In England and Wales the Health Act of 1999 placed a duty of partnership on the NHS to work with its social care colleagues in local authorities, and (for England) introduced the idea of Care Trusts as new organizations to which either party could devolve commissioning and delivery responsibilities for care at the health and social care interface.

Equity

Addressing inequalities in health status and the ending of GP Fundholding have already been identified as two of Labour's actions to achieve greater equity in health and health care. In addition a most significant, though highly technical, policy development in this area was the review of formulae for the allocation of NHS financial resources to health authorities. Historically, each country in the UK has had its own formula for this purpose based on the principles established in the 1976 report of the Resource Allocation Working Party (RAWP). Subsequently revised and refined these formulae guide the distribution of annual NHS spending in each country. Although intended to allocate funds in proportion to objective measures of need, they were criticised for failing to adequately account for the effects of social deprivation, and in Scotland, for the effects of population sparsity on the need for health care.

In coming to office Labour decided to review the formula in operation in each country, independently of each other. However, common to all countries was an attempt to include better measures of the health need consequences of social deprivation and to tackle the thorny issue of health status inequalities. Public debate about complicated resource allocation formulae tends to be limited, save for complaints from those parts of the NHS that enjoy lower rates of growth than more needy places as a consequence of them. But in taking forward these reviews Labour addressed a long-standing concern within the health service that its predecessors in government had suppressed discussion of and action to address social inequalities in health status.

Responsiveness

Improving the responsiveness of health services to the needs of patients was a central objective of the 'modernisation' programmes set out in the 1997 White Papers. They offered the vision of a health service that provides patients with high quality treatment and care 'when and where they need it'. All the papers are littered with initiatives to bring this vision to reality, including the use of information technologies to enable the electronic booking of hospital appointments. Perhaps the most innovative of all was the establishment of NHS Direct (in England) to provide patients with clinical advice from trained nurses located in telephone call handling centres. Within hospitals the extension of one-stop outpatient clinics was promoted to prevent patients feeling as though they were being 'passed from pillar to post'. But the centrepiece of Labour's efforts to have a responsive health service in the period between May 1997 and May 1999 was its policy on waiting lists. In its pre-election manifestos Labour committed itself to reducing hospital waiting lists in the UK by 100,000. This represented a shift in policy from the Conservative administration's concentration on reducing waiting times, though this is widely regarded as a better measure of access to services.

It is not clear why Labour selected the size of the overall waiting list as its policy target, other than its ease of comprehension and the attraction of lengthy NHS queues as symbols of NHS shortcomings. Fulfilling the ambition was to prove illusive. In the first 12 months after gaining office waiting lists went up, not down. In England the list increased by 17,600 between July and September 1997 (Department of Health 1997a) and similar increases were observed throughout the UK. The result was an injection of an extra £500 million into the health services (Department of Health 1998a) and all parts of the UK benefited according to their Barnett share. Some progress was eventually achieved in arresting the growth in lists, and indeed causing some of them to fall, but if this was welcome news to the Government it was accompanied by claims from within the medical profession that the policy was distorting clinical priorities as more complex surgery was delayed by large numbers of minor, non-urgent procedures undertaken to deliver a political target. Even so, the upsurge in emergency hospital admissions in subsequent winters undermined the capacity of the NHS to undertake routine elective surgery and the progress that had been made was rapidly lost.

Quality

If speed and ease of access to treatment are important components of a quality service so too are the physical conditions of clinical facilities and staffing levels. Traditionally these have been the focus of discussion about health service quality, and so they continued to be during Labour's first two years. Renewing hospital buildings has always been symbolic of an improving service. In opposition Labour had conveyed an impression of opposition to the Conservative administration's commitment to rebuilding hospitals through the use of private sector capital funding, though a carefully worded manifesto only committed Labour to improve the operation of the Private Finance Initiative (PFI) and to exclude the privatisation of clinical services from projects.

When Labour came to office many large projects were well advanced in various parts of the UK. There was little option but to continue with them, which in Scotland included the flagship Royal Infirmary of Edinburgh (Scottish Office 1998). Adjustments were made, however, to policy to ensure that no clinically related services or staff transferred to the control of the private sector facilities management companies involved in PFI consortia. Even the previous Conservative administration had been wary of proceeding down this route, but had explored the possibility in one PFI project intended to replace outdated community hospitals in Aberdeenshire, with a new hospital in the town of Stonehaven. In the event the local NHS Trust won the competitively tendered contract to provide clinical services. Ironically this enabled Sam Galbraith, the Labour Health Minister in Scotland at the time, to complete the building at a ceremonial topping-out removing any doubt in that country about Labour's commitment to the use of private sector capital to improve NHS services.

Buildings are only part of the service quality equation. The clinical effectiveness of the care provided is another obvious ingredient, though traditionally such matters were considered to be the preserve of the professions themselves. Labour policy after May 1997 began to challenge this through the introduction of 'clinical governance'. This policy was designed to reassure a public increasingly sceptical of the power of professional self-regulation to protect them. Mounting evidence from a succession of inquiries increasingly called into question the ability of the NHS to monitor the quality of clinical practice and deal with shortcomings when they were found. The statutory duties of NHS Trusts were amended to make it plain that chief executives carried ultimate responsibility for the services provided in their Trusts.

Subsequent papers in England and Scotland (Scottish Office Department of Health 1998b; Department of Health 1998a) took the systematic analysis of quality further, proposing the creating of national systems for assessing the quality of clinical services. This was done in different ways in each country. In England the Commission for Health Improvement (CHI) was established as an inspectorate of services, and the National Institute for Clinical Excellence (NICE) was set up to lead work on the assessment of health technologies, and the effectiveness of clinical practice. The remit of both of these organisations extended to Wales. In Scotland there was more of an existing organised base on which to build that led to the creation of the Health Technology Board for Scotland (HTBS), the nearest equivalent to the NICE, and the Scottish counterpart to CHI, the Clinical Standards Board for Scotland (CSBS).

Health and NHS policy in the UK 1999-2002

With such a substantial policy inheritance it was always unlikely that new politicians and new political institutions served by officials who had been involved in so much of what had gone before would depart immediately from the established direction of travel. Expectations however, were somewhat different. Devolution had been sold as an opportunity to break with the past, to usher in new policies suited to local needs, to construct policy through new processes built around partnership, openness, and transparency. In reality the first job for those involved was to breathe life in to new political bodies, a process admirably captured in the Constitution Unit's analysis of the first year of devolution (Hazell 2000). Inevitably, political horse-trading amongst the parties as they formed administrations, and within the various chambers as committees were constructed, tended to take the shine off the ambition. Combined with the inheritance of partially implemented policy, and pressing problems in the NHS there was little time and space left over for policy innovation on the health front in the first few months.

In every country serious financial pressures in the NHS surfaced quickly, notably in Wales. Alarm bells rang as waiting lists continued to defy attempts to control them, and delayed discharges clogged up hospital wards. Ministers wrestled with the twin problems of getting patients into hospital and then getting them out. By mid-winter, influenza-related illness and fears of the millennium bug effectively pinned down health ministers across the UK as they battled with political opponents and professional lobbies pressing their concerns, with a stream of examples of health services under pressure paraded daily in the media.

As the millennium turned, new health ministers could be forgiven if they wondered when they would be able to focus on the policy initiatives that had been set out in manifestos and programmes for government. Mainly consisting of commitments to complete the implementation of existing initiatives, and to extensions of inherited policy, it came as something of a surprise that the first piece of legislation enacted by any of the new administrations was in the field of mental health.

The explanation is found in the pressure of events rather than in plans: on this occasion a Scottish Sheriff Court had found the continuing detention of Noel Ruddle a patient at The State Hospital (for high security, mentally disordered offenders) was unlawful since his doctors had concluded he was no longer suffering from a treatable mental illness. Accordingly he was released, and in the face of massive public anxiety the Scottish Executive set about putting in place new legislation, the Mental Health (Public Safety and Appeals) (Scotland) Act 1999. It did so with all party support, and with great speed. Mr Ruddle was released in August; the Act was passed on 8 September and received Royal Assent within the week. Apart from being notable as an historical landmark the enactment of this legislation is notable for other reasons. First, it was introduced to the Parliament by Jim Wallace, leader of the Liberal Democrats, Deputy First Minister, and Minister for Justice on behalf of the coalition. Secondly, it was resolving a problem specific to Scotland that required primary legislation to be enacted quickly, one of the benefits which devolution was intended to bring.

Health and NHS issues figured prominently in the political discourse in each country during the first year after devolution. The details are captured in the monitoring reports of the Constitution Unit's monitoring project on health[1] and are not repeated in this paper. On the face of it the evidence indicates that health and NHS policy remained on its established trajectory, suggesting that devolution appeared to be making little difference, but this does not do justice to the changes occurring in the policy-making process and the growing confidence of the new institutions to chart their own course. There are three aspects within health that are worthy of particular comment. First is the emphasis given to 'partnership'; second is the impact of closer scrutiny; and third is the consideration of health policy through the new machinery for inter-government relations.

The first year: changing the production of policy

Partnership

With all of the administrations dependent on inter-party co-operation to achieve their goals the prominence of 'partnership' in the post devolution rhetoric is unsurprising, but it was also a key concept increasingly applied to the preparation and implementation of policy at national and local levels. In all countries the pursuit of public health objectives through 'joined-up' endeavours intensified, all administrations trying to place greater emphasis on the improvement of health status. The spadework for this had already been done by the previous administrations but it intensified in the period after mid-1999.

In Wales and Scotland especially, the new health ministers recognised that if devolution was to narrow health inequalities then galvanising the collective resources of national and local organisations around the theme of health improvement was an important way to do so. Moreover, they controlled many of the means to make it happen. The result was renewed vigour in the development of 'cross-cutting' policy, a significant challenge to central departments traditionally organised on strongly vertical lines, and local agencies that commonly spoke the language of partnership but lived separately behind the comfort of their administrative walls. The interface between health and social care came under close scrutiny; the portfolios of all the new health ministers combined responsibility for both, and they sought ways to bring the cultures, administration, and resources of different agencies into more effective combinations. For example, in Scotland, leaders of the health service were charged to pursue 'partnership with a purpose' with the aim of modernising policy, modernising service delivery, and modernising the governance of the NHS in Scotland (Deacon 2000b).

Did this ethos extend to working practices between the executives and their respective chambers? The evidence suggests not; in all countries there is evidence of tensions between health ministers and related committees. In common with other policy in Northern Ireland this was almost inevitable. In Wales and Scotland the initial optimism that some form of political consensus over health and the NHS might emerge from the new politics soon evaporated. The trigger in Wales was the familiar problem of budgets; proposals from the Assembly Committee to extend free eye testing were resisted by the Cabinet, though it subsequently relented to ensure the abstention of Plaid Cymru in the crucial vote authorising the Assembly budget. In Scotland, a bizarre episode on the back of the Parliamentary committee's consideration of the 'Arbuthnott Report' (Scottish Executive Department of Health 1999) concerning the distribution of NHS resources illustrated that older-style political rivalries remained alive and well. Having heard evidence from the Minister, the committee entered private session, but owing to a procedural failure in drawing the public session to a close their private conversation, including critical comments about the Minister, was duly entered in the official record (Scottish Parliament 1999). It was always unlikely that aspirations for a new style of politics would withstand the opportunities that committee meetings bring for political point scoring.

Scrutiny

Increasing the scrutiny of public policy was a fundamental objective of devolution, an indispensable process to remedy the perceived democratic deficit of government from Westminster. Its effects were quickly felt. In Northern Ireland the Sinn Fein Minister of Health found her decision to relocate a south Belfast maternity hospital to a hospital site in her own west Belfast constituency under intense, if expected, scrutiny having come to her view in the face of opposition from a majority of the health committee. It took several months for the process to run its course. Following a successful application for the judicial review of her decision, which found against her, the Minister had to suspend implementation of her plan and allow a period of consultation (Constitution Unit 2001a).

In Wales the early days of the Assembly Health Committee were taken up with the funding crises gripping hospital services, captured in one of the first papers prepared for it entitled 'Stocktake of NHS Wales'. However, the Assembly Committee has yet to extend its scrutiny to individual NHS Trusts (Constitution Unit 2001b) unlike Scotland, where additionally the Parliament's Audit Committee conducted a searching examination of financial problems in Tayside (Scottish Parliament 2001). In the first 18 months of the Scottish Parliament there were 50 debates on health and community care (Scottish Executive 2000a). During this time its Health and Community Care Committee moved on from its first big job considering the Arbuthnott formula and contributed to the scrutiny of legislation concerning Adults with Incapacity, and amongst others, two issues that illustrate a novel feature of the new parliamentary arrangements in Scotland, the Petitions Committee.

This enables citizens to present their concerns direct to the Parliament, and if it judges it appropriate the Committee can refer the issue for further inquiry to a subject committee. In this way concerns about the future of Strathcathro Hospital in Tayside and opposition to the proposed site of a secure unit for the mentally ill in Glasgow found their way on to the national political stage, requiring local health managers to account for the policies they were pursuing. On the back of their enquiries the Committee produced its own influential proposals for the conduct of public consultation about health care changes (Scottish Parliament 1999). As an illustration of the detailed nature of the Committee's interest in petitioner's concerns it recently asked, when considering delayed transfers of patients from the State Hospital, why the case of a particular patient had not been on the agenda of a health board meeting

(Herald 2002). Here are echoes of Aneurin Bevan's acid observation that the consequences of dropped bedpans would reverberate around Whitehall. The overlap of the Westminster and devolved electoral cycles adds to the intensity of political scrutiny; a general election for one or other of the chambers is never far away creating an almost permanent pre-election atmosphere. It would be a supreme irony of devolution if the institutions of devolved democratic accountability were to inhibit the discharge of responsibilities entrusted by them to local agencies.

There is little doubt that new political institutions have made a mark and in a chapter focussed on executive policy initiatives it is important not to lose sight of the contribution of the elected chambers. In all countries there was an upsurge in the amount of parliamentary related work. For instance in the first six months of 2000 there were 1100 parliamentary questions on health and related matters in Scotland, compared with 1500 on all subjects to the Secretary of State for Scotland in an average year pre-devolution (Scottish Executive 2000a). Media coverage of Holyrood took debate about health well beyond its immediate environs. Scotland enjoys a large and competitive national press that contributes much to the scrutiny of public policy, something less apparent in Wales (Osmond 2000). For some, the spectacle was less appealing than they would have liked. For instance, after a year Leicester concluded that the Scottish press continued to play 'the old game, and the politicians have done little to prompt anything different' (Leicester 2000). If this is a valid judgement it does not do justice to the simple fact that the proceedings reported are now 'local' rather than distant goings on at Westminster. As Curtice (2000) has shown, public opinion polling suggests that support for devolution in Scotland and Wales may not depend upon performance.

In quantitative terms the evidence indicates unprecedented scrutiny of health and NHS matters on the floor of the chambers, in the media, and in the volume of ministerial questions and correspondence. More difficult to judge is the extent to which this scrutiny generated light as well as heat. Has the powerful spotlight of parliamentary and public scrutiny illuminated the complexities of health and the NHS and led to a greater understanding of what can be achieved and what cannot? Has it made difficult decisions easier or easy decisions more difficult? Has it encouraged policy divergence? There is little doubt that there is now increased opportunity for pressure groups to influence the parliamentary decision-making process, and for local events to reach the national stage; resulting, according to taste, in either unhelpful delays, or greater participation in public policy. The architects of devolution imagined parliamentary scrutiny would lead to some policy divergence, but will the opposite occur? Will parliamentarians look to the actions of their close, and larger neighbours for ideas and comparators with which to challenge the executives, and counter to our intuition, cause policy to remain on a broadly similar course?

The intensity of political and media scrutiny of executive activities was accompanied by the introduction of new accountability systems for the health services. This was given great emphasis by the administrations in England, Wales and Scotland where revised performance management systems began to develop as governments pushed hard to accelerate policy implementation. Performance Assessment Frameworks (PAF) including numerous indicators of performance were devised to strengthen the 'centre's' ability to hold individual health service bodies to account for their use of public resources, accompanied by detailed monitoring systems intended to give ministers an ability to nip potential problems in the bud. Independent audit bodies grew in profile, and in England the Department of Health gave the Audit Commission and the Commission for Health Improvement responsibility for classifying NHS Trusts according to their performance, using a system of 'star ratings', though this practice was not followed by the devolved administrations.

Inter–government relations

In January 2000, as health ministers grappled with the problems of health services under enormous pressure from 'flu and related illness, the Prime Minister committed his Government to increase health spending in the UK so that it would reach the European average. The Chancellor of the Exchequer's subsequent budget (Brown 2000) and other related announcements set out the details of unprecedented growth (an increase of a third in real terms over a five year period) in NHS resources. This was probably the most significant health policy announcement in the period (though this was exceeded in the health spending increases announced in April 2002) and in its wake English health ministers announced the intention of publishing a 10-year plan for the NHS.

Subsequently, at the Prime Minister's invitation the devolved administrations joined with the UK Government in a meeting of a Joint Ministerial Committee on Health (JMC(H)). The facility to establish Joint Ministerial Committees is part of the new inter-government machinery created at the time of devolution, based on the Memorandum of Understanding and Concordats between Whitehall and the devolved administrations departments, though none of this has a statutory basis. Constitutionally, JMCs represent the coming together of partners. No administration can be bound by the decisions of the others in devolved matters, so Joint Ministerial Committees are a device for conflict resolution, co-ordination and discussion of common interests. They complement party political relationships and the day-to-day liaison that occurs between officials in the administrations and which ordinarily deals with most business. Significantly, it was through these channels rather than a JMC that the controversy over free personal care (see below) was conducted, thus keeping the dispute within the Labour family and preventing it from escalating to be a public test of the new constitutional arrangements.

Obvious questions are why the first JMC(H) meetings occurred when they did, what they reveal about the policy autonomy of the devolved administrations, and what they tell us about the reach of party influences across the UK? The communiqué (Scottish Executive 2000a) issued at the end of the (first) JMC(H) held in Cardiff shows the formal constitutional position of each country was carefully respected. The need for such sensitivity was evident at subsequent JMC(H)s held in London, Glasgow, and Belfast: occasions when the Ulster Unionist First Minister of the Northern Ireland Executive and its Sinn Fein Minister for Health attended, and the Scottish delegation was led by the Liberal Democrat Deputy First Minister in the absence (due to illness) of Donald Dewar.

There are, however, other dimensions to all of this. The Prime Minister's party held power in the devolved administrations in Scotland and Wales at the time of the first JMC(H) in Cardiff in April 2000 and as Northern Ireland was under direct rule from Westminster following the suspension of devolution Peter Mandelson, then Secretary of State, attended. At the time the bruising winter was still prominent in ministerial minds and with a Westminster general election expected during 2001 there was an obvious electoral need for the Prime Minister's party to deliver its NHS commitment throughout the UK. Secondly, as Barnett Formula beneficiaries of increased health spending in England, the devolved administrations had a significant interest in learning of Westminster's intentions, since they were bound to create expectations in their own back gardens. The JMC communiqués acknowledge the need for local variation in the process of policy design but there is also an emphasis on policy direction being driven by a common analysis of health service problems and a commitment to share experience in policy implementation. Is this the modern version of policy 'tartanisation' (Salmond 2000)?

As the second year of devolved government was to reveal, growing confidence on the part of some of the administrations to go their own way on some issues shed some light on this question. The extension of free prescriptions to the under-25s and free dental examinations to the over-60s in Wales are examples (Constitution Unit 2001c). At the same time it became increasingly apparent that NHS policy in England was moving in its own distinctive direction. Devolution was always intended to enable innovation by the new administrations and the possibility of policy divergence, but equally, it should be remembered that this divergence can occur when innovative policies developed in England are not adopted elsewhere. The issue of free personal care for the elderly is an example of the first; the role of the private sector in health care delivery an example of the second; and changes in the governance of the NHS are an example of both happening at the same time. These proved to be three of most important health policies in the second year of devolution.

The second year and beyond: changing policy directions

Long-term care of the elderly

No other health issue has demonstrated the power and consequences of political devolution than the issue of free personal care for the elderly, one of the recommendations of the Royal Commission on Long Term Care that had been set up by Labour in December 1997, its report appearing in March 1999 (Royal Commission on Long Term Care 1999). English ministers rejected the recommendation believing that the resources it would consume could be put to better, more targeted, effect on other services for the elderly. Wales adopted the policy in England with minor adjustment. In Northern Ireland, and especially in Scotland, the issue revealed the awkward choices that devolved administrations have to make when they step outside an English policy framework that has determined the resources transferred to them from the UK Treasury.

In Northern Ireland, the Executive wanted to adopt the policy (eventually) settled in Scotland, but claimed that because of the Barnett Squeeze it could not do so. Its initial intent to follow the policy in England that had extended free nursing care to residents of residential and nursing homes was subsequently dropped for the same reason (Constitution Unit 2001e). But it is the policy in Scotland and the political rows surrounding it that brought these issues in to sharp focus, opening up tensions within the Scottish Executive ministerial team, and giving the public a glimpse into the intrigues of inter-government relations. It brought the Executive in to conflict with its own coalition partners and produced remarkable political manoeuvres on the floor of the Scottish Parliament as the Executive sought to save face in the final minutes of a heated Parliamentary day on 25 January 2001.

It will take some years and several political memoirs to unravel all that took place and why. For the moment the essential points are as follows. In October 2000 the Scottish Minister for Health appeared to have settled policy on free personal care by adopting a very similar position to that in England. However, after Donald Dewar's death in October 2000 the issue was re-awakened by Henry McLeish following his election as First Minister. It is not clear why he did so, though it may have been an attempt to distinguish his leadership from that of his predecessor. But there had also been considerable support for free personal care in Scotland and the Parliament, stimulated in part by the presence in Scotland of the Royal Commission's Chairman (Sir Stewart Sutherland, Principal of Edinburgh University). If the change of policy was intended to spike the guns of political opponents who supported free personal care, it was a manoeuvre that did not enjoy the support of everyone in Mr McLeish's cabinet, a group that found itself at odds with its leader and the majority in the Parliament. Events suggest that the free personal care policy was made on the hoof by the First Minister (now resigned) rather than through a mature political process.

Over several weeks an expectation grew that free personal care was back on the political agenda and the Executive appeared to be on the verge of a policy 'U-turn'. But when the Minister for Health addressed Parliament on 24 January she only made moves to extend tax funded care to some additional groups, and remaining consistent with her October position and still close to the position in England, her statement avoided any commitment to embrace universal free personal care. This provoked a crisis with the Liberal Democrats (the Executive's coalition partners) who were aligned with the other political parties in support of free personal care. The following day the Executive continued to defend its position but it looked increasingly likely it would lose the vote at the end of a debate on a Scottish National Party motion demanding 'an unequivocal commitment' to free personal care. Accepting the Executive's request to make an emergency statement in the final minutes before the vote, the Parliament's Deputy Presiding Officer controversially opened the door for the Minister for Parliament to apparently shift the Executive's policy in support of free personal care and defeat the opposition motion. However, speculation on the nature of the Executive's position continued and the issue refused to go away.

As a result, on 29 January the First Minister made a statement at the launch of his (the Executive's second) *Programme for Government* in which he is reported to have said, 'We are embracing the principles of Sutherland in full....I don't want any doubts to remain in your mind as to which direction we are taking' (Scott 2001). Subsequently the Minister for Health published details of an expert 'Care Development Group' to be established under the Chairmanship of the then Deputy Minister for Health and Community Care, Malcolm Chisholm, to work out the details of the policy including its costs. When the report of the Group was published (Scottish Executive Department of Health 2001a) it revealed that the price tag for this commitment was approximately £125 million per year, though the precise costs may well turn out to be different as reality tests some of the assumptions and estimates made in the report.

No other policy issue better illustrates the dilemmas facing health (and other public) policy making in the devolved administrations. It is an issue that arises from a UK government enquiry; its proposals fall predominantly within the competence of the devolved administrations, but the resources available to them are the Barnett consequences of policy decisions taken in Whitehall. Once the First Minister decided to back free personal care, the (initially) estimated £125 million bill had to be found from within the Scottish Block, and by negotiation with Whitehall over a transfer of part of the budget controlled by the Department of Work and Pensions which remains a reserved matter. Enabling policy diversity is the purpose of political devolution but the tensions in the Scottish Cabinet and between it and Westminster exposed by free personal care have revealed other consequences of the devolution process. The decision in Scotland has encouraged pressure groups for the elderly to present the diversity in policy as an injustice, and they continue to campaign for its implementation elsewhere. Lord Lipsey, a member of the original Royal Commission and co-author of a minority report rejecting the proposal for free personal care suggested that the Scottish Executive's plans would lead to a flow of elderly people across the border to take advantage of the new entitlement (Constitution Unit 2001e).

It is tempting to see this wrangling as political infighting and rivalry (which it is) but to do so does not do justice to concerns about the opportunity costs of the decision. Could these resources be better utilised in improving services for the learning disabled or people with epilepsy or multiple sclerosis and so on? Or could they be put to better effect in transport or housing? The Executive's press release announcing the implementation of free personal care made the point well, if unintentionally, when the First Minister observed that the Executive had put its commitment to, 'older people at the very top of the Executive's priorities' (McLeish 2001).

In the middle of January 2002 the consequences of doing so became very clear and the issue became an extremely hot potato for the Scottish Cabinet once more. Failure to win the argument with the Department of Work and Pensions left a hole in the budget for free personal care reported to be about £23million at a time when private care homes were pressing for increased funding from local authorities and the number of delayed hospital discharges ('blocked beds') reached record levels (Chisholm 2002a). Ministers announced on 15 January 2002 that they were delaying the implementation of the policy from April 2002 until July because of the need for more time to sort out administrative difficulties, which immediately prompted widespread speculation of an imminent policy U-turn, something Ministers vigorously denied (Chisholm 2002b). It is unlikely that the final chapter has been written on this topic as the consequences of the policy will continue to impact on other health programmes as well as the Executive's overall plans. Whatever the arguments about the rights and wrongs of this policy, it is the policy that the Scottish Parliament wanted. The switches in the Executive's position suggest that the same cannot be said of it, but in bowing to Parliamentary pressure its actions brought the meaning of political devolution to life for the wider public, not only in Scotland, but throughout the UK. It also illustrated the effects of the new electoral system, its measure of proportional representation giving significant political leverage to the Liberal Democrats in the coalition administration.

Public-private partnerships

If personal care for the elderly discomforted Whitehall, the emerging policy position that extends the role of the private sector in health care in England has had a similar, if less marked effect in Scotland. In Northern Ireland and Wales the prospects of a more significant role for PPPs have been received with indifference at best and on occasion outright opposition (Constitution Unit 2001b). The first sign of a new policy direction came in the form of a 'concordat' between the Whitehall Health Department and the private sector that has no counterpart in any of the other administrations. This document begins with the statement 'There should be no organisational or ideological barriers to the delivery of high quality healthcare free at the point of delivery to those who need it, when they need it' (Department of Health 2000a). The concordat offered a framework for the NHS in England to call on additional hospital capacity in the private sector during periods of high demand, but it also removed any doubts about the political legitimacy of health authorities routinely using the private sector.

A report by the Institute for Public Policy Research (Commission on Public Private Partnerships 2001) and New Labour's election campaign in June 2001 gave further shape to these ideas in health. The policy is more than a repackaging of the previous PFI/PPP policy, resting on the idea that incentives and greater management freedom can improve performance in ways that have eluded the public sector. Predictably it is a policy that has brought the UK Government into open conflict with public sector unions fearful that the experience of contracting out hospital ancillary services will be repeated, their members bearing unfavourable changes in working practices, pay and conditions.

In Scotland, Labour politicians initially distanced themselves from the policy on the grounds that the private sector is comparatively small, arguing that the difference with London was more a consequence of local practicalities and pragmatism than any difference in political philosophy north of the border. Ironically, it is the need for pragmatic action that is also used to justify the extension of the policy in England: 'what matters is what works'. For the purposes of this chapter the central question is whether the ideas will remain an English policy or are they the thin end of a policy wedge that will end the public sector monopoly of health care delivery throughout the UK? Experience over free personal care suggests that Whitehall can resist the pressures of policy innovation in devolved administrations, but is the reverse true? Is it possible for small countries in the UK to steer a different course to England or are they still 'in bed with an elephant...no matter how even tempered and friendly the beast one is affected by every grunt and groan' (Scott 1985)? If administrations of different political colours were in power in each country would the same be true?

After some months of maintaining the position described above, the Scottish Health Minister Malcolm Chisholm, appointed in December 2001 by Jack McConnell, (Scotland's new First Minister following the surprise resignation of Henry McLeish) appears to have noticed the elephant's restlessness. His decision to set-up a national 'Waiting Times Unit' (Chisholm 2002c) includes the proposal to co-ordinate NHS use of private hospitals, including the HCI Hospital, Glasgow, set up (amidst controversy) with substantial public funding by the Conservatives in the early 1990s. This hospital is also the chosen location for NHS24 the Scottish equivalent of NHS

Direct though NHS staff will operate the service. It remains to be seen if ministers elsewhere are prepared to go as far as their English counterparts who have already struck a whole hospital deal with the private sector to deliver care to NHS patients (Milburn 2001a). The perennial problem of hospital waiting times is the key driver of these policies, and it remains the case in all countries that this is the biggest political headache for health ministers. 'Investment and reform' is the prescription in England, but so far other administrations have preferred the former to the latter, at least as it is conceived in Whitehall.

Governance of the NHS

For those people entrusted with responsibility for running health services in the UK most of 2001 was dominated by the implications of the various health plans produced by each administration (Department of Health 2000b; Scottish Executive 2000a; National Assembly 2001a). These plans emerged on the back of the additional resources allocated to health by the 2000 budget, and the discussion in the JMC(H) meetings referred to above. The initiative to prepare plans came from England, which explains why the English plan was published first in July 2000, those for Scotland and Wales appearing some months later, a delay that did not go unnoticed, nor uncritically, in the Scottish press (*Sunday Herald* 2000). No comparable plan was prepared for Northern Ireland though the Minister for Health published 'Priorities for Action in 2001/2002' described as 'a thin echo' of the papers in London and Edinburgh (Constitution Unit 2001a). A far reaching report recommending the restructuring of acute hospital services and administrative structures in the Province rests on the Executive's bookshelves awaiting action (Northern Ireland Executive Department of Health Social Services and Public Safety 2001).

There is a wider point to be made about the plans beyond their content, which is discussed below. It is concerned with the consequences of two of the devolved administrations deciding to follow the English lead. This would have happened as a matter of course in the era of administrative devolution, but with the transfer of political control both countries could have chosen not to do so. Had the devolved administrations produced plans in advance of England they would have acquired significant status as templates for distinctive action; did the fact that they came later feed a perception, whatever their content, that they were invented quickly as a response to developments in England?

The 'Celtic' plans have a greater emphasis on health than the English plan, which is very much a plan for the NHS. In both Wales and Scotland health ministers have been prominent in their support of public health initiatives, and the elected chambers have also devoted time to the debate of the adverse health record in each country, reflecting deep-seated anxieties about poverty and its impact on health. The 'Celtic' plans also emphasise the national identity of their proposals whereas the English plan omitted to say that it was a plan for England. Unlike its counterparts it also had comparatively little to say about the structure of the health services, apart from the controversial proposal to abolish Community Health Councils, the invention of a previous Labour Secretary of State for Health, Barbara Castle.

The Welsh Plan (National Assembly 2001) proposed the abolition of the existing five health authorities, to be replaced by 22 statutory Local Health Boards responsible for both commissioning and providing health care. These new bodies, which are coterminous with Welsh local authorities, are comparatively small and the successors of Local Health Groups themselves creatures of the recent past. Their limited size has required them to be gathered into 'consortia' for the handling of specialist issues. For some there is a sense of growing confusion and growing bureaucracy in the administration of NHS Wales (Constitution Unit 2001b). Implementing these changes requires primary legislation and attempts to achieve that through an NHS (Wales) Bill failed, and instead form part of the NHS Reform Bill published in November 2001. In Scotland, new NHS Boards were created, formalising the partnership of Health Boards and NHS Trusts in what are described as 'boards of governance' (not management) that also have much stronger involvement of local authority members (Scottish Executive 2001a).

In part these changes followed on from the policy developed between 1997 and 1999, indeed the Scottish plan presented itself as the completion of a post-internal market rewiring process. The differences which started to emerge in health service structures in that period were now beginning to become clearer, and became starkly so when the Secretary of State for Health in England surprised his NHS by announcing a wide-ranging restructuring aimed at the devolution of power to local organisations, particularly primary care trusts subsequently elaborated upon in a paper entitled 'Shifting the Balance Within the NHS' (Milburn 2001b). Its main proposals included the creation of 30 larger 'strategic health authorities' as replacements for district health authorities. The regional office structure of the Department of Health was reduced from a network of eight centres to four, covering different geographical areas to those of government offices for the regions (GO) and Regional Development Agencies (RDA), though public health staff from health regional offices have been moved to the GOs.

If these changes feel like the latest of many rearrangements of the NHS bureaucracy, subsequent policy statements (Milburn 2002) on the back of the April 2002 budget indicate that the English health minister is searching for stronger incentives for NHS management through for instance, the introduction of 'earned autonomy' and 'franchised management' for NHS Trusts. Those NHS Trust managements who are judged by independent inspection to be running high performing services will be rewarded with greater freedom to run their organisations independently of central controls, and also have the opportunity to take over poorer performing Trusts. Of course these plans should be seen alongside the expansion of the private sector in service delivery. Together they add to a radical programme of reform in the governance of the NHS England. The destination appears to be a publicly funded delivery system composed of a mix of existing NHS Trusts, not-for-profit, independent and for-profit providers, all of whom aim to win the right to provide care on behalf of Primary Care Trusts, delivered according to national service frameworks, overseen by strategic health authorities, and regulated by a new independent inspection body created from the merger of CHI and Audit Commission functions.

The structures of the health services in all of the countries are now developing quite differently and the process of change is not yet complete. In Northern Ireland, the Executive continues to wrestle with the replacement of GP fundholding; in Wales, the Liberal Democrats have had, at times, different views to the Minister on the restructuring of the health service (National Assembly 2001b); in Scotland the Minister for Health announced in December 2001 an 18 month period of further review that is believed by some to herald the formal end of NHS Trusts and the amalgamation of Scotland's 15 NHS Boards (Chisholm 2001). Organisational change does not capture the public imagination, but the reforms under way are far reaching and reveal a growing willingness on the part of each country to develop governance models with, apparently, limited reference to each other. In doing so they have created something of a natural research laboratory, but more importantly, they may have paved the way for their successors to make even bigger changes in the organisation and perhaps the scope of health services.

The future

The first three years of devolved Government can only be a pointer to subsequent possibilities. They represent the initial playing out of new roles, by new actors on a new stage. To an extent this was inevitable given the policy legacy inherited by the devolved administrations, but there is growing evidence in health of policy divergence taking place. It is customary to look for divergence on the part of the devolved administrations but the other side of this coin is that policy making in England has been developing independently of the devolved countries. As there is less need now for the English health department to share emerging policy across the UK it is entirely possible that any observed divergence of health policy has its explanation in the innovation of English ministers. They enjoy the support of the largest health policy-making machine in the UK and the No 10 Policy Unit takes a close interest in health matters. The health departments of the devolved administrations remain smaller than their English counterpart in spite of the broad equivalence of their responsibilities and if there is uncertainty about the 'right' policy there is some security for smaller countries to do what others seem to be doing. As one of a number of factors this could limit the possibility of further divergence. Four other factors are readily identifiable that may also decide if divergence accelerates or not: party political control and its alignment across the administrations; the identity of the NHS as a UK entity; the growing influence of the European Union; and resources.

Party policy

The interaction of party political loyalty and the exercise of devolved competence in health and NHS policy is one of the most intriguing aspects of post-devolution dynamics. So much of this takes place out of the public eye that it is difficult to unravel, and it is complicated further by new electoral systems that have produced greater diversity in the political makeup of government in the UK than ever before. In Scotland a coalition of Labour and Liberal Democrats formed the first Scottish Executive; in Wales Labour initially led a minority administration now replaced with a coalition with the Liberal Democrats; and in Northern Ireland there is an Executive that contains no Labour politician. It remains the case however that Labour is currently the dominant party in devolved administrations of Great Britain enabling its leadership to reach into devolved matters in a way that may not be possible in the future.

During the period of preparation for the new institutions distinctive health policies were brought forward in each part of the UK, though in this period ministers in each country remained part of the Westminster Government of Tony Blair, and bound to it. Have we been observing the same process post-devolution, albeit that some new inter-government machinery has been put in place? Is it possible to interpret the variation in NHS governance as a modern example of this tradition? On the other hand, the example of free personal care suggests a growing confidence, at least on the part of Henry McLeish if not his cabinet colleagues, to stamp a distinctive identity on the policy of long term care even when the same party controls both executives. Was the decision of Henry McLeish to go his own way a one-off? If so, it looks as though it will survive the change of First Minister and the reported pressure from Whitehall to think again. It is entirely possible that parties with common origins and similar names in each country will develop distinctive identities and policies, less beholden to the UK leadership. Thus the Conservative Party in Scotland also supported free personal care. With the passage of time more of the leading politicians in devolved countries will cut their political teeth in the devolved assemblies, and personal ties and loyalties to colleagues in Westminster will probably weaken.

The current pattern of political control will also change at some point. New elections take place in Wales and Scotland in 2003. Greater diversity in the political control of the administrations would almost certainly lead to greater diversity in policy. This possibility was obviously prominent in the mind of Helen Liddell, Secretary of State for Scotland who sought to make much of the advantages of Labour's dominant position during the UK general election. Writing in The Scotsman newspaper she claimed that political devolution would be most advantageous to Scotland with a Labour administration on either side of the border leading the paper's editorial to wonder why 'if devolution 'works best' only when Labour is simultaneously in office in the Scottish Parliament and at Westminster, what was the point of having devolution in the first place?' (Constitution Unit 2001f). The House of Lords has decided to explore this question through a select committee chaired by Lord Norton of Louth. The passage of time may reveal the early years of devolved government to have been relatively benign, and that the rows within UK political parties about policy in one country or another are nothing to the inter-government disputes which may follow.

Identity

After 50 years the NHS has survived as a concept; it has an identity across the UK and for all the public concern about its performance its founding principles still command substantial support. The values it embraces – equity, access to care according to need not income, public service – find favour in all parts of the UK. Indeed a case can be made for the NHS as one of the institutions that binds the UK together and contributes to its distinctive identity in the wider world. There is evidence that this is the case in longer established federal systems of government, Banting and Corbett (2002) suggesting that there is a special sensitivity associated with health care that constrains pressures to diverge. This appears to be the case in the UK as well. Michael Forsyth, during his time as Secretary of State for Scotland a determined opponent of devolution, proposed the replacement of the NHS in Scotland with the title 'The Scottish Health Service', arguing that the health service in Scotland had sufficient identity of its own to justify the change of name (Scottish Office Department of Health 1997). His successors, committed to devolution, never adopted the proposal such is the place of the NHS in the public mind. The British Medical Journal is still British even though its editor felt moved to caution against it becoming the English Medical Journal after devolution (Jervis and Plowden 2000). Throughout the UK the NHS remains a potent symbol of social solidarity and for many a remarkable political achievement.

There are also strong professional motivations for maintaining a UK identity for the NHS. Regulation of the professions remains a reserved matter (except in Northern Ireland), the medical royal colleges (including the three Scottish colleges) have memberships across the UK, medical research is managed on a UK basis, and major charities that are supporters of such research are UK organisations. Trade Union and professional associations, many of whom have distinctive leaderships in each country, remain nonetheless UK organisations with memberships who are part of UK labour markets (Smith 1999).

The negotiation of pay for doctors and nurses reinforces this. Pay is the largest element in health service costs and for some years government, in the light of recommendations from independent pay review bodies that cover the UK, has determined annual pay awards. Devolved administrations could abandon these arrangements if they wished, perhaps to take account of variations in local labour market conditions, but they have chosen to retain them, not least because they only receive the Barnett formula consequences of Treasury funding for pay factors in England. As the Scottish decision to increase teachers pay has shown, the additional costs of any move away from comparable practice in other countries has to be found from within the Block, which given the size of the health service pay bill could have profound implications for other programmes.

The European Union

Hitherto the European Union (EU) has played a limited role in health policy. There are signs that this is changing. The competence of the EU in health is defined in the Treaty of Amsterdam and is concerned with public health issues rather than the funding and organisation of health care systems. International aspects of health policy are within the competence of the Whitehall Department of Health acting for the UK as a whole (though the Scottish Health Minister represented the UK at a EU Health Council in June 2001), but this has not deterred the Welsh Health Minister seeking direct links with the EU's Commissioner for Health on public health matters.

Other parts of the European treaties, however, are having a growing impact on health services. Amongst them are the EU's competencies in the free movement of goods and services and in employment conditions (now exploited by English ministers seeking to recruit staff from other European countries). For example, the Working Time Directive (European Union 1993) has forced changes in the working hours of junior doctors. Meanwhile in the European Courts citizens of the EU have tested their entitlement to obtain health care without prior approval outside their country of residence under the EU's regulations permitting the free movement of goods and services (Watson 2001). The judgments in these cases have prompted the Secretary of State for Health in England to offer treatment in Europe to English patients suffering long waits, ushering in the prospects of 'health tourism', and the first patients traveled to France on 18 January 2001 (BBC 2002).

Human rights issues also have a growing impact, with the incorporation into domestic law of the European Convention on Human Rights (ECHR). As the implications of the ECHR are explored through the courts long established practices may be challenged, including in Scotland, for example, the compulsory detention of mentally ill patients (Lord President 2000).

It is hard to see how, in a Europe of growing harmonisation, some convergence in health care policy is anything other than inevitable. Increasingly, health threats require international action (for example, HIV and vCJD). Scientific advances in medicine are progressed through international networks; health care suppliers are organising themselves on a global basis; and health policy ideas are being transferred between countries through the activities of the WHO, OECD, the World Bank and the European Union (WHO 2000). Whether Beveridge ever 'meets' Bismarck is less important for this analysis than an acknowledgement that that there will be an interplay of the forces for convergence at a European level and the ambition for greater autonomy in health policy within the countries of the UK.

Resources

A final factor that will influence future health policy in devolved countries is the level of resources available to them. Whilst the Barnett formula continues administrations will make their health spending decisions within the totality of the resources transferred to them, and in the case of Scotland, the exercise of its discretionary tax varying powers of up to 3 pence in the pound. The exercise of this power is unlikely at a time when public expenditures are rising rapidly because of the adverse political consequences it would bring. Similarly, although administrations can choose to allocate the Block amongst their programmes as they think fit, any decision by them to move money into other budgets may prove controversial and politically impractical if growth in the Block derives from Whitehall decisions to increase NHS spending in England (McConnell 2002; Brown 2002).

The announcement of additional funding for the NHS in the Chancellor's pre-budget statement in November 2001 found its way to the health services in every country as has the unprecedented increase in health spending announced in the Budget itself in April 2002, though few commentators seem to have been much concerned that his statement of intent could only apply to England (Nelson 2001). The Chancellor's study (Wanless 2002) of long term health care funding was conducted on a UK basis, but it was a Treasury initiative inviting participation from devolved administrations rather than a review jointly commissioned by them. The decision to increase health spending in England at an average real terms rate of 7.5 per cent over five years stands out as the most significant of all initiatives in health since 1997. Such increases exceed the amounts that the Scottish tax varying power would yield, and no devolved administration could release equivalent amounts from other existing programmes without dire political and service consequences. If a reminder was needed these decisions illustrate that control over public expenditure and taxation remain highly centralised in the UK Treasury (see Heald and McLeod in Chapter 10).

There is, of course, the complication of the Barnett 'squeeze' described earlier, whereby similar per capita spending increases throughout the UK translate into smaller percentage increases in funding in the devolved countries, a matter of concern to them all. This begs the question of whether it can survive the scrutiny which devolution has brought to its operation. The House of Commons Treasury Select Committee considered the continuing validity of the formula in 1997 and concluded that a fresh 'needs assessment' was required to determine if total expenditure rather than annual increases continues to be allocated according to relative need. So far UK Government policy has been to retain the formula and no new needs assessment has been proposed by it, but rumours about and requests for such a review arise frequently. Rumbles of discontent are heard from both the devolved administrations concerned about the 'squeeze' and from parts of England who feel hard done by in comparison with neighbouring countries. Even the formula's 'inventor' Joel Barnett, now a member of the House of Lords, has made the case for a fresh examination of relative need (Treasury Select Committee 1997).

Any new assessment of needs is dependent on so many factors it is impossible to offer any measured comment on its consequences, though Bell and Christie have engaged in some modeling of relative need in the English regions and devolved countries. Long-term care of the elderly has brought these issues to prominence raising questions about the level of public expenditure in Scotland that seemingly enables the Scottish Executive to offer a level of security to the elderly that is unavailable elsewhere. Not so obvious is the price this policy extracts from other programmes. As Bell and Christie have pointed out Barnett is in theory a formula for spending convergence and the 'squeeze' may ultimately mean the costs of this policy will mean some other public service is less well resourced in Scotland than elsewhere (Bell and Christie 2001). Their conclusion is that the current arrangements are incompatible with the devolution of policy-making power and essentially unsustainable. If it seems to be more a matter of how and when the formula is reviewed than if, it is also probably true that the current Westminster government will not rush to undertake it. There is little doubt that such a review would ignite political debate across the UK and because of the significance of health spending as a proportion of devolved budgets could bring in its train a requirement for new thinking about how to fund and deliver health care.

Conclusion

It is impossible to predict with any certainty how the factors discussed in this chapter will interact in the future. Political 'events' and other considerations may come into play, for instance further constitutional change that extends the powers of the current administrations or perhaps the election of nationalist governments in some parts of the UK. Whatever the precise mix of factors there is undoubted potential for health related policy to take on a new and substantially different character in each part of the UK, but will this potential be realised?

After three years of devolved Government it appears that the forces of continuity – inherited policy, party political allegiance, the Barnett formula, a UK identity for the NHS, and a rapidly expanding health budget – remain dominant for all that some differences have emerged. This partly explains the nature of debate during the UK general election in 2001 when it did not seem to matter much to either politicians or the electorate that an argument about proposals for health in England (the role of the private sector) spilled over to the other countries. Perhaps this was because it is now recognised that such policy cannot be binding on the devolved administrations. Or could it be that Whitehall remains the biggest influence on devolved health policy? Could a new ebb and flow of policy ideas develop across the UK electorates? Just as some health policy ideas drifted northwards in the UK election of 2001 could some ideas from Wales or Scotland come ashore in England on the tide of the elections for the devolved assemblies in 2003? It is still early days post-devolution but increasingly new politicians and new political institutions are making their mark on health and health care. As the devolution process evolves, it seems increasingly necessary to speak of the UK's national health services rather than of its NHS.

Acknowledgements

I am grateful to a number of colleagues for their comments on this chapter; and to George France, co-editor of *Politiche Sanitarie* (an Italian public health journal) in which I presented an earlier analysis of health policy in Scotland and developed part of the analytical framework used in this chapter.

Endnotes

1   Available at www.ucl.ac.uk/constitution-unit

References

Armstrong P and Armstrong H (1999) 'Decentralised Health Care in Canada' *BMJ 318* 1201-1204

Banting K and Corbett S (2002) *Health Policy and Federalism* Montreal/Kingston: McGill-Queen's University Press

BBC (2002) 'English patients undergo surgery' 19 January 2002 BBC News Online

Bell D and Christie A (2001) 'The Barnett Formula: Nobody's Child?' in Trench A (ed) *The State of the Nations 2001* Exeter: Imprint Academic

Brown G (2000) 'Budget Statement' *Hansard* 9 March 2000 col 173

Brown G (2002) 'Budget Statement' *Hansard* 17 April 2002 col 577

Chisholm M (2002a) 'Bed Blocking figures released' 14 January 2002 Press Release SE5151 Edinburgh: Scottish Executive

Chisholm M (2002b) 'Free Personal Care timetable extended' 15 January 2002 Press Release SE5162 Edinburgh: Scottish Executive

Chisholm M (2002c) 'New Unit tackles waiting times' 8 January 2002 Press Release SE5129 Edinburgh: Scottish Executive

Chisholm M (2001) *Scottish Parliament Official Record* 12 December 2001 Edinburgh: Scottish Parliament

Commission on Public Private Partnerships (2001) *Building Better Partnerships: Final Report of the Commission on Public Private Partnerships* London: ippr

Constitution Unit (2001a) *Devolution and Health Monitoring Report* Northern Ireland, March 2001

Constitution Unit (2001b) *Devolution and Health Monitoring Report* Wales, September 2001

Constitution Unit (2001c) *Devolution and Health Monitoring Report* Wales, April 2001

Constitution Unit (2001d) *Devolution and Health Monitoring Report* Northern Ireland, September 2001

Constitution Unit (2001e) *Devolution and Health Monitoring Report* Scotland, March 2001

Constitution Unit (2001f) *Devolution and Health Monitoring Report* Scotland, June 2001

Curtice J (2000) 'The Peoples Verdict: Public Attitudes to Devolution and the Union' in Hazell R (ed) *The State and the Nations 2000* Exeter: Imprint Academic.

Deacon S (2000a) *Official Report* SW1-5574 24 July 2000 Edinburgh: Scottish Parliament

Deacon S (2000b) *Official Report* Vol7-1166, 6 July 2000 Edinburgh: Scottish Parliament

Department of Health (2002) *Delivering the NHS Plan* Cmnd Paper 5503 London: The Stationery Office

Department of Health (2000a) *For the Benefit of Patients: A Concordat with the Private and Voluntary Healthcare Provider Sector* London: Department of Health

Department of Health (2000b) *The NHS Plan – A Plan for Investment, A Plan for Reform* Cmnd 4818-1 London: The Stationery Office

Department of Health (1998a) *A First Class Service: Quality in the NHS* London: The Stationery Office

Department of Health (1998b) Press Release 18 March 1998. London: Department of Health

Department of Health (1997a) *A Service With Ambitions* London: The Stationery Office

Department of Health (1997b) Press Release 18 November 1997 London: Department of Health

European Union (1993) 'Council Directive 93/104/EC 23/11/93' *Official Journal of the European Community* 1993L 307/18.

Ham C (1999) *Health Policy in Britain* 4th edition Basingstoke: Macmillan

Hazell R (ed) (2000) *The State and the Nations 2000* Exeter: Imprint Academic

Hazell R and Jervis P (1998) *Devolution and Health* London: Nuffield Trust Series 3

The Herald (2002) 16 January 2002

Jervis P and Plowden W (eds) (2000) *Devolution and Health Monitoring Project: Annual Report* London: The Constitution Unit

The Labour Party (1997) *Because Scotland Deserves Better* London: The Labour Party

Leicester G (2000) 'Scotland' in Hazell R (ed) *The State and the Nations 2000* Exeter: Imprint Academic

Lord President (2000) *Anderson, Doherty, Reid v The Scottish Ministers* Opinion of the Lord President, Court of Session, X170/00

McConnell J (2002) 'Health spending to rise by almost 50 per cent' 18 April Press Release SENW007/2002 Edinburgh: Scottish Executive

McLaren G and Bain M (1998) *Deprivation and Health in Scotland* Information and Statistics Division, The Common Services Agency of the NHS in Scotland, Edinburgh

McLeish H (2001) 'Free personal care within seven months' 24 September 2001, Press Release SE4033 Edinburgh: Scottish Executive

Milburn A (2002) *Redefining the NHS: Speech to the New Health Network* 15 January, London: Department of Health www.doh.gov.uk/speeches

Milburn A (2001a) 'NHS partnership with private sector' 4 December 2001 Press Release 2001/0593 London: Department of Health

Milburn A (2001b) *Shifting the Balance of Power in the NHS: Speech at the launch of the NHS Modernisation Agency* 25 April, London: Department of Health www.doh.gov.uk/speeches

National Assembly (2001a) *Improving Health in Wales: A plan for the NHS and its partners* Cardiff: National Assembly for Wales.

National Assembly (2001b) 'Debate on Structural Reform in the NHS' *Official Record* 27 November 2001 Cardiff: National Assembly for Wales

Nelson F (2001) 'Thinking needs adjusted north of the border' 28 November 2001 Edinburgh: The Scotsman

Northern Ireland Executive Department of Health Social Services and Public Safety (2001) *Report of the Acute Hospitals Review Group* (Chairman, M Hayes) Belfast: Northern Ireland Executive

Northern Ireland Office, Department of Health and Social Services (1998) *Fit for the Future: A consultation document on the Government's proposals for the future of health and personal social services in Northern Ireland* Belfast: The Stationery Office

ONS (1999) *Regional Trends 34* London: The Stationery Office

Osmond J (2000) 'A Constitutional Convention by Other Means' in Hazell R (ed) *The State and the Nations 2000* Exeter: Imprint Academic

Royal Commission on Long Term Care (1999) *With Respect to Old Age, Report of The Royal Commission on Long Term Care* (Chairman Sir Stewart Sutherland), Cmnd 4192-1, London: The Stationery Office

Salmond A (2000) quoted in Hazell R 'Intergovernment Relations: Whitehall Rules OK?' in Hazell R (ed) *The State and the Nations 2000* Exeter: Imprint Academic

Scott D (2001) 'McLeish: I Stake my career on Free Care' *Scotsman* 30 January 2001

Scott P (1985) *In Bed With an Elephant* Edinburgh: Saltire Society Booklet – a title popularised by Kennedy L (1996) *In Bed With an Elephant: A Journey Through Scotland's Past and Present* London: Corgi Books

Scottish Executive (2002) *Review of Management and Decision Making in NHS Scotland* published on 3 April 2002 in a letter to the NHS Scotland from its Chief Executive Edinburgh: Scottish Executive Department of Health

Scottish Executive (2000a) *Our National Health: A Plan for Action: A Plan for Change* Edinburgh: The Stationery Office

Scottish Executive (2000b) 'Joint Ministerial Committee on Health' Press Release, SE01039/2000, Edinburgh: Scottish Executive

Scottish Executive Department of Health (2001a) *Fair Care for Older People – Care Development Group Report* 14 September Edinburgh: Scottish Executive

Scottish Executive Department of Health (2001b) *Rebuilding Our National Health* Edinburgh: Scottish Executive

Scottish Executive Department of Health (1999) *Fair Shares for All: Report of the Review of Resource Allocation for the NHS in Scotland* Edinburgh: The Stationery Office

Scottish Office (1998) *PFI Scotland* Edition 4, Edinburgh: Scottish Office

Scottish Office Department of Health (1997) *The Scottish Health Service: Ready for the Future* Cmnd 3551 Edinburgh: The Stationery Office

Scottish Office Department of Health (1998a) *Designed to Care* Cmnd 3811 Edinburgh: The Stationery Office

Scottish Office Department of Health (1998b) *Acute Services Review Report* Edinburgh: The Stationery Office

Scottish Office Home Department (1997) *Modernising Community Care: An Action Plan* Edinburgh: Scottish Office

Scottish Parliament (2001) *2nd Report: National Health Bodies in Tayside* Edinburgh: Scottish Parliament Audit Committee

Scottish Parliament (2000) *9th Report: Report on Strathcathro Petition PE13* Edinburgh: Scottish Parliament Health and Community Care Committee

Scottish Parliament (1999) *Official Report, Meeting of the Health and Community Care Committee* 27 October 1999, col 271-314 Edinburgh: Scottish Parliament

Smith R (1999) 'Editorial: Avoiding becoming the English Medical Journal' *BMJ 318* 1158-1159, May 1999

The Sunday Herald (2000) 30 July 2000

Treasury Select Committee (1997) *2nd Report The Barnett Formula* HC 341, 22 June Q211

Wanless D (2002) *Securing our Future Health: Taking a Long-Term View* April 2002, London: HM Treasury

Wanless D (2001) *Securing Our Future Health: Interim Report* November 2001, London: HM Treasury

Watson (2001) 'European Court ruling paves the way for cross border health care' *BJ 323* 128, July. European Court of Justice

Welsh Office (1998) *Putting Patients First* Cardiff: The Stationery Office

WHO (2000) *World Health Organisation Report 2000: Health Systems: Improving performance* Geneva: WHO

Woods K (2001) 'Sweden Today, Britain Tomorrow?' *British Journal of Health Care Management* 7.6 227 –230

3. Health policy: differentiation and devolution
Mike Sullivan

Kevin Woods' comprehensive chapter covers a wide range of issues relating to the impact of devolution on health. Within the limitations of the prescribed word limit for this piece, it is not possible to do justice either to the rich detail or to the broad scope of Woods' chapter. Rather, I intend to concentrate on a key feature of differentiation in health policy in the family of United Kingdom nations and to suggest that this differentiation (a) predates political devolution in the UK[1] and (b) is rooted in differently nuanced 'Labourisms'. In what follows, I consider the different emphases on involvement and participation in health policy before and after the devolution settlements. In brief, my argument is that these go to the heart of differing conceptions of the relationship between government and the citizen and that these differing conceptions are rooted in distinct Labour traditions and politics. As an example of pre-devolution differentiation, I consider the English, Welsh and Scottish White Papers (1997-98) as indicative of my argument.

Differentiation before devolution[2]

In the context of, and run up to, political devolution to Wales, Scotland and Northern Ireland, three White Papers appeared on the refurbishment and modernisation of the NHS. Each of them was informed by a set of values reflecting the key concerns of the Labour Government. While the foreword to the English White Paper (Department of Health 1997) talks of the importance of 'modernisation', the Welsh and Scottish versions focus on the need to 'restore' the NHS. In Wales, this was expressed as 'reaffirming its founding principles and devising new responses to the challenges which face it' (Welsh Office 1998, introduction to section 1) while in Scotland the aim was 'to restore the National Health Service as a public service working co-operatively for patients' (Scottish Office 1997, Foreword).

These aims are underpinned by a number of key principles, chief among them being a new emphasis in all three White Papers on accountability. This perhaps illustrates UK New Labour's emphasis on the 'third way'.

The 'third way'

As far as the NHS is concerned, this 'third way' is described in the foreword to each of the White Papers as replacing the internal market with integrated care, combining efficiency and effectiveness with fairness and partnership. There is, however, some difference between the English approach on the one hand, and the Scottish and Welsh on the other. Whereas the English White Paper identified the need for partnership between health and local authorities as one of six key principles (chapter 2), the need for partnerships at a number of different levels is spelled out in both the Welsh (paragraph 1.15) and Scottish (paragraph 8) versions, which describe the need for collaboration between:

- government and the electorate

- patients and professionals

- the NHS and other statutory and voluntary bodies

- NHS organisations

This difference in emphasis is best seen as reflecting the need to re-negotiate relationships between politicians, health and social services and the public in Wales and Scotland in response to the creation of the Welsh Assembly and the Scottish Parliament.

Involvement

The English White Paper laid emphasis on improving information and services *for* rather than *with* patients and the public. Great faith was placed in the ability of information and IT 'to create a powerful alliance between knowledgeable patients *advised* by knowledgeable professionals as a means of improving health and healthcare' (paragraph 3.15, emphasis added). Within what is an essentially passive model of patient involvement (Sullivan1994), information-giving is presented as a neutral technical exercise in which patients will be expected to comply with professional advice rather than actively sharing decision-making (Sullivan and Pickering 1997). The main emphasis here is on 'providing knowledge about health, illness and best treatment practice to the public' (paragraph 3.15). At the same time, health authorities were to engage the public more actively by 'ensuring public involvement in decision making about the local health services' (paragraph 4.19). The main mechanisms for this were Health Action Zones, which 'will offer opportunities to explore new ways of involving local people'; public involvement in the development of the Health Improvement Programme and National Service Frameworks (paragraph 7.8); and 'effective arrangements for public involvement' in Primary Care Groups (paragraph 4.9), which, however, are to shape services *'for patients'* (3.6, emphasis added). For their part, trusts will have to have public board meetings and publish information on trust performance, given that 'openness and public involvement will be key features of all parts of the new NHS' (paragraph 2.23). Once again, however, the emphasis is on giving information *to* rather than actively working *with* users and the public, and the White Paper has little else to say about 'involvement'.

In contrast, while the Welsh and Scottish White Papers share the English version's unquestioning faith in the transformative power of IT, information and advice lines, their approach implied a more pro-active model of user and public involvement. The Welsh White Paper, for example, is permeated by references to the importance of the patient focus and contains numerous *requirements* for involvement at all levels:

- 'Steps *must* be taken to find out what patients and communities want' (Wales 3.31, emphasis added)

- 'The NHS *should* give the highest priority to looking at services from the patient's perspective' as well as responding to their perceptions (paragraph 3.18, emphasis added).

- 'Service planning and delivery *should* be designed through the eyes of the patient' (paragraph 3.4, emphasis added)

- Particular emphasis should be placed on involving patients in clinical decision-making (paragraph 3.18) and 'NHS organisations are *required* to examine new approaches to care which focus on the patient's journey through the process' (paragraph 3.27, emphasis added)

- Patient evaluation of services is to be measured against the same criteria as those of professionals and managers (paragraph 3.20) and clinicians need to maximise the potential of audit by recognising the importance of patients' views/experiences' (paragraph 3.29)

The achievement of these aims was to be the responsibility of each part of NHS Wales. Health authorities were exhorted to:

> play their part in rebuilding public confidence by ensuring public participation in the development of Health Improvement Programmes; ensuring that Local Health Groups have effective public involvement; publication of their performance agreement with the Assembly and including a *requirement* in their agreements with local trusts that improved arrangements are established to represent the views of service users. (Introduction)

For their part, trusts were *required* to put in place new arrangements for patient representation (paragraph 3.33), they were *required* to improve communication with patients (paragraph 6.8) and 'oversee a programme for public liaison, co-ordinate the dissemination of information and respond to complaints and suggestions' (paragraph 6.18).

Much of this is echoed in the Scottish White Paper:

> Our starting point is that every aspect of the planning and delivery of services should be designed from the perspective of patients... The Government therefore expect all parts of the NHS to give priority at the highest level to the examination of services from the perspective of patients and to making changes designed to improve their experience of the NHS. *This will be a key test of organisational performance.* (paragraph 14, emphases added)

In stressing the need for services to be responsive to the needs of both individual patients and the public as a whole, the White Paper indicated the need for 'finding out what patients and communities want, and consulting them over proposals for change' (paragraph 36). At the individual level, patients were to be involved 'to a greater extent in decisions about their own care and treatment' (paragraph13), 'where possible allowing them to exercise choice, in consultation with their GP or the consultant to whom they have been referred' (paragraph 28). At the level of the community, the NHS was encouraged to work with Local Health Councils as well as finding 'other means of ensuring public involvement in the planning of services' and health boards were *required* to 'undertake thorough and imaginative consultation' on their Health Improvement Programme (paragraph 37). Responsibility for all this work will lie with a member of the executive team of health boards and trusts and progress will be part of their performance management (paragraph 38).

Devolution and differentiation

If differentiation characterised the politics of health policy in the pre-devolution period, this tendency has been sharpened since the formation of the Welsh Assembly and the Scottish Parliament. As evidence here, I cite the NHS Plans developed by the English, Welsh and Scottish administrations (Scottish Executive 2000, National Assembly for Wales 2001, Department of Health 2000). Here it seems to me, the differing conceptions and political traditions to which I have referred are writ fairly large.

Improving Health in Wales: a plan for the NHS with its partners seeks, *inter alia*, to put policy meat on the rhetorical bones of both public involvement and the need for the NHS to be part of the development of a new health policy trajectory in Wales which emphasises the primacy of public health (Greer 2000). In her Foreword to the

Plan, the Welsh Minister for Health and Social Services writes:

> I am delighted to introduce proposals, which place the citizen at the centre
> of the NHS and, building on an enviable record in Wales, establish firm
> lines of accountability to the people and communities of our nation. The
> NHS will, as part of its renewal, truly become the people's NHS. This
> involves not only maintaining the patient-centred focus of our services but
> also making the NHS answerable to all citizens – patients and potential
> patients alike. It also means involving communities in the collective
> development of policies for health and well being and makes the process of
> health policy making inclusive. Accountability to communities is thus
> integrated – with clinical and corporate governance – into a whole-system
> accountability system. We will enhance patient and citizen rights in the
> NHS. Not only will the NHS focus on patient need, it will also introduce
> new rights for citizens and communities. These will include the involvement
> of the public in NHS appointment panels, the creation of a more accessible
> complaints system and the strengthening and enhancement of the role of
> Community Health Councils. These new rights are part of a partnership
> between NHS Wales and the Welsh people. As in any partnership, rights
> also imply responsibilities. We are committed to ensuring health care of the
> highest standard and being accountable to the people. We are also
> committed to ensuring that citizens are actively involved in protecting their
> own health and the health of their community. To that end, this Plan looks
> to the active engagement of citizens in promoting their own health and well-
> being so that many health problems are prevented before they begin.

This dramatic commitment is given substance in Chapter 3 of the document –
interestingly entitled *The People's NHS* where the scope of and mechanisms for
involvement are addressed. A close examination of them indicates an interesting
emphasis on the nature of the contract between Administration, NHS and citizens in
Wales. Put simply, the contract implied in the Welsh renewal of the NHS is one
which stresses the connections between government, service planners and providers
and communities of citizens. This is enhanced by the Welsh Administration's
abolition of health authorities and the relocation of power closer to the citizen in
local health boards which have coterminous boundaries with local authorities.

The Plan is also intriguing as it is unique in its development out of an essentially
public health document which places the NHS at, or near, the centre of a partnership
network of policy actors engaged in the development of policy and practice rooted in
the social and economic determinants of health.

The Scottish Plan on the other hand – while rhetorically committed like its Welsh counterpart to consultation and involvement and to a public health agenda – retains existing structural arrangements substantially intact and sees the NHS, rather than the NHS with its partners, as driving the health policy trajectory. Interestingly, the ownership of the Service is couched in the language of participation while, to a great extent, the NHS is still regarded as the legitimate concern of three groups of stakeholders: politicians, professionals and managers. A close reading of the Scottish document also suggests an implicit contract. But, unlike the Welsh approach, it is a fairly orthodox contract between government and the individual citizen.

The English Plan, sometimes and unkindly seen as the master document as its writ runs, in some important respects, throughout the UK, is relatively straightforward. It encapsulates a commitment to improving the health service rather than health or health policy. It implies a contract between government, service and customer (rather than citizen or communities) and its horizons stretch little further than more effective service provision.

Some conclusions

What can be drawn out of this too brief response to Kevin Woods' chapter can be summarised as follows.

- Policy differentiation in relation to the NHS and health policy pre-existed political devolution, though it might well have been encouraged by a large measure of administrative devolution.

- Policy differentiation, and potentially its impacts, has been sharpened by political devolution.

- Implicit in the differentiation that has occurred, and is occurring, is a differentiated Labour Party and Labour dominated administrations in Scotland and Wales with different takes on the political philosophy of Labour.

- Put crudely, the fusion of an Old Labour tradition and a quasi-syndicalist impulse in Wales highlights the collective nature of the contemporary politics of health policy. In England, on the other hand, the Blairite emphasis on consumerism permeates the Plan and contributes to a individually – some say individualistically – focussed document. The Scottish approach sits, or so it seems to me, between the two.

- Collective ownership of the NHS, joint working with local government, voluntary organisations and communities – at all levels from problem identification through to policy solutions – is the golden thread that runs through the Welsh document and is based on notions of community enhancement and community capacity building substantially absent in the English and Scottish documents.

Finally, an irony. For the moment at least, the Welsh settlement is constitutionally the weakest of the devolved administrations. Indications are however that, notwithstanding this, policy differentiation from the English model is most obvious.

Endnotes

1   A large degree of administrative devolution existed in Wales from the formation of the Welsh Office in the mid 1960s while Scotland has historically had a policy-making role – particularly in relation to its legal and educational systems.

2   I am particularly indebted in this section to conversations with, and the work of, the late Dr Sue Sullivan.

References

Department of Health (2000) *The NHS Plan: a plan for investment, a plan for reform* London: The Stationery Office

Department of Health (1997) *The New NHS: modern, dependable* Cm 3807 London: The Stationery Office

Greer S (2001) *Divergence and Devolution* London: Constitution Unit

National Assembly for Wales (2001) *Improving Health in Wales: a plan for the NHS with its partners* Cardiff: National Assembly for Wales

Scottish Executive (2000) *Our National Health: a plan for action, a plan for change* Edinburgh: The Stationery Office

Scottish Office (1997) *Designed to Care: Renewing the National Health Service in Scotland* Cm 3811 London: The Stationery Office

Sullivan S and Pickering N (1997) *Patient and Carer Involvement in Clinical Decision Making: A Review of the Literature* Llandough: Clinical Effectiveness Support Unit Wales

Sullivan S (1994) *Involving the Public in Health and Social Care Planning* unpublished paper prepared for NHS Wales Cymru Public Engagement Group

Welsh Office (1998) *NHS Wales: Putting patients first* Cm 3841 London: The Stationery Office

III:
Economic
Development

4. Industrial and regional policy in a devolved United Kingdom

Andrew Gillespie and Paul Benneworth

In considering the implications of devolution for industrial and regional policy in Britain,[1] it is important first to clarify the distinction between these two policy domains, and to recognise the particular forms of industrial and regional policies that prevailed in 1997, when the election of New Labour opened the doors to devolution.

The distinction between industrial and regional policies is by no means straightforward, as industrial policies can be either 'spatially blind' or 'spatially sensitive', in the latter case of which they can become congruent with regional economic policies. Examples of spatially blind industrial policies would include nationalisation, privatisation, sectoral policies, technology policies, science policies, enterprise policies, competitiveness policies, cluster policies and so on, which are framed primarily as *national* industrial policies. Such policies may, indeed almost invariably do, have differential regional impacts and implications, but these are effectively unintended consequences. The same types of policies can, however, be framed with regional differentiation and differing regional needs in mind, or indeed they can be framed specifically to reduce the degree of regional variation in industrial performance, in which case they become synonymous with regional policies: an example would be a 'national' industrial policy which had as its primary objective raising the industrial performance of lagging regions.

In situations in which national industrial policies are primarily spatially blind, which was the situation prevailing in 1997, we can anticipate that devolution is clearly likely to lead to industrial policies in the devolved territories becoming differentiated from the policies of the English remainder, in that industrial policies for Scotland and Wales are likely to come to reflect the specific needs, problems and potentialities of the Scottish and Welsh economies, which for historical reasons are very different from the UK economy (and, indeed, from each other). Further, we can anticipate that 'national' (or English?) industrial policies will have become more spatially sensitive since 1997, with the result that, together with the effects of devolution to Scotland and Wales, we can expect an increasingly spatially differentiated set of industrial policies to be emerging. Effectively, therefore, the distinctions between industrial policies and regional policies will be blurring.

The election of New Labour in 1997 signalled a marked change in both industrial and regional policy, though the direction of change has certainly not involved a return to the industrial and regional policies of 'Old Labour'. If we take the mid-1970s as the 'high water mark' of interventionist industrial policy, a policy paradigm can be discerned which involved state ownership of a number of key industries, the subsidisation and bailing-out of politically or strategically important industries which got into difficulties, policies of attempting to 'back winners' in terms of the industries of the future, and encouraging mergers so that 'national champions' could be created. A number of these policies were spatially sensitive, unsurprisingly given that the nationalised industries (such as coal and steel) tended to have clearly demarcated geographies of production, and the 'lame ducks' that were bailed-out, such as British Leyland, were also often concentrated in particular cities and regions. These relatively spatially sensitive industrial policies were complemented by strong regional policies, which had the aim of steering industrial investment to the regions of northern England, Scotland and Wales which were suffering from the run-down of (nationalised) coal-mining, steel and other traditional staple industries. The main mechanisms of this interventionist regional policy included the Regional Employment Premium and automatic capital investment subsidies in the form of the Regional Development Grant.

The election of a radical free-market Conservative government in 1979 heralded the dismantling of interventionist industrial and regional policies. The *laissez-faire* approach to industrial policy reached its apotheosis in the wholesale privatisation of previously state-owned industries, while regional policy, if not entirely abandoned, was relegated from an economic to a social, ameliorative role, with the reduction in scale of the assisted areas and the replacement of automatic grants with much more selective forms of assistance directed at capital investment in the assisted regions.

In the early 1990s, the beginnings of the re-creation of industrial policy can be traced to the (re-)arrival of Michael Heseltine at the DTI in 1992. He was responsible for initiating the 'competitiveness' agenda which has dominated the UK's industrial policy landscape for the ensuing decade. The basis of this approach was to offer a middle way between intervention and *laissez-faire* economics, assisting on the supply-side to overcome market failures in areas such as high technology skills. The intention was to increase the competitiveness of UK businesses and generate national wealth; as such, it was very much a spatially-blind national industrial policy.

With the election of New Labour in May 1997, there has been no return to the interventionist industrial policies of the 1970s, with 'anything redolent of corporatism, picking winners and rescuing lame ducks [being] off the agenda' (Coates 2001). Instead, a 'non-interventionist activism' has been espoused, which aims to refocus the competitiveness agenda of the previous government towards knowledge-based competitiveness. The rhetoric contained in the key documents of this approach, the 1998 and 2001 White Papers and the 2000 Science White Paper emphasised this 'light touch' approach:

The present Government will not resort to the interventionist policies of the past. In the industrial policy making of the 1960s and 1970s, to be modern meant believing in planning. Now, meeting the requirements of the knowledge-driven economy means making markets work better. (DTI 1998)

This then is the context within which, for the remainder of the chapter, we examine the implications of devolution for the development of industrial and regional economic policies in Scotland, Wales and the English regions. Although, for the reasons outlined above, we anticipated that devolution is likely to have created the conditions for policy divergence, our findings suggest that, while there are certainly elements of divergence discernible, paradoxically one can also point to some examples of policy *convergence*. The paradox is explained by the fact that industrial and regional policies had already diverged considerably in the period from 1975 to 1997, and that the beginnings of a re-invigoration of English regional policy since 1997 (and particularly since 2001) has seen the first signs of a 'closing of the gap' between Scotland and Wales on the one hand and England on the other, though admittedly from a widely divergent set of starting points.

Policy divergence 1975-97

The Scottish Development Agency (SDA) was created in 1975 in response to the rising popularity of the Scottish Nationalists, and as an attempt to address some of those structural problems facing Scotland which were beginning to manifest themselves in rising unemployment. The Welsh Development Agency (WDA) was created the next year as a similar response to the electoral pressures posed by Plaid Cymru. Although the 1970s devolution 'project' was ultimately to prove abortive, the presence of these large strategic bodies in Scotland and Wales during the 1980s and 1990s – when UK national industrial policies had changed considerably away from intervention and regional policies had been substantially down-graded – acted to focus and give coherence to their territorial development policies.

The SDA and the WDA, congruent with the Scottish and Welsh Offices respectively[2] were keen as being seen as strong advocates for their regions (Danson *et al* 1992). As development agencies responsible to territorial ministries, they were able to gain sanction to deviate from the official prescriptions of the centre. By contrast, in the English regions there were no state bodies that could effectively 'campaign' for policy implementation more sensitive to regional needs; in the 1976 White Paper outlining English options for devolution, both an English development agency and English regional development agencies had been ruled out as policy options (Office of the Lord President of the Council 1976).

Both the SDA and the WDA were originally created as organisations to focus on the attraction of flagship inward investment projects. Initially, there was a separation of powers between the development agencies and the centre, with the latter retaining control over designation of the areas for assistance and the allocation of grants for employment and investment support, whilst the two RDAs provided factories, industrial estates and environmental improvement. Inward investment became important to them, because the projects which inward investment brought were comparatively productive in terms of employment creation, and were useful in justifying their continued existence.

Subsequently the exercise of powers under the Industrial Development Act shifted from the Department of Industry to the Scottish and Welsh Offices,[3] and the development agencies, representing the government, could entice, and at times coerce, other local and regional actors to join coalitions offering packages of support to investors. In England, meanwhile, the hurdles to obtaining investment support in the assisted areas were being raised by the replacement of automatic grants by more selective (and hence politicised) decision-making, while the bodies established to attract inward investment, institutions of variable scale and quality, had to attempt to assemble local coalitions of supportive actors without the incentives the heavily funded SDA and WDA could offer.

This divergence represents the first devolution-led tension within industrial policy, and arose because administrative devolution, leading to the establishment of Scottish and Welsh development agencies and to the transfer of responsibility for regional selective assistance to the Scottish and Welsh Offices, permitted Scotland and Wales to compete more aggressively with the English regions to attract inward investment. This became particularly contentious towards the end of this period, when authorities in English regions became aware that Scotland and Wales were proving disproportionately successful in the promotion of inward investment (Trade and Industry Select Committee 1997). Whilst the Government Offices in the English regions (which had been established in 1994) were assembling local partnerships to support investors once they had arrived, Scottish Enterprise (as the SDA had become in 1989) and the WDA were pro-actively seeking to increase their share of investment at the expense of other regions.

This divergence in the 1975-97 period in the effectiveness of industrial and regional policies between England on the one hand and Scotland and Wales on the other, was also accompanied by a divergence in policies and powers between Wales and Scotland. Scottish Enterprise had not limited itself as a development agency to the attraction of inward investment, but had begun to seriously address questions of endogenous regional capacity, helped by an accretion of powers. When, in the late 1980s, the Training and Enterprise Councils (TECs) were being created in England and Wales, a quite separate set of arrangements were introduced in Scotland. They gave Scottish Enterprise control over Restart and work-based training and local economic development, to be delivered through a network of Local Enterprise

Companies. This provided an institutional basis in Scotland for policy integration and 'joining up', in that there was a single body with responsibility for training, enterprise, local economic development, regeneration, innovation and land reclamation.

Scottish Enterprise later capitalised on the opportunity this provided for joined-up policy by publishing in 1996 an integrated economic development strategy for Scotland spanning training, business advice and land assembly: *Competitive Locations* (Scottish Enterprise 1996). Another powerful example of the different path being pursued in Scotland, permitted by its relative administrative autonomy from the centre, was the adoption, in the early 1990s, of 'clusters' to drive Scottish industrial policy.

Although driven partly by an attempt to reinvent itself by importing external expertise in strategy development, the strategic clusters approach initiated by Scottish Enterprise broadened its view of industrial policy beyond the attraction of inward investment. The Scottish model was to identify key sectors, and enact appropriate cluster policy processes, mapping clusters, tailoring support policies to the clusters' needs, ultimately to boost innovation and the territorial attractiveness of Scotland. As Scottish Enterprise was in possession of a broad-based set of responsibilities covering education and training besides inward investment attraction and support, the cluster approach was able to fit more closely with the needs and potential of the Scottish economy.

By the mid 1990s then, Scottish Enterprise had established itself as an effective regional body, and used the latitude in its relationship with the Scottish Office to begin to pursue a number of quite distinct agendas, promoting both clusters and entrepreneurship several years before they were to appear on the English agenda. The 1996 Competitiveness White Paper made it clear that Scotland was (and had the freedom so to do) pursuing its own policies, and explained how these policies were compatible with the economic development philosophy the DTI was promoting (DTI 1996).

The situation in Wales was different to the situation in Scotland, but also to the English regions. Administrative devolution to Wales was less comprehensive than to Scotland, with two countervailing effects. The first was that the WDA lacked the broad range of policy tools such as education and training which Scottish Enterprise had joined up through their various strategies. However, because the WDA was the main institution for economic development, it enjoyed a pre-eminent and privileged relationship with the Welsh Office, who realised that Welsh economic development was dependent on the success of the WDA. In its heyday, the WDA enjoyed a close working relationship with the Welsh Office who put a wide range of planning and industrial support tools at its disposal. The strength of the coalition was demonstrated in the ill-fated LG project,[4] where the WDA and Welsh Office provided a perfect environment for the inward investor. Certainly, the failure of that project to realise its potential was no consequence of the strength of institutional relationships in Wales.

Although the extent of administrative devolution in Wales prior to 1997 was undoubtedly less advanced than that of Scotland prior to 1997, it is important to note also the structural differences between the Scottish and Welsh economies; by the mid 1990s, Scotland had recovered to a GDP level comparable with the UK average whilst Welsh GDP had continued to decline in relative terms. This placed a greater imperative on employment creation in Wales, so it is important not to ascribe all the differences in outcome to the relative strength of the devolved administrations. What the case of LG does illustrate is the much greater latitude that Wales enjoyed with respect to the English regions (insofar as they had any latitude at all).

In England, regional policy was characterised by the virtual absence of regional networks until the late 1990s. When the requirement to formulate regional 'single programming documents' (SPDs) was introduced for the European Structural Funds, the European Commission was extremely unwilling to accept the documents which came out of the English regions because they showed evidence of having been written centrally. From 1994 onwards, Government Offices began to assemble regional coalitions, but these were primarily oriented towards writing SPDs acceptable to the Commission rather than taking any wider decisions. When the Government Offices produced their Regional Competitiveness Strategies in early 1997, they likewise lacked the imprimatur of any regional decision-making capacity, and were quietly abandoned after the elections that year.

Thus even prior to the formal devolution in the 1997-2001 Parliament, it had become clear that the divergence of administrative and institutional arrangements in the territories of the UK had unleashed tensions which undermined the notion of a single, nationally-determined industrial policy. These tensions had manifested themselves in the divergence of industrial policy approaches and activities. Scotland had moved furthest towards a regionally-determined industrial policy, whilst Wales' situation was more centrally influenced and negotiated: the WDA had latitude, but only to deliver centrally-determined economic development priorities (the attraction of inward investment). Conversely, in England industrial policy was arguably less regional than at any time since the passing of the 1936 Special Areas Act.

Industrial policy under devolution: Scotland and Wales 1997-2002

The contemporary situation in both Scotland and Wales reflects the fact that devolution was enacted by giving new political bodies oversight of existing administrative structures. This meant the political divergence which devolution engendered was very different in each of the territories, taking as its starting point the existing administrative situation. It is possible to argue that there were very different outcomes in Scotland and Wales, and that these differences arose from the different ways devolution was framed between the two.

In our view, these differences do reflect a pre-existing divergence, as we have argued above. Scottish Enterprise and the WDA had already begun to pursue very different agendas and interests prior to 1997. It is therefore unsurprising that they have achieved very different outcomes since devolution. What devolution has enabled is the continuing divergence of structures away from the current Westminster and Whitehall policy networks, notwithstanding the work of the Joint Ministerial Committee (JMC). In Scotland, where Scottish Enterprise has long been independent of Whitehall, tangible evidence of divergence is discernible in terms of policy outcomes. By contrast, the situation in Wales has seen a partial divergence, which we characterise as mainly structural, but which is likely to be a necessary precondition of more tangible outcomes.

Scotland: new political choices in a stable administrative environment

The main impact of Scottish devolution has been to encourage continued divergence. An important part of devolution has been a redefinition of the boundaries of what the 'state' does. In that context, one of the most important policy statements to come out of Scotland has been the Framework for the Economic Development of Scotland (FEDS), published by the Ministry of Enterprise and LifeLong Learning in 2000, which explicitly made the case for progressive/redistributive public policy in the field of economic development. It is hard to envisage HM Treasury or the DTI writing anything as candid or as interventionist as the FEDS position:

> Indeed, intervention in market activity will be considered – irrespective of whether the markets operate efficiently or inefficiently – if they fail to deliver the equity outcomes that are desired. (Ministry for Enterprise and Lifelong Learning 2000)

This bold statement is part of a more general tendency towards a distinctive style of Scottish industrial policy. Economic development policy is a devolved matter, and so the Executive has wide ranging competence to decide on the strategic thrust and direction of economic development policy. The Business Birthrate Strategy (BBRS), the retention of the Scottish Enterprise Network model and the introduction of community planning in the post-devolution period would be listed by Scottish practitioners as evidence of a distinct Scottish policy style.

However, it is important to stress that these policies have continued divergent paths begun under the Scottish Office regime, and implemented by bodies which evolved prior to the current round of devolution, such as Scottish Enterprise. Scotland has been a remarkable laboratory for policies which have later been adopted in England. The BBRS is the latest in a series of distinctively Scottish competitiveness policies which have only latterly been taken up in England. Through the work of Scottish Enterprise in *Competitive Locations* and the Scottish cluster strategies, Scottish interest in the competitiveness agenda has been heavily focused on entrepreneurship, which is arguably a reflection of poor rates of formal entrepreneurship in Scotland.

By contrast, Scotland appears not to have been particularly innovative in its use of the powers of industrial intervention (particularly Regional Selective Assistance). These have been re-badged and stream-lined rather than more comprehensively re-aligned with the interventionist approach alluded to in FEDS. The Scottish Executive has been criticised by some for failing to really do anything more substantive in terms of regional policy than re-badging old policies and departments. In other areas, there has been the persistence of the existing situation: there remain strong sub-national pressures for a Scottish regional policy to address the cleavages between the East and West coast urban areas, between the Central Belt and the rest of Scotland, and the unique situation of the Highlands & Islands.

The case of Scotland illustrates the different changes which devolution involves that are likely to lead to substantive policy divergence between the territories of the UK. First, institutions are necessary in order to make a difference, and those institutions which have had the greatest impact in the short period of devolved government are those that were already operational, such as Scottish Enterprise.

Second, the change of scale of government has led to a resurgence of what could be termed 'sub-regional' issues within Scotland. The dynamic and logic of these debates are specific to Scotland, and so over time the political debate over the direction and nature of policy can be expected to lead to a divergent Scottish industrial policy because of the way these specificities and internal sub-regional tensions become incorporated.

Third, Scotland demonstrates that for policy divergence to occur, a propensity to be experimental and to try new policy approaches has to be well developed. We would contend that, for a no doubt complex set of reasons, Scotland has demonstrated such a propensity, and has remained extremely innovative in the field of public industrial and regional policy. The development of a new Scottish science strategy, to take a recent example, is leading to a change in the way university research funding was allocated in Scotland (Scottish Executive 2001). It aims to increase the investment potential of the expenditure and to capture an increased share of the UK science budget (which is allocated on the basis of scientific excellence). This has attracted interest from English regions with below average public sector science budgets who see similar potential for increasing their own share of the science budget, particularly the North East and the North West. This has happened despite the fact that 'UK science policy' *strictu sensu* remains a reserved matter.

Wales: finding the limits to new opportunities

Devolution to Wales has been limited by the restriction of its legislative powers to secondary legislation, although there are a significant range of devolved powers relevant to the promotion of Welsh economic development. Undeniably, there is a rhetoric in Wales that devolution has led to something significant happening, although there is some debate over the nature and consequence of that 'something'. Commentators have remarked that devolution has at least led to the formation of 'Team Cymru' for any particular project or activity, a much clearer sense of the Welsh interest has led to much more effective ways of co-operation and delivery.

Under the terms of the Government of Wales Act (1999), the National Assembly for Wales (NAW) has considerable latitude to use the economic development powers as part of its delivery of an overall strategy for Wales. There has been some concern that the 'employment creation' policy community would be too strong for those with an interest in encouraging a focus on knowledge-intensive activities over mass employment creation. However, devolution has led to fairly comprehensive structural change, with a reorganisation of the management of the Welsh Development Agency, and the introduction of new local forums to provide sub-national input into economic development policy.

The main substantive critique that can be made of post-devolution industrial policy in Wales is that these new opportunities have been matched to only a limited extent by correspondingly new thinking. There has been a tendency to regard the winning of public sector support (notably Objective 1 funding) as an end in its own right rather than considering what needs to be done with that funding. The political and business establishment appears to have retained a tight control over strategic documents, with the economic development strategy appearing to argue that greater selectivity over inward investment will be sufficient to close the considerable gap between Welsh GDP and the rest of the UK.

However, some would argue that this is perhaps an unfair judgement on a political infrastructure which is innovating in a number of ways. Expecting radical outcomes is optimistic given that new institutional arrangements and relationships are being constituted, and that the degree of budgetary discretion is extremely limited in the first instance. In this situation, it becomes necessary to judge the achievements of the Welsh Assembly against what could reasonably have been achieved in such a short space of time, which is relatively little.

For this reason, the fact that a number of commentators have noted 'something afoot' in Wales becomes important, as a proxy outcome which could conceivably be trailing the real divergences which emerged in Scotland in the longer term. In Scotland, the SDA evolved its thinking over a 20-year period in concert with the development of a Scottish political penumbra. By contrast, Wales has been relatively lacking in those institutions – the think tanks, political lobbyists and special advisors – which perhaps are instrumental in driving policy innovation. Although the Welsh Assembly could be criticised for failing to deliver a Welsh style of industrial policy, it would perhaps be more worrying had that policy changed significantly in so short a time, given the experience of Scotland, as such rapid change would represent a 'short-circuiting' of the necessary institutional learning seen in Scotland.

Lessons from the devolved territories' experience

From the cases of regional and industrial policy in Wales and Scotland given above, there are a number of lessons for the way that a devolved industrial policy emerges and is managed. The first point is that devolved institutions can initially lack critical mass, not as a flaw of the devolution process, but because an element of devolution is building that critical mass. Scotland was lucky to have a reasonably strong political community which arose around the allocation of the Scottish Office budget, with a distinctive policy style which continued under devolution, whereas in Wales, political community formation in advance of devolution had been much more limited.

The second and related point concerns the formation of the political community: in Scotland it emerged in response to a need to be able to deal with and resolve distinctly Scottish issues on a Scottish agenda, such as sub-Scottish disparities and the uneven impacts of Scottish industrial restructuring. These policy communities were not a function of devolved powers, but of decision-making needs. Furthermore, there is some evidence that a distinctly Welsh agenda may be emerging in Wales, for the same reasons; political issues emerge in forms which leads to Welsh politicians and civil servants needing to take their own decisions, which requires their own resources, knowledge and legitimacy. It is this which will drive the formation of a broader community, the political penumbra, and whose early stages are being seen in the 'something afoot' which commentators have noted.

Competitiveness post-1997: a UK industrial policy applied to England

It might have been expected that, alongside devolution to Scotland and Wales, the UK's industrial policy post-1997 would have become much more sensitive to regional needs. However, evidence would suggest that the spatial insensitivity of the Department of Trade and Industry prior to 1997 has continued to this day. Indeed the 1998 Competitiveness White Paper (DTI 1998) adopted a far more strident pro-market tone than the softer, 'interventionist-lite' approach of the Heseltine-era department. This spatial insensitivity was reiterated in the outcome of the reorganisation of the DTI following the 2001 election, in which activities were grouped into three areas: science, technology and innovation, competitive markets and business support services. Regional policy falls under business support services and has become a subset of industrial policy activities underpinned by the philosophy that they apply to all parts of England.

Consequently, all the tools which are deployed in support of industrial policy apply to all parts of the policy territory. Thus, every region has a Regional Development Agency (RDA), all regions are drawing up cluster strategies and promoting clusters, and all regions are getting a Manufacturing Advisory Service. The only real regional inflection is the differential level of funding provided; in some cases (for example, the RDAs) this correlates with the need for regional industrial policy (using GDP as a crude proxy), whilst in other areas (the Small Business Service) it does not.

The 2001 Enterprise, Skills & Innovation White Paper makes clear that the DTI's over-riding aim is to promote the UK knowledge economy (DTI and DfEE 2001). Because of the way that the DTI and its expenditure is organised and the way it chooses to deliver its services, many of those policy tools promoting the knowledge economy have a profoundly anti-regional policy impact. One key area where this is true is the science budget. There is a large body of research which has demonstrated the economic development pump-priming effect of public R&D, which Scotland has tacitly acknowledged in its integrated science strategy. And yet public expenditure on R&D is highly regressive in regional terms, in that it favours those regions that have existing strong economies (Charles and Benneworth 2001).

This highlights one of the main limitations to the DTI: their poverty of ambition in creating an England of knowledge-driven regions. Although there is a rhetoric of 'widening the winners' circle', the current supply side approach is reinforcing the existing contours of the English knowledge economy, which is heavily concentrated in London and its surrounding regions. The knowledge economy is integral to the economic success of the UK, but the DTI's ambition seems limited to widening the scope of this economy rather than encouraging alternative regional centres of excellence.

As for policies which are labelled as regional policies rather than industrial policies, the main policy innovations in the period since 1997 have been the strengthening of the Government Offices so as to better deliver joined-up central government policies in the regions, and the creation of a Regional Development Agency in each region of England. The eight English RDAs came into existence in April 1999, with the aim of injecting a higher degree of territorial specificity into the design and content of economic development policies. As non-departmental public bodies (a form of appointed central government agency or quango), it has been argued that they 'run the risk of being seen as the creatures of central government' (Morgan 1999).

In their implementation, they were created as rather a 'hotch-potch' of largely unrelated organisations, including elements of English Partnerships, the Rural Development Commission, DETR (as it then was) and the regional development offices, and they were required to write regional strategies covering a broad range of social, environmental and economic issues. Over time, their main emphasis has been re-focused towards being 'strategic drivers of economic development'. The Treasury formalised this link in the Spending Review of 2000 through Public Service Agreements which regarded the RDAs as a tool to raise regional trend GDP growth rates. This process culminated in the assignment of RDA sponsorship to the DTI (from the DETR previously) in June 2001.

The extent to which they act effectively as drivers of economic development in their regions is open to question, given the relatively modest scale of their budgets. Although there is some correlation between the scale of these budgets and regional economic development needs, this arises not as a rational outcome of allocating RDA funding in line with reducing GDP disparities, but is instead a quirk of the way the RDAs were created. The budgets originated in specific funding streams; the largest of those budgets related to physical redevelopment, and so those regions which had the largest need for regeneration have been those with the biggest absolute and per capita budgets. Table 4.1 below quantifies the contribution that RDA expenditure makes to regional expenditure.

Table 4.1 Indicative RDA contribution to regional identifiable expenditure, latest years available

Region	RDA Budget 2001-02, £m	Identifiable regional expenditure 1999-2000, £m	RDA budget as % IRE
North East	162	12485	1.3%
North West	281	31840	0.9%
Yorkshire	245	21317	1.1%
East Midlands	97	16861	0.6%
West Midlands	170	22428	0.8%
East of England	62	21226	0.3%
South East	109	30163	0.4%
South West	92	20113	0.5%
London	298	36683	0.8%

Source: Commons Hansard 28 January 2002 Col 68W, PESA 2001-02

Regional policy is a very small element of inter-regional transfer payments (far less than welfare payments), and the specific measures promoted by RDAs are limited to the supply side. In lagging regions, there are problems in stimulating demand for Government support for knowledge-intensive activities, which regional policy as currently constituted in England is unable to address. The current policy framework is thus decidedly problematic: spending delivery for regional policy is channelled through the Department for Trade and Industry, a department that appears to remain extremely insensitive to the possibility of divergent regional needs.

However, an unlikely counterweight to the supply-side prescriptions has emerged in the form of the Treasury, which has begun to articulate a rationale for all national policy to be more regionally inflected. It is this which could well have quite profound consequences for regional and industrial policy in England, and shift the centre of gravity of a highly national policy back towards the more regional end of the spectrum.

The strange rise of the Treasury as regional champion

The Treasury has long been concerned with UK productivity, particularly the view that the UK's long-term industrial decline resulted from a consequence of poor productivity, and sustainable economic growth therefore requires higher levels of productivity to be attained. Previous industrial policy documents have made extensive reference to the need to raise productivity in the UK as a whole, and a range of fiscal instruments have been deployed to achieve this aim, the latest of which being the R&D tax credit, devised to increase the innovativeness of UK business.

This pre-occupation with productivity has been, since the late 1970s, encapsulated in a neo-classical approach to economics, which stresses the need to maximise market efficiency and eliminate distorting externalities produced by state intervention. Active/interventionist regional policy has thereby been eroded because of a pre-occupation with the negative effects of distorting the spatial externalities that *dirigisme* causes.

However, the received wisdom that the Treasury is the main barrier to a more active and joined-up regional industrial policy took a setback in November 2001 when HM Treasury published *Productivity in the UK: 3 – The Regional Dimension*, the third ('Chapter 3') in a series on productivity in the UK (HM Treasury/DTI 2001). This report managed to put together a very spatially sensitive set of recommendations within the language of neo-classical economics, stressing for example the negative spatial externalities which arose from the over-concentration of economic activity in the South East of England. In line with that report, the current spending round is taking submissions from regional partners on their own perceived priorities, and departments are being asked to report the spatial implications of their spending plans.

This could potentially introduce significant spatial sensitivity into expenditure planning, with quite profound ramifications for regional and industrial policy in the UK. If the DTI is asked to account how its expenditure in each of the regions is promoting the knowledge economy or economic convergence, then spatially-inflected policy becomes more attractive as a policy style. The Chapter 3 report is reasonably sensitive to the fact that different policies might be necessary for different regions, and this would present an opportunity for some divergence of policy applied across the regions of England. The DTI retains importance under this scenario, ensuring that the regional inflection promotes economic convergence.

It is perhaps unsurprising that the Treasury, rather than DTI, has emerged as the champion for the English regions, because of its promotion and management of a number of elements of regionally-oriented public finance. The Treasury has for a long time been used to dealing with the separate 'regions' of Scotland, Wales and Northern Ireland, and the different funding arrangements applicable in each territory. The Treasury has been disaggregating spending on a regional basis for the last four years, with only 30 per cent of total managed expenditure unallocated between regions. It has also successfully managed the introduction of the Single Programme Budget (the so-called 'single pot' arrangements) for the RDAs, and negotiated the requirements this raises for accountability through Parliament.

Conclusion

How then can we characterise the changes to industrial and regional policy which have taken place during the process of devolution since the 1997 election? The first observation is that industrial and regional policy in the UK was hitherto structured by the DTI, who seem incapable of any kind of regional policy that is explicitly redistributive. In working to promote UK competitiveness, the DTI has seemingly lost the language to articulate the view that imbalanced economic development in the UK might be a problem, which seriously undermines the importance it attaches to regional policy.

Its regional policy measures are seen as short term correctives to market failures, so the potential for them to affect longer-term knowledge and productivity investments are ignored. Similarly, the contributions made to regional productivity by supposedly non-regional expenditure are overlooked (for example, the science budget, military procurement, the NHS prescription bill). One of the first observable outcomes from devolution has been the shift in the devolved territories to use permitted policy tools to promote regional investment in the interests of the territory rather than addressing local market failures to improve UK competitiveness. In Scotland, this preceded political devolution because of the high degree of functional autonomy, whilst in Wales, this process is beginning to now emerge as distinctly Welsh issues appear on the political agenda.

There are signals that there might be some degree of convergence towards this position by the English regions. Both the Chapter 3 report and the recently-published regional governance White Paper (Cabinet Office/DTLR 2002) have stressed the importance of local knowledge and decision-making for national policy making. This local/regional dimension is deemed necessary to deal with deep seated regional problems which undermine national competitiveness. However, it remains to the outcome of the Treasury's Spending Review of 2002 to decide whether regional considerations have had a significant impact on Whitehall expenditure planning.

Although there has, for much of the period under investigation, been considerable divergence, as regionally-blind policies have been applied in England and regionally-sensitive policies applied in Wales and, particularly, Scotland, this new convergence represents a shift of the centre of gravity of industrial policy towards greater regional-sensitivity. Moreover, this reinforces Keating's point (Chapter 1) that central pressures towards convergence are so strong that divergence in policy style is usually a temporary phenomenon.

The way in which industrial and regional policy has evolved following devolution in Scotland and Wales raises a number of issues for understanding the process of UK devolution more generally. Devolution has involved a range of different changes, political, administrative, organisational, but devolution tends to be judged on the difference made to territorial administration; the incubation period for radical divergence of industrial policy in Scotland demonstrates that outcomes are not the only way of judging the success of devolution.

The DTI does appear to be fighting a losing battle to inhibit regional inflection of England-wide policies, given the degree to which the devolved administrations have adopted such powers as they have been granted for their own use. This situation will only increase into the future as the proportion of 'clean money' in their own incomes increases with the 'single pot' arrangements. However, the DTI retains a role to ensure that there are not beggar-thy-neighbour consequences from the way the devolved administrations pursue their own interests. This obviously has to be handled with some sensitivity, because devolution means that the DTI has relinquished some of its powers. It would be extremely risky (although entirely possible) for the DTI to shift its emphasis to promoting English competitiveness, although this has the dual risk of failing to address intra-English differences (as great as any in the UK) as well as failing to deal with any negative spatial impacts from the devolved territories.

The experience of recent years suggests that divergence in industrial policy should not materially affect its delivery. Although devolution has led to temporary divergence, the sub-national pressures which such asymmetries have engendered have led once more to a reconvergence, albeit at a different point to the pre-1997 position. Devolution does create pressures which the centre needs to respond to in order to prevent the devolved territories' success dominating the political agenda, which in the case of industrial and regional policy has led to increasing the degree of regional input in the regional and industrial political process. Indeed, it is ironic that perhaps the greatest responsibility for the maturing of industrial policy in the English regions can be lain at the door of the devolved institutions of Scotland and Wales.

Endnotes

1   Industrial and regional policies in Northern Ireland have been driven by a very different logic to those in the rest of the United Kingdom, and in this chapter we concentrate on Scotland, Wales and England.

2   This is not entirely true: both territories had their own development agencies for the remote rural hinterlands, Highlands & Islands Enterprise and the Development Board for Rural Wales respectively.

3   However, the DTI retains to this day responsibility for the designation of assisted areas, which set the spatial boundaries for assistance under the provisions of the Industrial Development Act.

4   Lucky Goldstar (LG) are a Korean company who solicited financial support bids from Regional Development Agencies across Europe for the siting of an electronics complex which was supposed to encompass domestic electronics to semi-conductors. The WDA won the contest, reoriented their entire business support programme to support LG, and then market conditions caused LG to abandon plans for a semi-conductor fabrication plant, the only really desirable element of the project.

References

Cabinet Office/DTLR (2002) *Your Region, Your Choice: Revitalising the English Regions* Cm 5511 London: The Stationery Office

Charles DR & Benneworth PS (2001) 'Are we realising our potential? — joining up science and technology policy in the English regions' *Regional Studies* February 2001 pp71-78

Coates D (2001) 'Industrial policy: where next?' *New Economy* 8.3 London: ippr p134

Danson M, Lloyd MG and Newlands D (1992) 'Regional development agencies in the United Kingdom' in Townroe P and Martin R (eds) *Regional Development in the 1990s: The UK in Transition* London: Jessica Kingsley

Department of Trade and Industry (2000) *Excellence and opportunity a science and innovation policy for the 21st century* Cm 4814 London: The Stationery Office

Department of Trade and Industry (1998) *Our Competitive Future: Building the Knowledge-driven Economy* London: The Stationery Office p11

Department of Trade and Industry (1996) *Competitiveness – creating the enterprise centre of Europe* London: The Stationery Office

Department of Trade and Industry and Department for Education and Employment (2001) *Opportunity for all in a world of change: a white paper on enterprise, skills and innovation* London: The Stationery Office

HM Treasury/DTI (2001) *Productivity in the UK: 3 – The Regional Dimension* London: HM Treasury

Ministry for Enterprise and Lifelong Learning (2000) *Framework for the Economic Development of Scotland* Edinburgh: MinELL (para 4.2)

Morgan K (1999) quoted in Roberts P and Benneworth P (2001) 'Pathways to the future? An initial assessment of RDA strategies and their contribution to integrated regional development' *Local Economy* 16.2 pp142-159

Office of the Lord President of the Council (1976) *Devolution: the English dimension: a consultative document* London: Her Majesty's Stationery Office

Scottish Enterprise (1996) *Competitive Locations* Edinburgh: Scottish Enterprise

Scottish Executive (2001) *A Science Strategy for Scotland* Edinburgh: Scottish Executive

Trade and Industry Select Committee (1997) *Co-ordination of inward investment: first report of the Trade and Industry Select Committee* London: HMSO

5. Industrial and regional policy: a London perspective

Ian Gordon

Gillespie and Benneworth effectively combine two lines of argument. The first is essentially analytic, about the difference that institutions make to policies and their implementation. The second is more normative, about more and less effective or equitable approaches to industrial and regional policy – which then colours judgements about how well institutions are performing.

Broadly, their value judgements are in favour of more active industrial and regional policies, and with each seen as enhancing the other. Thus the best forms of industrial policy emerge as ones which are regionally 'inflected', while the best forms of regional development policy are those with a strongly interventive 'industrial' element to them, in contrast to the simple pursuit of inward investment. I would not quarrel greatly with these judgements, though writing from a London rather than a Newcastle perspective it seems to me that the real economic benefits of regional-scale agglomeration and the actual competitive advantage of core regions for many activities are not given their full weight. However this is primarily a paper about institutions and their effects, rather than about policies, and it is on some of these issues that I shall focus.

In relation to Scotland and Wales significant differences are identified in the way industrial policies have evolved in the two nations since political devolution which are traced back to differences in forms and extent of administrative devolution operating over the previous 20 years. Broadly, Scottish policy has been more interventionist in relation to indigenous business while Welsh policy has concentrated more on attraction of assistance and inward investment. This difference is attributed partly to the relative strength of the Scottish economy, and in part to the greater strength of the Scottish administrative institutions and policy community.

What this might imply for the potential character and effectiveness of devolved regional institutions within England is ambiguous, however, depending on how far the Scottish/Welsh difference is seen as reflecting the effects of learning-by-doing, given effective administrative devolution, or those long-run differences in political development which led to Scotland securing a stronger form of devolution. In either case, most English regions would clearly start a long way behind Wales in their potential to develop effective industrial and spatial policies. Gillespie and Benneworth also argue that the initial step of administrative devolution has been more significant than the political follow-up in development of regionally/nationally-inflected policies;

and that in the Welsh case at least political devolution may have increased government's vulnerability to chasing relatively low technology, potentially transient investment projects.

Interesting points are also made about the role of central departments in the context of regionalisation. Predictably the DTI is seen as judging the value of regional initiatives essentially in terms of their capacity to promote national growth and being rather resistant to 'regional-inflection'. Less predictably, the Treasury is seen to have recently become more sympathetic to what regionally-differentiated policies could contribute to national productivity growth. In this contrast, it is tempting to see some relation with the fact that DTI remains in part an English government department, whereas the Treasury is more straightforwardly a UK government department with a better developed vision encompassing the three territories with devolved administrations. As far as the Treasury is concerned, however, the new regional interests would also seem to reflect some quite traditional 'territorial' competition between Whitehall departments, with the Treasury confident that it has brought the macroeconomy under control but dissatisfied with the failure of growth, competition and DTI policies together to effect significant improvements in productivity. Furthermore, in this case the Treasury is untrammelled by any pre-existing involvement on its own part in this field.

Beyond the ground that Gillespie and Benneworth very effectively cover, there are two general issues that I would like to raise, with a footnote then about the more recent experience of limited devolution in London, as my own patch.

First, I should like to push further points which Gillespie and Benneworth make about the relationship between industrial and regional policy, and how devolution affects these. At a national level a key difference has been that industrial policy is essentially conceived in efficiency terms whereas regional policy has been essentially about (spatial) equity issues. In practice it has never been quite that simple, regional policy commitments have often been rationalised in efficiency terms – though national government never seems to have taken these seriously enough to commission close examinations of the key arguments – while industrial policy has always been vulnerable to special pleading for support invoking spatial equity concerns, as well as more specific business and employment interests.

However, regional policy in particular has been essentially a top-down exercise, both because it has been designed to avoid potentially wasteful competition between regions, and because it depends on notions of fairness within what has been perceived to be a single national polity. Indeed, as with the EU's concern with 'economic and social' (read political) cohesion, the essential function of post-war regional policy can be seen as of seeking to sustain that polity and the national (two) party system through which it operates (Gordon 1999). From this perspective there are a couple of inherent tensions in the devolution process in relation to these policies. One is that devolution itself seems to weaken the basis and motives for spatially redistributive regional policies, indeed in some respects to be an alternative to these as a strategy of political management. The second is that devolution inevitably involves a promotion of bottom-up forms of territorial competition. Currently this operates in an asymmetric way, with Wales and Scotland having substantially greater autonomy to pursue competitive initiatives than the more prosperous regions of the south. Establishment of the RDAs in England may only have changed this situation rather marginally, but the moves toward more full-blown political devolution contemplated in the 2002 White Paper on the English regions will give them too a stronger base to participate in territorial competition. If they too can develop an effective capacity in this field, the outcome will be to make spatial redistribution of activity and regional convergence less likely.

Second, is the politics or political economy of these policies and how these work out in the context of devolution. As I see it, there are a number of implicit aims associated with devolution of responsibility for these policies, several of which have political as well as economic dimensions to them. Among these aims are: an improved ability of policies to respond to different local circumstances – and/or to regionally differentiated values and preferences; a by-passing of some of the 'forces of conservatism' (in New Labour terms) associated with established bureaucracies, through opening up policy-formation more directly to market forces and pressure from affected interests; enhancing the legitimacy of governance; and reducing the gap between policy and implementation. There may well be others, and differences of relative importance among these, but this listing should at least suggest the importance of questions about *who* it is who effectively comes to express regional interests and concerns in these specialised fields of decision-making.

This is, of course, an issue at UK level, but there at least there are established channels of representation and consultation involving a number of countervailing forces, most of which are likely to be rather undeveloped at a sub-UK scale – especially when economic interests have tended to be aggregated in sectoral rather than spatial terms. There seems to be an important collective action problem at this scale, which is liable to create a rather biased pattern of economic representation (Cheshire and Gordon 1996). As well as the issues covered in this chapter, I think then that we need to know a lot more about how Scottish, Welsh or Northern Irish national/provincial 'economic interests' get to be constructed, in relation to local policy decisions, and not simply to external lobbying. At the most general level, we also need to understand more about ways in which devolution (and its different forms) may have affected the balance between business and other affected interests.

As a final footnote from London, it is appropriate to make a couple of early comments about the functioning of the new London institutions in this policy field, particularly the London Development Agency. The LDA has the form and responsibilities of a Regional Development Agency, with a few possibly significant differences: members of the LDA are appointed by the (directly elected) Mayor, who takes responsibility for its Economic Development Strategy; policy objectives and targets are nominally set independently, rather than by central government, though since funding comes from the centre it has been prudent to adopt, and add to, the standard RDA targets, rather than reject them; and the Chief Executive has a more political background than his peers elsewhere.

In practice, for different reasons, neither the Mayor nor the (scrutinising) Assembly seem to have a great direct impact on formulation of the LDA strategy, though there were a lot of participatory inputs. Another significant issue in the first two years has been the limited professional capacity available for development and implementation of the strategy. However, a notable outcome has been – reflecting some of the key issues in London – that the Economic Development Strategy has been more 'social' in its orientation than many elsewhere, and (surprisingly) less 'global city' focused, with more interest in diversity, than the city's own Spatial Development Strategy.

References

Cabinet Office and DTLR (2002) *Your Region, Your Choice: Revitalising the English Regions* Cm5511 London: The Stationery Office.

Cheshire PC and Gordon IR (1996) 'Territorial competition and the predictability of collective (in)action' *International Journal of Urban and Regional Research* 20 pp383-399

Gordon IR (1999) 'Regional policy and national politics in Britain' *Environment and Planning C: Government and Policy* 8 pp427-438

IV:
Education

6. Developing differently: educational policy in England, Wales, Scotland and Northern Ireland

David Reynolds

Education in the United Kingdom has been vested with the goals of increasing economic prosperity, of enhancing 'social inclusion', of aiding the development of national solidarity through an emphasis upon 'citizenship' and of generating skills not just of a 'basic' variety but additionally the 'learning to learn' skills that a modern society is argued to need in an age when information is deemed to be redundant every twenty years or so.

For the three nations having some form of devolved powers in the United Kingdom, Wales, Scotland and Northern Ireland, the attraction of seeking to use the formal, compulsory education system that takes children up to age 16 to deliver valued social and economic goals is understandable. There are the economic imperatives to generate a changed attitude to 'wealth creation' amongst children in societies where historic economic insecurity has generated a desire for employment in the service sector or in local/national state employment. There is the need to enhance levels of GDP per head to English levels, particularly important in Wales given the reduction in Welsh standing relative to that of the other three nations of the United Kingdom in the last ten years.

There are those who have argued that the 'human capital' theory that motivates virtually all governments of modern industrial societies is misplaced (Robinson 1997) and that education does not possess the power of returns it is believed to have. Nevertheless, this 'return' to education measured as the extent to which additional increments of educational achievement are associated with enhanced earnings through the life span is now at the highest level that it has ever been historically (Stringfield 1995). The contemporary enthusiasm for education as a 'driver' of economic, and potentially social, outcomes may be excessive but it is not unreasonably so, and it is particularly understandable of course that Scotland, Wales and increasingly Northern Ireland have been drawn to distinctive educational and training related policies as a possible solution to their long term social and economic problems.

It is also noticeable that the three peripheral nations (Wales, Scotland and Northern Ireland) have taken a different stance to England on the relative importance of 'Education' as against 'Training'. Paradoxically, given the historic emphasis in the three nations upon education as a means of individuals attaining their social mobility, even if that social and likely geographical mobility disadvantaged the society as a whole, there is a contemporary emphasis upon a 'training' orientation, reflected for example in the 'Training and Education' title of the Educational Department in Wales. 'Training' implies ensuring an individual's education is orientated to collective rather than individual goals, and that wealth production rather than wealth consumption is the macro-policy orientation.

This 'training' orientation is of course easier to 'sell' politically in the three nations than in England, given their widely acknowledged need to generate economic development. In England, by contrast, the need to court traditional middle class populations that have seen education as an individual right rather than a collectively defined solution to societal needs, makes any such 'training' emphasis more difficult.

It is perhaps this greater prevalence – in educational administrative circles if not in the wider societies of the three nations – of a commitment to training that explains why these societies are widely regarded as producing more effective policies in relation to Information and Communication Technologies than England. The quantity of total 'spend', the pervasiveness of policies (which go beyond the concentration upon hardware and software that is characteristic of England) and the importance attached to this policy area can all be seen as additional evidence of the presence of this 'training' orientation.

Education in England, 1995 to 2002

Education has been one of New Labour's key policy areas, with policies being radically redrafted after the arrival of Tony Blair as Opposition Leader, and David Blunkett as Shadow Education Spokesperson in the mid 1990s. Their diagnosis of the problems of the compulsory sector of education has included the following key points.

First, achievement outcomes from English schools have been seen as too low by comparison with our industrial competitors, particularly in Mathematics which was viewed as tightly related to the capacity to produce wealth (Reynolds and Farrell 1996). The Third International Mathematics and Science Study (TIMMS) published in 1996 (Keys, Harris and Fernandes 1996) showed a particularly disappointing UK performance in Mathematics, although of course the recent PISA (The Programme for International Student Assessment) study, using outcome measures that reflect more on the capacity of students to *apply* their knowledge in addition to the capacity to *possess* it, has shown a considerably better performance (Department for Education and Skills 2002).

Secondly, variation between schools has been seen as large relative to that of other societies (see Reynolds et al 2002 for confirmation of this view), with perhaps 12-15 per cent of pupil variance in academic achievement being due to the quality of schools attended (see Teddlie and Reynolds 2000, for a review). Whilst family background and the individual characteristics of pupils have clearly been the major determinant of school outcomes, the 'competitive edge' possessed by 'effective' rather than 'ineffective' schools is not inconsiderable in policy terms, amounting at secondary school stage for example to the difference between 7 GCSEs at grade C and 7 at grade E, if we compare the schools in the top and bottom deciles of effectiveness (Sammons 1999).

For Labour, probably validly, the UK's educational problems were seen as not being the absence of knowledge of how to educate children effectively (the 'validity'), it was that society did not try to ensure that all schools did as the effective ones did (the 'reliability'). Given that in all kinds and categories of catchment areas some primary schools, for example, succeeded in virtually universal attainment for all children of high quality educational outcomes, then policy was seen as simply a matter of getting this reliably distributed, as was the goal of the English Numeracy and Literacy Strategies from the late 1990s (see the evidence in Department for Education and Employment 1997 and 1998).

Thirdly, students' life chances were seen as closely circumscribed by their social class of origin, given the very high correlation that exists between individual student home backgrounds and their achievement (a correlation of 0.8 between reading score at age 8 and GCSE total points score being the 'normal science' of the school effectiveness field for example, as in Sammons 1999). There are also hints that this relationship may become 'tighter' over students' life times in the United Kingdom, by comparison with other societies like those of the Pacific Rim. There it becomes weaker as what are 'powerful' education systems distance children from their social origins as the strength of system influence allows talented children to reach their 'natural' levels (see Reynolds *et al* 2002 for evidence and speculations on this theme).

Fourthly, the early years of schooling were seen as paramount in terms of affecting later achievement, partly reflecting on the school effectiveness evidence that primary school effects between ages 5 and 11 were more substantial, and longer lasting, than secondary school effects (Teddlie and Reynolds 2000). The decision to focus upon the primary sector rather than the secondary sector was also influenced by the potential political opportunities that were presented by widespread concern amongst public and professionals about the methods being employed in primary schools, their effects and the general disillusionment that existed with the primary 'progressive experiment' that had been in operation since the 1970s.

Related to this diagnosis of the educational system's problems was a view that the structure and processes of the teaching profession was part of the 'problem' and that 'root and branch' reform was necessary. It was seen as inflexible in its reluctance to differentiate between teachers in remuneration rates; even though school governors had the power to offer individual bonus or merit payments since the early 1990s, only 0·5 per cent of teachers in 1998 were receiving them. It was believed the profession needed to be differentiated out, for example into those of 'advanced skills' and the others, which was to encourage the marking out of those with more effective behaviours to enable others to learn from them. Many other policies concerning teachers and Headteachers could be seen as offering the 'support' rather than the 'pressure' from the well known Labour 'pressure and support' phrase (including the English CPD strategy announced in Autumn 2001, the Headteacher qualifications that were updated/revised, the National College for School Leadership that began in 2001 and the encouragement of teacher researchers through the 'Best Practice' Scholarships). However, much of the emotional and personal energy in terms of the reform of the profession went into the organisation of the Threshold system of performance related pay, in which all teachers at the top of the 'main grade' were offered the chance of gaining an additional salary payment of approximately £2,000 per year plus access to a new pay scale that ceilinged in the high £30,000s. As England and Wales were yoked together in this, and as there were no Welsh Assembly powers in the area of teachers' pay and conditions of work, this was to have major effects on the relationship between the Westminster and Cardiff administrations.

There have been a number of analyses of Labour policies in England, attempting to ground them in the explanatory variables that have generated them, looking at the influence of biographical factors, international economic pressures, and those that attempt to explain them as above all tactically, rather than strategically, driven responses to the political imperatives of winning elections (see the contributors to Daugherty, Phillips and Rees 2000).

Perhaps neglected by most analyses is the extent to which Labour policies relate to and build upon many of the contents of the old Fabian paradigm, associated with the 'right wing' of the Labour Party in the years following the Wilson governments of 1964 to 1970 and 1974 to 1976. The Fabian paradigm believed not in changing capitalism in terms of changing the ownership of the means of production but more in planning capitalism to be more productive and thereby generating more wealth for distribution to all. 'At heart', someone once remarked 'its leaders were bureaucrats not democrats' and indeed it was nicknamed 'the Institute for Social Engineering' by critics. In its educational goals, the Fabian paradigm never went beyond the perceived need for 'equality of opportunity' to a more radical 'equality of outcomes' between social groups that marked out the beliefs of many on the left. Nor did it ever suggest any need for the major changes in the outside-school social and economic structures that are clearly the most important influences upon how children achieve, and which would have to be changed if 'weak' or 'strong' definitions of education were to be reached.

From Fabianism, then, came some of Labour's orientation to planning (school development plans, local educational authority plans), and to gradualism, in its approach to the better management of state services that has been the hallmark of its approach over the last five years. Crucially, though, Labour added a number of other ideological components to its educational paradigm that would not have been any part of the Fabian paradigm. First, given its analysis of the popularity of Thatcherism's historic 'anti-statism' and related distrust of public sector (and private sector in some cases) professions, Labour 'spun' against teachers as partially responsible for the condition of schools, against social workers for the condition of social welfare services and to a lesser extent against the medical profession for the condition of health services, although the latter has appeared to be very recently markedly attenuated. Secondly, it kept in its virtual entirety the 'market based' educational policies introduced by the Conservative government from 1988 to 1997, involving the systematic tightening of central control on the nature of the curriculum and on assessment outcomes, combined with devolution to schools of the determination of the 'means' at school and classroom level to determine outcomes. Parents and OFSTED were used as monitors of quality and a substantial 'reward system' in the form of direct transfer of resources to schools where the quality was perceived to be high helped the market operate through the presence of incentives.

Education in the three nations

Whilst Labour's educational policies were developed to reflect the perceived needs of the English educational system, the policies involved have always been seen to have less salience in the other three countries. These settings historically exhibited adherence to a different educational philosophy that often went beyond that of 'equality of opportunity' to embrace 'equality of outcomes', which given the importance of outside school factors would have necessitated considerable positive discrimination in the 'quantity' of resources allocated to the schools of poorer communities and perhaps something closer to 'equality' in the outside school communities.

These non-English settings were also, historically, higher spenders on education per pupil than England, exhibited customarily higher levels of achievement at the 'top' end of the ability range (especially in Wales and Scotland) and had a historical commitment to state education as a means of personal and collective advancement. These non-English settings were also not necessarily appropriate for the exercise of what was still seen as a 'market based' solution to the historical British problem of poorer educational standards, since in all three countries a much higher proportion of the population lived in rural areas or small towns in which there was effectively no choice of school than in England, since schools other than the local neighbourhood school were often fifteen to twenty miles distant at secondary school stage in many parts of the three countries.

The 'specialist schools' developed in England (Science and Technology Colleges or Language Colleges for example) had not been developed outside England, nor had any 'Beacon' provision whereby some schools were differentiated out of the system to specifically 'spread good practice' been developed either (a policy which has now spread to encompass training and advanced training schools involved in professional training). The absence of differentiation within the state school sector and the absence of any potential for creating a market in many geographical areas of the three nations, combined of course with the historically low level of pupils at private schools, made the exercise of educational markets much less possible than in England. Additionally, of course, the absence of published performance data in Scotland and Wales on the achievements of primary schools made 'consumer information' less persuasive. In Wales, indeed, although not in Scotland or Northern Ireland, the national government has ceased to publish national performance tables for secondary schools as well.

The inability of existing market based solutions to, in the much used phrase, 'lever up' standards is not the only distinguishing factor in the three nations. In all three, there has been an absence of the harsh rhetoric that has characterised England, where the period of office of Chris Woodhead was marked by attacks on the quality of education being offered, on the trailing edge of teachers that were assumed to be lowering standards and on the so called progressive methods that were assumed to have pervaded primary education. No Chief Inspector of Schools of the three nations has lacerated the teaching profession in this way, and associated with a more favourable public perception of schools in the three nations has been an emphasis upon school based review as the way of driving up standards. Even the very disappointing performance of Scotland in the TIMMS study of 1996/7 (Keys *et al* 1996) did not generate the criticism of the education system in Scotland that was present in England at the same time: the tone of the debate was more of sadness that Scotland had done apparently poorly, rather than of apportioning blame. The proposal to cut teachers' hours of work considerably, improve their level of pay and improve their conditions of work in Scotland as proposed by the McCrone Committee could only have come in a relatively supportive educational climate. Wales, of course, is tied to England in pay and conditions (although not in the nature of teachers' professional development which is determined by the Welsh Assembly), so what seems to be a more supportive and less polarised educational climate in Wales cannot at the moment impact on these 'structural' issues to do with pay and conditions.

The final distinctive features of education in the three nations has been the absence of any central prescription of methods that has been a central plank of the 'standards agenda' in England, originally in primary schools but now in secondary schools through the Key Stage Three initiative. The Numeracy Strategy, the Literacy Strategy and the Key Stage Three Strategy are much more accurately categorised as initiatives that specify the *curriculum* and make it more systematised for learning purposes than as initiatives that specify *pedagogy* (since there is little detail proposed in this area other than the three part lesson). However, even this limited degree of prescription of methods is in stark contrast to the acceptance in the three nations that varied methods may be equally appropriate in different circumstances and that the teacher is to be empowered with choice as to what is appropriate. Beyond the rejection of the specific strategies, it is clear from the publications of the Welsh and Scottish school inspectorates that a 'blend' of methods is often preferred to the more 'either/or' tone that has marked English prescription, as represented by, for example, the major shift from individualised learning to whole class 'interactive' teaching in the three strategies.

Finally, it is clear that the private sector is clearly to play a more limited role in the three nations than in England, and the decision has been made to keep a role for local education authorities that is now more difficult to keep in England, where 90 per cent of funding is to be devolved to schools by 2004. In all three nations, local education authorities retain a more central role than that envisaged in England

Building on difference

Distinctiveness in the educational policy provision of Scotland of course reflects not just on a lack of desire to follow the English policy paradigm but on the considerable differences in the curriculum and in assessment systems that are a consequence of the existence of a separate Scottish nation. In Wales, historical distinctiveness came through the development of the Welsh language schools, and an associated set of policies related to Welsh in the national curriculum of Wales, and in Welsh life. Development of policies in other areas only came with the publication and implementation of the groundbreaking *The Learning Society* document (as for example in the abandoning of the publication of national school league tables, and of the statutory assessment tests at the end of Key Stage One).

The capacity of Wales, Scotland and Northern Ireland to originate policies that are more internally consistent and more potentially appropriate than policies in England, has been enhanced by a number of successful initiatives in these three countries in areas of considerable importance in policy terms, which combine of course with the opportunity provided by a reluctance to follow the English agenda, to make possible interesting and distinctive policies.

In Wales, for example, there is a clear desire that early years education should be freed from some of the pressure that testing at age 7 has put upon both teachers and pupils, with the future absence of assessment in academic achievement at this age being used to generate firmer social foundations for learning (see National Assembly for Wales 2001). Interestingly, there are increasing numbers of adherents to the thesis that a delay in the academic demands of formal school to permit the development of social competencies, social skills and group consciousness amongst children is associated with a very steep learning curve when academic demands start. This is the situation that exists in the Pacific Rim societies, for example, and which is one of the distinctive features of the Finnish education system that had probably the best results in the 2002 PISA survey.

In Wales, Scotland and Northern Ireland, the potential of ICT to change the nature of the classroom experience seems to be being realised in ways unknown in England. The quality of the analysis in the well known Welsh 'Harries report' (Harries 2000), the attention given to the *support* of ICT in schools and communities rather than to the *content*, and the pilots into the potential formative use of on-line assessment in classrooms in both Scotland and Northern Ireland all suggest a discourse, policies and practices ahead of those prevalent in England.

The area of post-16 education and training also shows promise in the three nations, (ETAG 1999) and indeed there is evidence that the Welsh agenda on these issues concerned with 'joining up' the administrative systems of education and training that was pursued in the late 1990s has had an impact upon the English policy formulation of Learning and Skills Councils. The Welsh Baccalaureate, now being piloted in a dozen schools and colleges, also has potential to advance curriculum provision beyond the historic compromise that is represented by England's introduction of vocational GCSEs and a 'vocational route' that is still running, in parallel, with the existing high status 'educational' route.

The specialist policy committees in both Wales (Egan and James 2001) and Scotland seem to have given substance to the assertions of those supporters of devolution that a more inclusive politics would result from the different systems of governance. In Scotland, several committees dug deep into the examinations fiasco of 2001, and in Wales there is a clear, evident line from committee discussion to *The Learning Country* document. The proposals in the latter for education for children up to age 7 were trailed in committee documents, and the publication of specialist reports. Interestingly, in both Wales and Scotland it is practitioners, such as former Directors of Education and headteachers, who have been seconded to be specialist committee advisers rather than the academics who have filled this role in England, in a deliberate attempt in the two countries to be inclusive of *professional* opinion.

Conclusions

Any assessment of the potential to develop post-devolution, distinctive educational policies in Wales, Scotland and Northern Ireland would be misplaced without acknowledgement of the blocks that stand in their way. There are issues to do with the educational research communities' capacity in both Wales (Furlong and White 2001) and Scotland, and issues to do with the relative capacity of the Welsh Assembly and the Northern Ireland Assembly to generate the research and intelligence required on educational matters with their current resources of staff. The fertile breeding ground for ideas created by the Scottish 'think tanks' stands in stark comparison with the situation historically in Wales and Northern Ireland, although in both the latter countries the situation may be changing.

It is also important to point out that the advantage that may have been possessed by not adhering to the English paradigm in terms of deciding what *not to do* may be minimised if there is not further work on, and understanding of, what *to do*, in terms of distinctive policies. In at least four global areas of the educational system/societal interaction the three nations need to formulate some answers:

- What is the 'driver' of educational change to be, and how can that 'driver' be resourced? If we eschew the use of a critical body politic to raise standards, if we eschew market competition/parental choice and if we make our systems' internal variation less obvious through restricting performance data (or not having it in the first place as in primary education in Wales and Scotland), how will standards improve? If the sole remaining driver is the profession of teachers themselves, how can they be motivated and resourced?

- Where does the knowledge to improve standards come from? If we eschew the provision by the State in the form of prescription, how do we ensure that the system itself chooses valid knowledge rather than invalid? In a situation where the educational research communities may be historically less well developed than in England and where the systems of advice may be fragmented across a large number of small local education authorities (as in Wales and Scotland), where does valid knowledge come from?

- If the OFSTED style of inspection regime is unacceptable in the three nations because it is summative, simplistic and discouraging of the professional community of teachers, what is an alternative? Since the only alternative is some form of 'school based review', how can this be made more rigorous, effective and potentiating of school/teacher improvement than the existing versions of this currently in Wales and Scotland?

- If the involvement of central government in the increasing determination of educational matters is seen as counterproductive and disempowering, what governance arrangements maximise (rather than minimise in a 'zero-sum' way) the power available to the various partners in education? What balance of local education authority, parental, professional and central government influence is most productive of educational advance?

Thinking about these issues is only in its infancy in the three nations but is seen to be moving towards a 'new producer-driven' set of arrangements to replace the 'consumer-driven' policies that predominated in England. It is the teaching profession itself that is to be 'trusted' with the roles of knowledge generation, implementation, inspection and the general role of improving standards, whereas in England the profession is still heavily steered by the Department for Education and Skills and heavily monitored by an empowered consumer movement of parents.

No doubt this 'trust' in the three nations reflects their historic commitment to education, as well as the existence of the Labour coalitions in government that have always been politically close to the teaching profession, and in particular to the public sector teaching unions. However, it is difficult to square a commitment to 'inclusion', locally based decision making and 'openness' in at least two of the three nations with policies that make more opaque the operation of the educational systems because of a restriction of information to consumers. In both Wales and Scotland, in education at least, the inclusion may be of local elites from the usual gang of suspects in local organisations, rather than of the populace.

Whether or not the three nations can further develop 'new producerist' policies is at the moment unclear. It is also unclear the extent to which any variation in policies in the three nations will have effects upon the key factors of pupils' outcomes, their employment prospects/potential and indeed on the wider societies around them, given the evidence we possess about the limited effect of educational provision upon macro-societal structures.

It is finally unclear the extent to which distinctiveness in the educational arrangements of the three countries may encounter blocks that will impede change. Indications are that the cost of the McCrone Committee recommendations may pose difficulties that may only be solved by additional funding from the Exchequer. Indications also are that any attempt by the Welsh Assembly to acquire responsibility for the pay and conditions of Welsh teachers will be resisted, given that England benefits substantially from the cross border flow of teachers trained in Wales to posts in English schools, a flow that is eased by equivalence in this area. Whether the 'Devolution Settlement' can itself be re-negotiated in the area of education as the interests of the three nations, and of England, change remains to be seen.

References

Daugherty R, Phillips R and Rees G (2000) *Education Policy-Making in Wales* Cardiff: University of Wales Press

Department for Education and Employment (1998) *Numeracy Matters* London: DfEE

Department for Education and Employment (1997) *The Implementation of the National Literacy Strategy* London: DfEE

Department for Education and Skills (2001) *Press Release on PISA, 4 December.* London: DFES

Education and Training Action Group (ETAG) (1999) *An Education and Training Action Plan for Wales* Cardiff: Welsh Office

Egan D and James R (2001) 'A promising start: the pre-16 Education, Schools and Early

Learning Committee' in Jones JB and Osmond J (eds) *Inclusive Government and Party Management* Cardiff: Institute of Welsh Affairs, Welsh Governance Centre

Furlong J and White P (2001) *Educational Research Capacity in Wales* Cardiff: School of Social Sciences

Harries N (2000) *Information and Communications Technology in Education* Cardiff: Education and Lifelong Learning Committee, The National Assembly for Wales

Keys W, Harris S and Fernandes C (1996) *Third International Mathematics and Science Study National Report – First Part* Slough: National Foundation for Educational Reseach

Mortimore P, Sammons P, Stoll L, Lewis D and Ecob R (1988) *School Matters: The Junior Years* Salisbury: Open Books (Reprinted in 1995 by Paul Chapman: London)

Muijs D and Reynolds D (2001) *Effective Teaching* London: Sage

National Assembly for Wales (2001) *The Learning Country* Cardiff: The National Assembly for Wales

Reynolds D, Creemers BPM, Teddlie C, Stringfield S and Schaffer G (2002) *World Class Schools: International Perspectives on School Effectiveness* London: Routledge Falmer

Reynolds D and Farrell S (1996) *Worlds Apart? – A Review of International Studies of Educational Achievement Involving England* London: HMSO for OFSTED

Robinson P (1997) *Literacy and Numeracy and Economic Performance* London: London School of Economics, Centre for Economic Performance, Working Paper 888

Sammons P (1999) *School Effectiveness: Coming of Age in the Twenty-first Century* Lisse: Swets & Zeitlinger

Stringfield S (1995) 'Attempting to improve students' learning through innovative programs – the case for schools evolving into high reliability organisations' in *School Effectiveness and School Improvement* 6.1

Teddlie C and Reynolds D (2000) *The International Handbook of School Effectiveness Research* Lewes: Falmer Press

7. Devolution and the restructuring of post-16 education and training in the UK
Gareth Rees

Analysing the impacts of the latest phases of devolution in the UK on policy development of any kind is necessarily only preliminary. There can be little doubt that the creation of a Parliament in Scotland and Assemblies in Northern Ireland and Wales, with their respective administrations, marked a sea-change in British constitutional arrangements. The activities of central government in the three territories have been opened up to much greater public scrutiny and, potentially at least, accountability to their electorates. However, the advent of what has been termed 'democratic devolution' is very recent. Accordingly, the devolved bodies have had very little time to develop new policies in any field, let alone implement them effectively. In consequence, the evidential basis for drawing conclusions about the policy effects of the new pattern of devolution is pretty limited at the moment.

These constraints of chronology are compounded by the relative absence of systematic research on *the effects* of democratic devolution. Most of the work which has been carried out so far has focused on the mechanisms and operation of the devolved institutions themselves (for example, Bogdanor 2001; Hazell 1999). This is not surprising, of course, in light of the previous point. Inevitably, therefore, the arguments which follow tend to be rather general and, some would say, speculative. They also reflect in some measure my own greater familiarity with developments in Wales (and to a lesser extent England) than elsewhere.

These difficulties are exacerbated still further by the complexities of the post-16 education and training sector, the particular topic of this chapter. Far more so than the compulsory sector of education, post-16 provision is highly heterogeneous. It embraces both what has recently been termed the Learning and Skills Sector (LSS) and Higher Education (HE) (Piatt and Robinson 2001). The former, in turn, includes – in institutional terms – Further Education colleges, sixth form colleges, school sixth forms, work-based learning for young people and adult and community learning. Moreover, this categorisation does not take account of work-based provision for (older) adults, let alone a vast array of less formal types of adult learning. Clearly, it is not possible to cover everything in a short chapter such as this.

This is especially so, given that the different elements of the post-16 sector have radically divergent relationships with the devolved institutions, in terms of both the formal devolution settlements, as well as the day-to-day reality of policy development and implementation. For example, HE – unlike other parts of the post-16 system –

occupies a somewhat ambiguous position in relation to the devolved administrations, not least because of its continued dependence on UK-wide systems of resource allocation, such as the Research Assessment Exercise (RAE). The latter allocates resources to universities across the UK to reflect the quality of their research activity; and this implies that the devolved administrations are required to accommodate to funding levels for HE which lie largely outside of their control. Hence, in 2001-2002, Scotland 'earned' RAE-derived resources somewhat higher than its proportion of the British population (11 per cent compared with 9 per cent); whilst Wales got slightly less than its population proportion (4.5 per cent compared with 5 per cent).[1]

Whilst the allocations for 2002-2003, based upon the new RAE conducted in 2001, will change these proportions (especially as the Scottish universities have made considerable strides in terms of their RAE scores and the Welsh ones rather less so), the external control of the allocation procedure remains. Nevertheless, the ways in which allocations are distributed between institutions can be adjusted to reflect the different circumstances in the various countries. For instance, the Higher Education Funding Council for Wales is making RAE-based funding available to a wider range of university departments (in terms of RAE 'scores') than its counterparts in England and Scotland, presumably to take account of the historical pattern of lower levels of RAE-based funding in Wales.

For these kinds of reasons, therefore, what follows is highly selective in its treatment of the post-16 sector. Further analysis will be required as the contours of the policy landscape after the advent of democratic devolution become clearer. The argument here is therefore intended to raise questions about the nature of the impacts of democratic devolution, rather than to present an exhaustive analysis of what has been happening in this part of the education and training system.

The diversity of devolution

In considering the impacts of devolution on education policy, there is a danger of obscuring by simplification. Quite simply, devolution has embodied a diversity of different processes in Scotland, Wales and Northern Ireland; and this diversity constitutes a significant parameter in any analysis of effects on policy development and change.

At one level, this diversity is reflected in the well-known differences between the three devolution settlements in formal terms. The real inequalities in power which derive from these divergent settlements have already resulted in quite significant contrasts between policies. Most notably, perhaps, the restructuring of arrangements for student fees in Scotland, following the recommendations of the Cubie Report (Independent Committee of Inquiry into Student Finance 1999), has been significantly different from what has happened in Wales, following the recommendations of the Rees Report (Independent Investigation Group on Student Hardship and Funding in Wales 2001).

Hence, the Scottish Executive was able to use the powers vested in the Parliament to abolish up-front tuition fees and replace them with a graduate endowment scheme, requiring Scottish graduates to pay back £2000 once their earnings reach £10,000 per annum.[2] Bursaries for Scottish students from low-income families were also introduced, broadly akin to the old maintenance grants. In Wales, the National Assembly simply does not have the powers to abolish tuition fees. However, the recently announced alternative of introducing a means-tested Assembly Learning Grant (up to a maximum of £1500 per year) for all students who have been resident in Wales for three years or more is regarded by many as a highly imaginative alternative. In particular, the inclusion for eligibility of students in both HE and Further Education (FE) and those studying part-time as well as full-time is especially innovative. Moreover, the extension of funding to support access and to support students at Welsh institutions in hardship has also been widely welcomed.

In part, of course, these divergences reflect the differences between the two Reports and their political reception by the respective executives. Certainly, the fact that the Liberal Democrats had made the abolition of tuition fees a 'non-negotiable' element of their election manifesto and subsequently found themselves in the Labour-Liberal Democrat coalition running the Scottish Executive, was a key factor in explaining events in Scotland. Similarly, the shift to a Labour-Liberal Democrat coalition in Wales greatly enhanced the ability of (what is now termed) the Welsh Assembly Government to pursue a coherent policy programme. Equally significant, however, have been the straightforward discrepancies between what the two devolved administrations are empowered to do.

However, the diversity of devolution embodies more than this differentiation between the formal settlements. Hence, the divergent institutions of democratic devolution have been inserted into contexts in Scotland, Wales and Northern Ireland which were already radically different. A number of separate points need to be made here.

Administrative devolution

It is important to remember that devolution did not begin with the establishment of the Scottish Parliament and the assemblies in Wales and Northern Ireland. In each of the three territories, there were established patterns of 'administrative devolution' (complicated in the case of Northern Ireland by the existence of Stormont up until the instigation of Direct Rule in 1972) long before the advent of democratic devolution. In particular, the three territorial departments – the Scottish, Welsh and Northern Ireland Offices – had accumulated major powers over considerable time periods. Certainly, each exercised responsibility for the LSS, even if HE remained more closely attached to central UK government and a succession of intermediary bodies (the University Grants Committee and the Universities Funding Council).

It is also clear that administrative devolution took quite distinct forms in the three territories. Certainly, it has been argued that the Scottish Office had far greater resources on which to draw and was thus able to instigate new policies, as well as implementing them. It was also of sufficient size to allow for the career development of Scottish civil servants. In Wales – and probably in Northern Ireland too – it was characteristically the interpretation and perhaps adaptation of policies which originated in Whitehall and Westminster which occupied the much smaller civil service (Raffe *et al* 1999).

'Assumptive worlds'

This, in turn, led to the development of quite different 'assumptive worlds' both amongst politicians and civil servants (McPherson and Raab 1988). What is meant here is that the ways in which roles and powers were understood within the respective devolved institutions differed significantly and this became self-reproducing. Moreover, the ways in which substantive policy issues came to be conceived and conceptualised also reflected what became conventional ways of thinking. Hence, as Paterson (1994) has argued, even in Scotland and much more so in Wales and Northern Ireland, policy-making was essentially 'technocratic', with little or no attempt to challenge the political assumptions upon which established policy trajectories were based. More specifically, particular policy issues came to dominate 'official' thinking; and these substantive policy issues were viewed in characteristic ways.

The significance of these arguments for an analysis of the impacts of democratic devolution on education and training policy is that the 'assumptive worlds' which emerged during the era of administrative devolution have persisted (at least so far) into the new era associated with the new forms of devolution. Hence, for example, considerable interest was expressed over the establishment in Scotland in 1999 of a Department of Enterprise and Lifelong Learning, bringing together policies for many aspects of economic development with those for post-16 education and skills development. Whilst this arrangement was different from those in Wales (Education and Lifelong Learning) and Northern Ireland (where the Department of Higher and Further Education, Training and Employment has recently been renamed the Department for Employment and Learning), it is pretty much consistent with what existed in Scotland prior to democratic devolution, through the Scottish Office Education and Industry Department, as well as through Scottish Enterprise and the Local Enterprise Companies, which explicitly combined responsibilities for economic development with those for skills development. This is not to suggest, of course, that these Scottish arrangements under administrative devolution always worked smoothly; and neither have those under the current system, as the surprising resignation of the Minister for Enterprise, Transport and Lifelong Learning, Wendy Alexander, may indicate. At the moment, it also remains to be seen, of course, whether the Scottish configuration of departmental responsibilities will produce significant divergences in policies from what happens in Wales and Northern Ireland.

In Wales too there are clear indications of the persistence of 'assumptive worlds' from one form of devolution to another. Hence, one of the major policy initiatives in the field of education has been the restructuring of the organisational framework for the LSS in Wales through the establishment of the National Council-ELWa, which has taken over the responsibilities formerly discharged by the Further Education Funding Council for Wales and the Training and Enterprise Councils, as well as for the funding of school sixth forms. It is important to remember here that the Education and Training Action Group (ETAG), whose Plan (ETAP) presaged much of the reorganisation, was established before the inception of the National Assembly, in the immediate aftermath of the 1997 General Election. Indeed it reflected major concerns about the quality of post-16 education and training in Wales which had been expressed throughout the 1980s, as the collapse of the traditional industries of coal and steel prompted the prioritisation of skills development as an essential precursor of Welsh entry into what would now be called the 'knowledge economy' (OECD 2001).

What is intriguing in this context, however, is the extent to which the form that this restructuring of the LSS took was changed as the ETAP was debated in the National Assembly. In particular, the role of business interests in the new arrangements was significantly constrained in face of the capacity of local education authorities and other educational groupings to persuade the then Post-16 Education and Training Committee to broker changes to the ETAP proposals with the Cabinet. In part, this reflected quite fundamental features of civil society in Wales, where the role of the public sector (and local authorities, in particular) has historically been extremely powerful. However, it is clear that the new mechanisms through which policy-making occurs provided a vehicle through which these social groupings in civil society were able to exert important influences over the policy-making process, in ways which had not been possible under administrative devolution. Although the power of the Committee was undoubtedly enhanced by the fact that at this time there was a minority Labour administration, these events may also indicate the emergence of a somewhat more open form of policy formulation. However, whether this produced better policy outcomes remains a moot point (Morgan and Rees 2001).

Economic and social structures

The latter discussion also raises the issue of the wider influence of the economic and social structures within which policy-making within the new institutions of democratic devolution takes place. It has frequently been argued, for example, that the Scottish experience of working in the Constitutional Convention during the years preceding the establishment of the Scottish Parliament provided a basis of political consensus which was largely absent in Wales and certainly in Northern Ireland. However there are also much longer term influences at work too. The point here is that again what these new institutions are able to do is shaped by relatively enduring features of the economies and societies of which they are part.

Most obviously, this is illustrated by the situation in Northern Ireland. Not only has the functioning of the Northern Ireland Assembly itself been disrupted through temporary suspension, but also the development of thinking about policy innovation in the area of post-16 education and training (as in many other areas of 'normal' policy-making) has been constrained by the dominant place in Northern Ireland politics of the political troubles and the need to develop effective strategies for conflict resolution (Osborne 2000). Equally, however, it is not wholly fanciful to suggest, for example, that the Scottish initiative with respect to student fees in HE owes much to the well-established traditions of relatively equitable access to university education in Scotland (Anderson 1992); although, of course, the specific circumstances of political coalition within the devolved government was a crucial factor too.

Similarly, it is very striking that the recently published recommendations on the restructuring of the University of Wales, produced by the Assembly's Education and Lifelong Learning Committee (2002), have been roundly condemned and a 'Save the University of Wales Campaign' mounted; whilst the Committee's other recommendations on, *inter alia*, widening student access, strengthening Wales's research performance and the role of HE in economic, social and cultural regeneration have received far less attention. It is impossible to understand this seemingly perverse response without a knowledge of the role which the University of Wales has played historically in shaping patterns of Welsh national identity (Paterson 2001).

However, it remains to be seen how far this mobilisation within civil society will produce significant impacts on the direction of policy for Welsh HE. Certainly, in the Welsh Assembly Government's own statement of strategy for HE, some of the more radical proposals for restructuring made by the Education and Lifelong Learning Committee were toned down considerably (National Assembly for Wales 2002). Nevertheless, the need for change in the face of significant economic pressures remains clearly recognised. Indeed, as Paterson (2001) has argued, it is likely to be a general feature of devolved institutions – especially in territories which are less-favoured in economic terms – to seek to mobilise HE in the cause of economic regeneration. More specifically, given the widespread adoption of the 'knowledge economy' as the model for regional economic development, the role of universities as producers of research which can be transformed into innovation and of graduates who can become key 'knowledge workers' is crucial (OECD 2001).

In summary, therefore, these arguments suggest that what has happened in terms of policy development for post-16 education and training since the inception of democratic devolution owes as much to the residue of previous eras – and of administrative devolution in particular – as to the constitutional changes themselves.

Policy divergence and the process of 'policy learning'

Despite the preceding emphasis on the continuities in policies for post-16 education and training, it remains the case that there are emergent indications of increasing divergences in both policy-making and policies between the constituent territories of the UK. This is especially striking in Wales, where previously approaches originating in England have exerted much more powerful influences than in Scotland and Northern Ireland. Hence, for example, the recently published Paving Document, *The Learning Country*, attaches considerable importance to the development of a policy programme which is specifically geared to what are defined as the distinctive needs of Wales (National Assembly for Wales 2001). As the Minister for Education and Lifelong Learning, Jane Davidson, puts it in her Foreword:

> We share strategic goals with our colleagues in England – but we often need
> to take a different route to achieve them. We shall take our own policy
> direction where necessary, to get the best for Wales. (p2)

Whilst the policy divergences are perhaps most striking for the compulsory sector of education, it is significant that Wales now has administrative arrangements for the LSS which are distinct from those in England, although how far this will produce differences in policies for the sector remains to be seen. Equally, the coming together within Education and Learning Wales (ELWa) of both the National Council (with responsibility for the LSS) and the Higher Education Council[3] offers the potential for the development of policies which are more effectively integrated than elsewhere in the UK. Again, however, it is too early to judge the extent to which this potential will be fulfilled.

It is important to emphasise, however, that these emergent divergences cannot be 'read off' from the existence of new institutions of democratic devolution. To put this another way, it is by no means *inevitable* that the new forms of devolution will produce policy outcomes which are increasingly specific to the constituent territories of the UK. Policy outcomes continue to reflect highly complex processes of negotiation and brokering between, for example, political parties, professional bodies, interest groups, civil servants and so forth. Whilst the new constitutional arrangements have opened up new mechanisms through which such negotiation and brokering can take place, they have not removed the indeterminacy of the outcomes which emerge.

Hence, for example, the operation of the Assembly Committees in Wales has provided much more open access for interest groups of all kinds to influence the process of policy development. And it has been argued that the Committees have provided a more potent source of policy innovation than the Welsh Assembly Government itself. This may reflect, of course, the fact that for the first year or so of its existence, the devolved administration in Wales did not have a majority in the Assembly. However, in Scotland too, it is suggested that the Parliamentary Committees provide an important arena for policy development (in ways that are very different from the Westminster model of Select Committees). For example, the recently published *Interim Report on the Lifelong Learning Inquiry* by the Enterprise and Lifelong Learning Committee promises to effect significant changes in the organisation of the post-16 sector in Scotland, especially in respect of new definitions of 'entitlement' to learning (Scottish Parliament Enterprise and Lifelong Learning Committee 2002). Nevertheless, the substantive content of policies which emanate from this process remain largely dependent upon contingent factors: the actions of individuals; the formation of what may be transitory political alliances; and so forth.

Moreover, there are important pressures which continue to exert an influence in the direction of *convergence* of policy outcomes. The example of the reorganisation of the LSS in Wales, for instance, raises the possibilities for 'policy learning' in the reverse of the traditional direction. As mentioned earlier, historically at least, policies have tended to originate in Westminster and Whitehall and have been implemented in Wales. ELWa offers the prospect of the transmission of effective practice in the opposite direction. Indeed, it has been claimed that ETAG's proposals for the restructuring of the administration of the LSS provided the blueprint for the development of the Learning and Skills Council (LSC) and its associated bodies in England. What is ironic here, of course, is that the model implemented in England was far closer to ETAG's proposals than what was done in Wales, largely as the result of the amendments to these proposals which were made as a result of scrutiny and debate within the National Assembly (Morgan and Rees 2001).

It has also been suggested that 'policy learning' in a technocratic sense does not exhaust the range of possibilities for this kind of process. For example, it is arguable that Scotland's decision to 'abolish student fees' – as it was very widely if not wholly accurately portrayed – produced a kind of 'domino effect' in Wales and Northern Ireland, culminating in the Westminster government's current investigation into the options for the reform of student finance. Certainly it is very likely that the Scottish initiative had significant political effects amongst voters in England (and in Wales), whom New Labour election strategists are very keen to retain. Equally, however, it is difficult to under-estimate the significance in this context of the general instability in the system of student finance – and, indeed, university financing more generally – which derives from a failure to come to terms with the 'massification' of the HE system in the UK as a whole (Rees and Stroud 2001).

More generally too, the extent to which policies for post-16 education and training can diverge between the territories of the UK is restricted by the continuing influence of a

'British system'. Hence, the UK Parliament retains important reserved powers which affect education and training policy, including employment and social security policy. Most crucially, it continues to control spending; and whilst the devolved administrations may reallocate spending between policy areas, their realistic freedom of manoeuvre is limited. In this context, it is instructive, for instance, that the 'Scottish solution' on student fees operates within fairly rigid parameters and certainly falls far short of some of the more radical proposals for changing student financing (for example, Piatt and Robinson 2001).

Equally, there remain important policy initiatives which have a UK competence, often giving rise to some confusion over the responsibilities of the devolved administrations. For example, the Sector Skill Councils (SSCs) and the Sector Skills Development Agency (SSDA) are currently being established as *UK-wide* organisations. They will be developed by groups of influential employers in industry or business sectors of economic or strategic significance and will involve trades unions, professional bodies and other stakeholders in the relevant sector. It is intended that they will function to increase productivity and business and public service performance, through increasing opportunities to boost skills, improving learning supply and thereby reducing skills gaps and shortages. The licensing of the SSCs is by the Secretary of State for Education and Skills, although in consultation with the Lifelong Learning Ministers of the devolved administrations. What this means in practice for the functioning and, perhaps more significantly, the funding of the SSCs remains to be seen.[4] What is clear, however, is that UK policy has not simply disappeared with the advent of even democratic devolution.

In short, therefore, the question of divergence or convergence in policy for post-compulsory education and training is an extremely complex one. On the one hand, there is some emergent evidence of policy divergence, although this should not be seen as an inevitable outcome of democratic devolution, but rather reflects the working out of complex policy-making processes. On the other, there remains a strong 'British system' for policy-making which limits the differentiation which can take place. Moreover, to the extent that 'policy learning' between the territories of the UK develops as a major element in policy-making, then this is likely to reinforce tendencies towards policy convergence.

Devolution and educational outcomes

The discussion so far has focussed on the policy-making process and the policies which emanate from it. It is important to emphasise, however, that whatever the divergences between the UK territories in these terms, there is currently very little evidence to suggest that there are significant changes in the ways that post-16 education and training actually operate on the ground. Hence, there are no indications that, for example, rates of participation in post-compulsory learning are undergoing contrasting patterns of change in the constituent countries. Similarly, there are no suggestions that the quality of teaching and learning in the LSS or HE is being improved (or worsened) more radically in one territory rather than another. Still less can it be argued that the advent of democratic devolution has brought about differential progress towards the achievement of wider policy aims such as greater social inclusion (however measured) or more rapid economic growth. In short, to the extent that there are divergences between the constituent territories of the UK as a result of democratic devolution, they remain at the level of policy, rather than discernible effects of those policies on educational outcomes.

In part, of course, this is explicable in terms of the modest nature of policy divergence so far and the very short period of time that has elapsed during which policies have been able to exert an influence. More fundamentally, however, it serves as a salutary reminder that the impacts of policies on educational outcomes are generally rather modest. Hence, it is well established that patterns of participation in post-compulsory education and training and the quality of learning that is achieved within the latter, are fundamentally shaped by the wider social and economic structures within which they take place. Family background, gender, previous educational experience, employment opportunities, levels of economic activity (and so forth) are all factors which exert profound effects upon people's access to learning after they leave school. However they are factors on which post-16 education and training policies have very little, if any, impact (Gorard and Rees 2002).

This is not to suggest, of course, that the influences of education and training policies are non-existent; but it does serve to warn against expecting too much from them. The effects of these policies are profoundly constrained by the economic and social conditions within which they operate; and so are the devolved institutions which are increasingly responsible for making them.

Endnotes

1   Northern Ireland is excluded from these figures.

2   This was widely regarded as a significant watering-down of the Cubie recommendation to pay back £3000 when annual earnings reached £25,000.

3   Its statutory name remains the Higher Education Funding Council for Wales (HEFCW).

4   Perhaps the commitment to devolution is best illustrated in the fact that the documents relating to establishment of the SSCs all have versions in Welsh.

References

Anderson RD (1992) *Universities and Elites in Britain Since 1800* London: Macmillan

Bogdanor V (2001) *Devolution in the United Kingdom* Oxford: Oxford University Press

Education and Lifelong Learning Committee (2002) *Policy Review of Higher Education* Cardiff: National Assembly for Wales

Gorard S and Rees G (2002) *Creating a Learning Society? Learning careers and policies for lifelong learning* Bristol: Policy Press.

Hazell R (1999) *Constitutional Futures* Oxford: Oxford University Press.

Independent Committee of Inquiry into Student Finance (1999) *Student Finance: fairness for Scotland (The Cubie Report)* Edinburgh: Scottish Executive.

Independent Investigation Group On Student Hardship and Funding in Wales (2001) *Investing in Learners: coherence, clarity and equity for student support in Wales (The Rees Report)* Cardiff: IIGSHFW.

McPherson A and Raab C (1988) *Governing Education: a sociology of policy since 1945* Edinburgh: Edinburgh University Press.

Morgan K and Rees G (2001) 'Learning By Doing: devolution and the governance of economic development in Wales' in Chaney P, Hall T and Pithouse A (eds) *New Governance – New Democracy?* Cardiff: University of Wales Press

National Assembly for Wales (2001) *The Learning Country: a comprehensive education and lifelong learning programme to 2010 in Wales* Cardiff: National Assembly for Wales

National Assembly for Wales (2002) *Reaching Higher: Higher Education and the Learning Country* Cardiff: National Assembly for Wales

OECD (2001) *Cities and Regions in the New Learning Economy* Paris: OECD

Osborne B (2000) 'The Implications of Constitutional Change for Education and Training: Northern Ireland' in Raffe D and Croxford L (eds) *The Education and Training Systems of the UK: convergence or divergence?* Edinburgh: Centre for Educational Sociology

Paterson L (2001) 'Higher Education and European Regionalism' *Pedagogy, Culture and Society* 9, 133-60

Paterson L (1994) *The Autonomy of Modern Scotland* Edinburgh: Edinburgh University Press

Piatt W and Robinson P (2001) *Opportunity For Whom? Options for the funding and structure of post-16 education* London: ippr

Raffe D, Brannen K, Croxford L and Martin C (1999) 'Comparing England, Scotland, Wales and Northern Ireland: the case for "home internationals" in comparative research' *Comparative Education* 5, 9-25

Rees G and Stroud D (2001) 'Creating a Mass System of Higher Education: participation, the economy and citizenship' in Phillips D and Furlong J (eds) *Education, Reform and the State* London: Routledge-Falmer

Scottish Parliament Enterprise and Lifelong Learning Committee (2002) *Interim Report on the Lifelong Learning Inquiry* Edinburgh: Scottish Parliament

V:
Rural Affairs

8. Devolution and the governance of rural affairs in the UK

Neil Ward and Phillip Lowe

Rural character and rural crisis

The UK's rural areas are diverse in their socio-economic and landscape and cultural characteristics. As a result, there have been long-standing differences in emphasis in the rural policy agendas of England, Scotland, Wales and Northern Ireland. However, these differences have been given new salience and new opportunities for expression since the devolution reforms of 1999. Devolution has led to a greater openness and transparency in rural policy-making among the devolved administrations of the UK and has given greater public and political prominence to rural issues. At the same time, devolution has brought new types of tensions between the different parts of the UK in policy areas such as agriculture where European common rules require that a single UK position and framework be adopted.

The UK is a relatively urbanised country in European terms, with four-fifths of the population living in urban areas, and with a relatively high population density of 242 persons per square km. However, this overall figure conceals wide disparities in population density from 376 persons per square km in England to 140 in Wales, 122 in Northern Ireland, and 66 in Scotland. Even in England, population density falls below 30 persons per square km in the most isolated rural districts of the north (for example, Tynedale in Northumberland), a similar density to mid-Wales, and falls below 10 persons per square km in the Scottish Highlands.

Many rural areas in the UK can be characterised as being one or other of two broad types. On the one hand, more accessible rural areas have been experiencing population and employment growth since the 1960s, and there the development pressures for housing, roads and businesses confront the social forces of countryside preservation and greenfield protection. These types of rural area are found around most cities, but also across much of southern and central England. On the other hand, more peripheral rural areas still face the traditional rural development problems of economic stagnation and low incomes – associated with dependency on the primary sector (as well as tourism) – and poor access to services. These areas are more prevalent in northern and western England and Wales and Scotland. The national territories and regions of the UK thus include somewhat different mixtures of these two types of rural area.

The UK's rural areas are also crucially shaped by their regional contexts. England comprises essentially a set of urban-centred regions whose economic and social geography is an important influence on the local pressures and priorities of the rural areas in their hinterlands. In Scotland, in contrast, there are more extensive rural regions, far more marked by geographical peripherality than is the case anywhere in England. These are areas that are peripheral in a UK and a European context, but also in relation to the urbanised central belt of Scotland. In Wales, the most rural areas are in the centre of the nation, with urban Wales occupying the geographical fringes of the north and south. Although Mid-Wales is sparsely populated and agricultural in complexion, it is also subject to socio-economic processes of change driven, in part, from across the border in the English West Midlands.

In addition to differences in geography, population density and peripherality is the varying importance of agriculture. Agriculture accounts for about three-quarters of land use, but less than two per cent of the national working population. In England, even in the 150 most rural districts, agricultural employment amounts overall to less than five per cent of the workforce. Only in a small number of rural districts in England – mainly in the north, the south west and the Welsh Marches – does agricultural employment exceed ten per cent. However, in much of rural Wales farming represents more than 15 per cent of the workforce, while the proportion is over a third in Scotland's Western Isles (Ministry of Agriculture, Fisheries and Food 1999, pp63-64). The conditions for farming also vary, as reflected in the fact that only ten per cent of England's agricultural land is designated as Less Favoured Area compared to 70 per cent in Northern Ireland, 77 per cent in Wales and 84 per cent in Scotland.

There are differences too in the role and connotations of rural culture. The rural environment – 'the countryside' – is very much part of the identities of England, Scotland and Wales, but with varying aesthetics, from the pastoral of the English downs to the sublime of the Scottish Highlands. The popularity, status and contention surrounding country living and country pursuits ensure that an urban-rural divide remains a central feature of the class structure and politics of English society. In Wales, the urban-rural distinction has a different significance and complexion due in large part to the status of the Welsh language. What holds rural Wales at the heart of the Welsh nation is the fact that it is a repository of native Welsh speakers. In Scotland, the history and presence of the large estates coexisting with small farmers and crofters contributes a much greater sense of class conflict *within* the countryside that has shaped Scotland's national consciousness. Finally, in Northern Ireland, the Loyalist/Republican divide is one that runs deep through rural areas.

Recent years have seen a rising sense of crisis surrounding rural affairs across the UK. Campaigning groups have worked to draw attention to rural hardship, including the long decline in local services, the drop in farm incomes since the mid-1990s and the problems that arose from the Foot and Mouth Disease crisis of 2001. However, it has been the legislative threats to hunting that have provided a platform around which campaigners have been able to mobilise the largest numbers of protestors nationally and locally in defence of what they see as valued rural traditions under threat. At the core, therefore, is a crisis of *identity*. Rural areas and their economic and social bases have been subject to a profound set of restructuring processes that are driven externally and are undermining and eroding the distinctive features that define the role and character of traditional rurality (see Ward and Lowe 1999). They threaten to leave the 'rural' as a residual category, affected by change but with little scope to influence it.

Nevertheless, rural agendas have been stubbornly refractory. Arguments for recognition of the distinctiveness of rural sectors and localities have continued to hold sway, driven by increasing public interest in the provenance of food on the one hand, and the continuing appeal of rural areas as distinctive living, consumption and ecological spaces on the other. Thus we have seen the re-emergence of agriculture and 'the rural' as key cultural categories in the UK. In the past, rural distinctiveness was derived from the productive role of the agricultural economy, the prominence of other primary forms of production, and from the contrast between remoteness and accessibility. Now the agricultural and the rural derive their distinctiveness from socio-cultural factors – from notions of lifestyle, tradition, authenticity and nature. This cultural potency has raised the profile of rural issues in public and political debate to levels greater than might be warranted by their economic significance alone.

Two key policy challenges have emerged as a result of this new cultural potency. The first centres upon what we call the *re-territorialisation* of food production. This challenge stems from the question of how to ensure the integrity of farming as a prime source of value in the food chain (whether it be organic, welfare friendly, conservation grade, quality assured, GM free, guaranteed origin, locally produced, or whatever). This is a particular challenge given the many decades in which agriculture has developed as a national industrial sector, producing relatively undifferentiated commodities for a globalised agri-food system. The second challenge is to redefine the role of the rural in the regional and this concerns the distinctive value of rural places in an urbanised society. What particular attributes do rural localities contribute to the economy and quality of life of the regions of the UK – regions that inevitably tend to be understood as urban-oriented, but which increasingly look to their rural areas to define their distinctiveness?

Long-standing rural differences and traditions are thus a feature of the UK and have found expression even in a centralised unitary state. New rural agendas that stress the significance of territory and place potentially have new avenues of expression in the devolved and decentralised governance of the UK post-1999. The rest of this chapter[1] explores the difference devolution and decentralisation have made to the dynamics of rural affairs. The chapter first describes the distinctive rural agendas in the component parts of the UK, both in terms of the continuity of long-standing traditions and the changes stimulated by devolution and decentralisation. It then examines the recent politicisation of rural policy-making, the role of the new devolved administrations and the emergence of new quasi-federal structures within the UK. Two case study 'episodes' are briefly explored to shed light on the post-devolution governance of rural affairs. These concern the financing of CAP reform and the handling of the recent Foot and Mouth Disease crisis.

The chapter's central argument is as follows. Pre-devolution structures of governance allowed some leeway for different emphases in rural affairs in the different parts of the UK, reflecting the distinct rural and regional geographies at work. The two key sets of changes since 1999 have been, on the one hand, the introduction of accountability to elected representatives and a devolved framework for policy devolution in Scotland, Wales and Northern Ireland and, on the other, the gathering pace of English administrative regionalism. The results of these changes to date have been a heightened public and political profile for rural affairs in Scotland, Wales and Northern Ireland and the beginnings of a consciousness about the role of agriculture and the rural environment in regional development in England. In Scotland, Wales and Northern Ireland, devolution has enabled voice to be given to a variety of rural interests and concerns with the effect of raising rural issues up the public and political agendas. However, any acceleration in policy divergence is generally less evident. Common European frameworks have acted as a brake on divergent trends in important areas such as agriculture, and have raised particular problems in devolving crucial spending and resourcing decisions. Future European reforms to rural and agricultural policies between 2003 and 2007, and greater devolution and decentralisation to the English regions, are likely to bring more tensions around these spending and resourcing issues, as pressures for increased differentiation in the governance of rural affairs in the UK grow.

Pre-devolution structures for rural policy and administration

Prior to 1999, the governance of rural affairs involved different models in different parts of the UK. The UK Ministry of Agriculture, Fisheries and Food (MAFF) worked with the Scottish Office Agriculture, Environment and Fisheries Department, the Welsh Office Agriculture Department and the Department of Agriculture in Northern Ireland. The Whitehall Minister was *primus inter pares*, taking the lead especially on European and budgetary matters, but the territorial ministers had substantial responsibilities. Non-departmental public bodies also played important roles in the territories, including Highlands and Islands Enterprise, the Development Board for Rural Wales, the Countryside Council for Wales, Scottish Natural Heritage and the various tourist boards. Rural affairs were thus already characterised by a relatively highly decentralised administrative state for Scotland and, to a certain but lesser extent, for Wales. Decentralisation was less evident for England, but a set of rural quangos – the Countryside Commission, English Nature and the Rural Development Commission – gave expression to an English rural policy, although the term was not generally used. Significantly, the predecessors of each of these agencies had once had a wider UK or England and Wales remit.[2] As they had become split territorially, the English-based agencies had had to come to terms with their sister organisations in the territories and some proto-federal structures had emerged, most notably the Joint Nature Conservation Committee which co-ordinated conservation policy across the UK. In addition, bodies such as the Land Use Policy Group of the statutory conservation and countryside agencies of Great Britain and the Countryside Recreation Network emerged to help share policy intelligence and co-ordinate lobbying among statutory agencies in the fields of rural land use and recreation respectively. To complete a confused picture there was at least one field of policy – forestry – where England and Wales were administered from Edinburgh by the Forestry Commission.

The structure of rural interest groups reflected the different degrees of decentralised administration, but here too there were different models. A set of London/England-based groups have typically taken the lead on UK policy matters in their field, even though their formal geographical remits may have been more circumscribed (for example the Council for the Protection of Rural England, for England; the National Farmers' Union, for England and Wales; and the National Trust for England, Wales and Northern Ireland). Some groups – such as the Royal Society for the Protection of Birds and the Worldwide Fund for Nature – have dealt with their UK-wide responsibilities and membership through offices and branches in Scotland, Wales and Northern Ireland. Others – such as the wildlife trust movement – have adopted a federal structure with the Scottish and Ulster Wildlife Trusts part of a family of trusts which in England and Wales cover one or more counties. Then there is the situation where the devolved administrations have their own autonomous bodies, such as the Campaign for the Protection of Rural Wales and Friends of the Earth Scotland.

It is in Scotland where there has been the most distinctively autonomous rural lobby, with its own NFU, Scottish Landowners' Federation, National Trust, Wildlife Trust, Association for the Preservation of Rural Scotland and so on. Although typically more poorly resourced than their English counterparts, these groups have nevertheless had a significant presence in the smaller policy world of Edinburgh, and have benefited from its greater cohesion and specific focus on 'Scottish interests'. Wales and Northern Ireland in more instances have had to make do with branches of England or UK organisations, but this has not always suited local sensibilities. At the height of the Troubles, the Northern Ireland headquarters of the National Trust were bombed by the IRA, and the NFU in Wales has faced opposition from the Farmers' Union of Wales which sees the NFU as too dominated by English farming interests and agendas.

These variegated UK national administrative and lobbying structures have evolved over the years. One of the significant exogenous forces shaping their evolution has been the gathering process of European integration. The effect has varied between policy fields. Agriculture is highly Europeanised and indeed for a long time it was the only significant common policy of the European Community. Environmental protection became strongly Europeanised in the 1980s, although certain fields – such as land use planning – are still subject to local and national policy frameworks. In the 1990s, rural development was also drawn into a European framework through the expansion of the Structural Funds, especially the Objective 5b rural development programmes and the introduction of the LEADER Community Initiative. In general, the effect of Europeanisation has been to centralise, reinforcing a hierarchy between London or England-based organisations involved in Brussels/UK policy making and other organisations involved in domestic implementation (Lowe and Ward 1998). This has certainly been the case in the agricultural and environmental fields, but there has been a somewhat contrary effect in the rural development field.

Scotland, Wales and Northern Ireland have benefited disproportionately from the European Structural Funds and this has both fostered direct links (bypassing Whitehall) between the devolved administrations and Brussels and promoted regional partnerships of mainly local and sub-national interest groups and agencies (as prescribed by Brussels) to implement regional development programmes. Partly in consequence, Scotland, Wales and Northern Ireland have their own distinctive rural development programmes. Northern Ireland's is the most extensive, with a strong community development focus, financed through a combination of domestic funding, Objective 1, LEADER, PESCA and INTERREG funding, as well as support from the International Fund for Ireland and the Special Support Programme for Peace and Reconciliation. In addition, the Scottish Highlands have had Objective 1 designation and there have been four other Scottish Objective 5b programmes. In Wales, Rural Wales benefitted first from Objective 5b status, and subsequently, West Wales has become an Objective 1 area. Several Objective 5b programmes also ran in England from 1994 to 1999. These programmes helped facilitate the development of nascent structures and networks for expressing regional interests in rural development that have, in some cases, gathered momentum since the programmes ended (Ward and McNicolas 1998).

Before the devolution of the late 1990s there was therefore scope through the decentralised administration of the territories (including England) for different emphases and approaches to be pursued in rural affairs. The scope for decentralised decision-making varied between policy fields, set not only in UK frameworks but also

European policy frameworks. The extent and limits to which policy could practically diverge were revealed in a set of rural white papers for England, Scotland and Wales produced in 1995/96 by John Major's government. Though common in many respects, the Rural White Papers showed notable differences in the relative priority accorded to economic or community development and to environmental protection. For instance, in the Scottish White Paper, *Rural Scotland*, the primary aim was to ensure that 'Scotland's identity as a nation is enhanced', while in the English version, *Rural England*, it appeared to be to 'conserve the character of the countryside'. The differing concerns were reflected in the different policy goals. The Scottish and Welsh documents were preoccupied with the question of how to sustain rural communities – how to ensure their cultural and economic vitality – whereas the English document was preoccupied with sustaining the countryside as 'a national asset, reconciling economic and environmental objectives and ensuring that the rural environment and way of life are not 'submerged in our predominantly urban culture' (see Department of the Environment and MAFF 1995; Scottish Office 1995; Welsh Office 1996; and Lowe 1997, p390). Distinct policies and priorities for rural services, transport, community development and public participation are all clearly evident from the White Papers.

The consequences of devolution

How can we assess the difference that devolution has made to the situation? First, devolution has a number of components. One is the politicisation of policy development and accountability through the introduction of an elected political class in the form of the Scottish Parliament, the National Assembly for Wales and the Northern Ireland Assembly. Another is the transformation of the respective former territorial ministries into national executives with devolved policy-making authority. A third is the requirement for new structures of a proto-federal or intergovernmental kind to mediate formally between the different national executives (including Whitehall) in the UK. We examine each of these in turn to draw out some of the early implications for the conduct of rural affairs.

The politicisation of policy development and accountability

The formal politicisation of territorial governance has considerably raised the profile of devolved matters. Decision-making is now much more directly subject to political accountability, with a huge increase, for example, in the number of questions from politicians that civil servants in the devolved administrations have to answer. There are now many more ministers to publicise policy-making: for example, the former Scottish Office had five ministers, but there are now 22 ministers in the Scottish

Parliament plus three UK ministers with Scottish responsibilities in London. Party competition heightens interest in particular issues, and the proceedings of the new Parliament and assemblies give prominence and bring contention to policy debates. Finally, disagreements or tensions between London and the other UK national capitals are more evident and open to political challenge.

Rural and agricultural issues have not been exempt from this politicisation. Indeed, they have figured particularly prominently in the new political agendas of Scotland, Wales and Northern Ireland. A number of factors seem to be at work. *First*, rural issues have generally risen up the political agenda in the period, including at Westminster. This relates to the widespread sense of rural crisis discussed earlier. Farming groups highlight the marked fall in farm incomes since 1997, and the new Parliament and assemblies have provided them with additional fora through which to expose their plight and grievances. The farm income crisis has elicited a succession of emergency aid packages,[3] but has also focused attention on what should be the long-term strategy for agriculture.

Second, agriculture and other rural sectors are more significant for the economies of Scotland, Wales and Northern Ireland than for the UK overall. Economic problems, subsidy reforms or policy changes affecting rural sectors will potentially have disproportionately greater consequences for them. This has always been the case, but now there is greater scope and political necessity to express different priorities and needs publicly. Thus, while MAFF issued a series of consultation documents during 1999-2000 on certain policy options for UK agriculture in relation to CAP reform, the Scottish Executive produced its own strategy for Scottish farming in June 2001, as did the National Assembly for Wales for Welsh farming in November 2001.

Third, the establishment of the new Parliament and assemblies represent new episodes in the expression of national identities. Given the defining role of rural cultures in Scottish and Welsh identities, it is not surprising that rural affairs have figured prominently in the proceedings and in the efforts of the parties to define their Scottishness or Welshness. Some of the issues raised and debated have also been highly symbolic, such as the role of agricultural supports in maintaining the Welsh language and the possibilities for keeping Welsh agriculture GM-free. In Scotland, several important rural bills have gone through the Parliament, including a number relating to historical struggles over land. For example, the Land Reform (Scotland) Bill was introduced in 2001 to establish rights of public access to the land and the Abolition of Feudal Tenure (Scotland) Bill received royal assent in June 2000. The National Parks (Scotland) Bill establishes powers to create National Parks in Scotland and received royal assent in August 2000, and the Protection of Wild Mammals (Scotland) Bill includes a ban on hunting with hounds and received royal assent in March 2002.

Fourth is the geography of party competition in the new Parliament and assemblies. In Scotland, Labour is in a coalition government with the Liberal Democrats, and the main opposition comes from the Scottish Nationalists and the Conservatives. The rural cleavage is of particular significance in the relationships between the parties given that the Liberal Democrats have rural affairs as one of their Cabinet posts and the opposition parties draw more support from rural areas. In Wales, the Labour Party faces competition from three other parties – the Liberal Democrats, Conservatives and Plaid Cymru – all of whom draw more of their support from rural areas.

Finally, agricultural and rural policies are in essence largely redistributive in nature. They involve the spending of public monies raised through taxation among particular social groups and economic sectors. Inevitably devolution sharply politicises such redistributive policies around the issue of the resource flows to or from devolved administrations. This applies not only to policies that are geographically redistributive by intent, such as regional aid, but to other policy fields where geographical redistribution is an indirect, and until recently little considered, consequence. In this way the development of agricultural and rural policy has become deeply embroiled in arguments about the fairness of funding arrangements.

The national executives and devolved policy-making

Another component of devolution has been the transformation of the respective territorial ministries into national executives with their own policy-making powers and responsibilities. The opportunity has been taken to re-label departments. The previous Scottish Office Agriculture, Environment and Fisheries Department has been renamed as the Scottish Executive Environment and Rural Affairs Department, overseen by a 'Minister for Rural Affairs'. In Wales, rural responsibilities are split between an Agriculture Department and a Department for Economic Development, the former now headed by a 'Secretary for Agriculture and Rural Development'. In Northern Ireland, the old Department for Agriculture, Northern Ireland has been replaced by the Northern Ireland Executive's Department for Agriculture and Rural Development, headed by a Minister with the same title. Despite these name changes, the bulk of spending and activity goes on agriculture, although the scope for 'doing things differently' lies more in other areas of rural policy.

In rural affairs, the CAP is by far the largest spending programmes. MAFF estimated that in 1997-98 total CAP support amounted to £5.27 billion (including £3.63 billion in England (69 per cent of the UK total), £716 million (14 per cent) in Scotland, £473 million (9 per cent) in Wales, and £453 million (9 per cent) in Northern Ireland. The 'intensity' of CAP commodity support also varies across the UK. Measured on a per hectare basis it is highest in Northern Ireland (£425 per ha), followed by England (£395 per ha) and Wales (£320 per ha) and lowest in Scotland (£140 per ha) (MAFF 1999, pp60-61). In 1999, the Agenda 2000 CAP reforms saw the establishment of the new Rural Development Regulation (RDR) hailed by the European Commission as the 'second pillar' of the CAP. The RDR finances agri-environment schemes, support for Less Favoured Areas and for the wider rural diversification and development. Under the Regulation, four rural development programmes have been submitted and agreed: one each for England, Scotland, Wales and Northern Ireland.

One of the key tensions around rural affairs in the UK centres upon what should be the rationale for financial support for the agricultural sector. Given the impetus towards the reduction in market supports in line with moves to further liberalise world trade, the relative emphasis placed on a *social* rationale vis-a-vis an *environmental* rationale becomes an important determinant of the nature and purpose of rural and agricultural policies. A classic economic argument is that support should be for the provision of public goods (usually understood to imply *environmental* public goods such as landscape, soil and water quality and biodiversity). However, this leaves unresolved the question of whether, over and above these environmental resources, the farming population itself constitutes a public good, to be financially supported *for its own sake*. Not only is this tension unresolved, but it is also geographically variable, with more emphasis on this social rationale for farm support in Wales and Northern Ireland, followed by Scotland, and less in England, particularly in the English lowlands. Linked to this geography is that of the relative scepticism around alternative strategies for agricultural competitiveness such as value-added, marketing, diversification, with suspicion about the potentials of such strategies notably stronger in Wales and Scotland. Differences in resource priorities also follow. Questions of the resourcing of Less Favoured Areas (LFA) and agri-environment measures within the rural development programmes depend on how this balance is struck, and in Scotland and Wales there have been greater allocations to simple social payments to farmers through LFA schemes, while in England proportionately more resources are allocated to agri-environment schemes (Dwyer and Baldock 2000).

A further tension is between the traditional institutional sectoralism of the agricultural policy-community, and the imperative of a more territorial and integrated approach to agriculture's role in wider rural development. Government intervention in rural areas and land management has long been highly skewed towards the agricultural sector through a classic 'functional chimney' or 'policy silo': that is, a dedicated Ministry. The establishment of national executives that cut civil servants loose from these silos and demand a corporate approach might be expected to weaken this type of sectoralism. In Scotland and Wales, cross-boundary working is generally regarded to be easier to achieve than in England because the rural policy communities are smaller and so officials have more contact with each other. The main constraint on policy-making capacity lies in the volume of work facing officials in the Scottish Executive and National Assembly for Wales. A longer and more extensive experience with Structural Fund programmes has also meant that cross-sectoral rural development partnerships are more widespread and better established than in England.

In Wales, a more cross-departmental and holistic approach to sustainable development is evident since devolution. This is not least because Section 121 of the Government of Wales Act 1998 established a duty for the National Assembly for Wales (NAW) to promote sustainable development in the exercise of its functions. The duty has been a catalyst for the NAW to develop a sustainable development scheme – 'Learning to Live Differently' – to 'mainstream' sustainability issues across government in Wales. The scheme includes a review of all policies, programmes and grant schemes over a five-year period to align them with sustainable development objectives and an overhaul of appraisal mechanisms and criteria. At the same time, the development of new approaches to spatial planning in Wales are leading to much more sophisticated analyses of the spatial impacts of different NAW policies.

In Northern Ireland, the sensitivities of the Troubles have always made the province a special case in the governance of the UK. As in Scotland and Wales, devolution has altered the dynamics of decision-making. Ministers of the Northern Ireland Assembly are now required to take decisions in consultation with their respective Statutory Departmental Committees of the Assembly. These Committees have a scrutiny, policy development and consultation role. They consider and advise on departmental budgets and plans, approve relevant secondary legislation, initiate and report on enquiries, and consider and advise on matters brought to them by the relevant minister. Rural issues come under the remit of several Departments: Environment, Regional Development, and most importantly Agriculture and Rural Development. However, this arrangement does pose challenges for an integrated approach to rural issues in the Northern Irish context. The Northern Ireland government is in a four-party coalition by design rather than choice, and some ministers are less inclined to co-operate with each other across party lines because of the depth of party differences. As a result, overarching themes such as sustainable development have little profile and are difficult to pursue.

There is evidence that devolution has reinforced agricultural sectoralism, rather than fostered 'joined-up working' in parts of the UK. Far greater attention seems to have been given in public and political debate to farming rather than rural problems, and the processes of policy review in Scotland and Wales have focussed on the preparing of agricultural strategies rather than wider strategies for rural development. In addition, the implementation of the RDR in Scotland, and to a lesser extent in Wales, is such that it has become a narrow instrument to supplement agricultural sectoral support, rather than to strengthen the links between farming and other aspects of rural development. Furthermore, reforms to LFA policy have been conservative in Scotland, Wales and Northern Ireland, where the primary concern is to minimise the losses to those farm businesses most threatened by a move from headage to area-based payments. As a result, there have been complaints from Scottish environmental groups about a farming dominated agenda for rural affairs north of the border, most vividly encapsulated in the lack of enthusiasm in Scotland for modulation to finance an expanded rural development programme.

There are two possible explanations for this reinforcement of agricultural sectoralism. The first is that Scotland, Wales and Northern Ireland are net beneficiaries of the CAP and therefore have less to gain from CAP reform than England. However, also important is the enhanced scope for Scotland-wide or Wales-wide interest groups (such as the farming lobby) to influence their national policy processes through effective lobbying of the new national institutions. In other words, the decentralised administrative structure fostered the development of the territorial farming unions and they have been well placed to shape the policy and political debates post-devolution. Officials in Wales are quick to acknowledge that it is the farming lobby that has been by far the most effective in adapting its lobbying to the post-devolution system.

New 'inter-governmental' structures and relations within the UK

Under the post-devolution arrangements since 1999, the UK remains the Member State of the EU, and so negotiating changes to EU legislation is still a UK-level responsibility, rather than one for Scotland or Wales. It is Margaret Beckett, the Secretary of State for Environment, Food and Rural Affairs, who sits in the Council of Ministers and participates in negotiations. Representatives from the devolved administrations may attend EU meetings, but they accompany the Secretary of State, and then only at her invitation. However, much policy change is in the sphere of interpretation and rule-making by Commission officials, especially desk officers, and here it has long been usual for Scottish, Welsh and Northern Irish officials to liaise with EU officials in Brussels.

Scottish, Welsh and Northern Irish officials and politicians have been able to develop and strengthen direct relationships with European institutions. However, pro-devolutionists in Wales have sometimes been sceptical about the differences that the new Assembly is able to make. For example, an attempt to introduce a Welsh Calf Processing Scheme failed in part as a result of what was widely felt to be a lack of support from the UK Minister of Agriculture (Morgan and Mungham 2000).

EU frameworks have been a particular constraint on the scope for divergence in agricultural policy since devolution. However, their importance has also meant that the dialogue between the four ministers and between their officials has become more structured and formalised through the establishment of a quasi-federal system of intergovernmental structures. Meetings between ministers are held every month, a week before the Agriculture Council, with officials meeting the week before that. These meetings effectively serve as a 'special committee on agriculture for the UK', and have the authority to set up working groups. (A current one is looking at the prospects for CAP reform in the mid-term review, for example.) These arrangements have resulted in a more collaborative, intimate and delicate set of relationships around agricultural policy in the UK. From a Northern Ireland perspective, the meetings are seen to have a formal basis in the Good Friday Agreement (para 31) that led to the establishment of the Northern Ireland Assembly. A memorandum of understanding (MOU) between the UK Government and the devolved administrations sets out the principles upon which the relations between them are based (Lord Chancellor 2000), and a series of concordats between MAFF and the devolved administrations outline more detailed working arrangements (p18-19). Neither the MOU nor the concordats represent legally enforceable contracts: both are intended to be binding in honour only. Therefore, although, *de jure*, the arrangements do not quite go so far as to require unanimity between all Ministers and establish a veto on agricultural policy decisions for each Minister, the crucial importance attached to the maintenance of 'goodwill' means that, *de facto*, every effort is made to secure consensus.

One further dimension to intergovernmentalism post devolution is the new North-South Ministerial Council which means that Northern Ireland Ministers now co-operate on agricultural and rural policy issues with their counterparts in the Republic of Ireland. This arrangement has become an increasingly important influence upon rural affairs in Northern Ireland.

Devolved rural affairs in practice

In this section we turn to two specific policy issues that help shed light on the difference that devolution has made to the governance of rural affairs. These concern the financing of CAP reform and the new European Rural Development Regulation, and the handling of the recent Foot and Mouth Disease crisis. They both deal with agriculturally related matters, for it is here where European frameworks are most constraining and tensions between divergent tendencies within the UK require most careful resolution.

Financing of CAP reform and rural development

This first case illustrates the operational limits of intergovernmentalism within the UK in the context of European frameworks. The Agenda 2000 reform deal gave Member States the discretion, if they so choose, to apply a 'redirecting' measure, called modulation, to the direct payments to farmers under the CAP. The system of direct payments was introduced following the 1992 CAP reforms to 'compensate' farmers for reductions in levels of commodity price support. They provide UK farmers with some £2.0-£2.5 billion a year. The Agenda 2000 reform deal means Member States can claw back up to 20 per cent of these payments, and recycle these savings into expanded European financing for the accompanying measures in the RDR, including LFA and agri-environment schemes. The modulated expenditure under these measures requires domestic match funding, and so in order to 'green' the CAP in this way, additional funding has to be agreed by the Treasury.

Modulation proved the most contentious aspect of the implementation of the Agenda 2000 reforms in the UK. Its main proponents were the environmental lobby and statutory countryside conservation agencies, and the momentum for modulation was generated first and foremost within an English rural environmental agenda. It can be applied using any one, or a combination, of three criteria which allow Member States to selectively apply the measure, discriminating against the more prosperous farms or those that receive the most aid or employ fewer workers (Falconer and Ward 2000). How the burden of modulation is distributed across the farming community – as well as the decision whether or not to modulate at all – is at the discretion of the Member State. To date, only the UK and France have chosen to use the measure.

The then Agriculture Minister in Whitehall, Nick Brown, announced the decision to apply modulation in December 1999 to greatly expand the funding for the implementation of the RDR. He talked in terms of 'a major switch of farm spending from production aids to support for the broader rural economy' which represented a 'radical redirection of support' (MAFF 1999a, p1). The move flew in the face of conventional wisdom that no major additional public resources should be allocated to agriculture prior to a fundamental reform of the CAP that would include the dismantling of most of its price supports and direct payments. It therefore marked a major departure for UK public policy. It was a necessary step, though, if the UK was going to make anything at all of the potential of the new RDR. (Allocations for RDR financing from the EU were based on historical patterns of spending under the old accompanying measures, and so the UK fell foul of low levels of past uptake of these schemes.) However, modulation starting at 2.5 per cent and rising to 4.5 per cent by 2006, with matched funding from the UK Treasury, will increase the total budget for the RDR by about 60 per cent in this period, including a doubling of the resources for agri-environment schemes in England.

There has been much less enthusiasm for modulation in Scotland, Wales and Northern Ireland where the measure is continually referred to by farming groups as a 'tax on farming' (despite the fact that modulated receipts bring in additional match-funding). The NFU in Scotland has strongly opposed the measure, and many in Wales have been uncomfortable with a UK-wide system having to be 'imposed' on Welsh farmers. However, the strength of opinion in Whitehall that modulation represented a progressive step in the modernisation of the UK's approach to the CAP meant that the Scots, Welsh and Northern Irish had to go along with the measure. After legal opinion was sought, it was considered that modulation would have to be applied in a single standardised way across the whole of the UK, otherwise the Government may have been vulnerable to legal challenge from farmers on the basis of unfair competition. The decision could only be sold to the Scots and Welsh by the Treasury conceding that it would provide the match-funding element rather than it coming from the devolved budgets. (In the case of Northern Ireland, the modulation decision was taken during a period of 'direct rule' from Whitehall.)

In Scotland, the Rural Affairs Minister has tried to placate farmers by assuring them that the additional resources in the RDR that result from modulation will go back to farmers. He said:

A number of bodies consulted suggested that some of this money should be used for wider rural development purposes, other than farming. I have rejected that. Half of this money comes from farmers and it is right that this money plus the matched funding goes back to them in ways that will benefit their industry.[4]

More recently, the Policy Commission on the Future of Food and Farming (2002), established after the 2001 General Election under the chairmanship of Sir Don Curry, contained a set of recommendations about accelerating the use of modulation as the centre-piece of its proposals for reform of agricultural policy. The Commission recommended that the rate of modulation be raised to ten per cent by 2004 and if substantive reforms to the CAP were not agreed during the coming mid-term review, then the rate of modulation be upped to 20 per cent. Much of the comment and coverage of the Curry Commission focused on the relative merits of this aspect of its analysis.

The Curry report provoked a strong response from farming groups in Scotland, Wales and Northern Ireland who attacked the Commission for straying beyond its remit, which was confined to England. Scottish NFU President, Jim Walker, complained:

The Policy Commission was given a very specific remit to consider future food and farming strategy in England alone. But its sweeping recommendation on modulation, if implemented, would have a substantial impact on the incomes of all farms across the UK. To make such a major recommendation shows a serious disregard for its brief and a failure to understand devolution. In Scotland, Wales and Northern Ireland, where agriculture plays an even more important role than in England, farming and rural strategies have already been drawn up by the devolved administrations working with farming and rural organisations. The Policy Commission has no right to stray into these areas (quoted in Wright 2002).

For modulation to be deepened, as recommended by Curry, is likely to require that UK ministers agree a *quid pro quo* for the devolved administrations. Ratcheting up modulation could prove a real test for devolution, and for the management of a single co-ordinated line on CAP reform.

Linked to the contentious issue of CAP financing has been the implementation of the Rural Development Regulation which illustrates the operation of the national executives. Four plans have been produced in the UK, and each is different in terms of the process of plan formation, the balance of priorities, and the general profile the plan has within the wider framework for rural policy.

In England, the Plan contains a national framework of measures, accompanied by nine regional chapters. Measures for agri-environment schemes, Less Favoured Areas, and an energy crops scheme are programmed nationally. Other measures are administered at the regional level. These are the Rural Enterprise Scheme (which includes measures for village improvement, tourism, farm diversification and environmental protection), a new Processing and Marketing Scheme, and a rural development training scheme. The Plan was drawn up after a wide ranging consultation exercise involving a national strategy group and regional stakeholder groups. However, the national and regional consultations operated simultaneously, and the extent to which the two lines of thinking gelled is rather limited. Put simply, the regional consultation and drafting produced regionally-tailored draft plans that were quite broad in scope. Once these were fed into the national structures, they were streamlined and simplified and the final regional chapters have a stronger element of national steer and less regional diversity in the measures they include.

In Scotland, the consultation process on which the Plan was drawn up has proved more contentious than that in England, with several rural development and environmental organisations left bitter and disillusioned. The process was criticised for the very limited consultation on the contents of the Plan, with timescales that were prohibitively tight. A draft plan was published and circulated to interested parties on 14 December 1999, with comments requested for 21 December and submission to the European Commission by 3 January 2000. The draft plan included three core accompanying measures (Less Favoured Areas, agri-environment and forestry) with additional proposals for measures covering processing and marketing, diversification, promoting public access and some other Article 33 measures (to promote the adaptation and diversification of rural areas). However, in the final plan submitted to Brussels, these additional measures had been removed. The narrow scope of the plan, with its strongly agricultural focus, angered some of the participants on the team responsible for drafting the plan.

In Wales, the three core accompanying measures (Less Favoured Areas, agri-environment and forestry) also dominate the programme's finances, although it does contain processing and marketing, training and Article 33 measures. Consultation in Wales was structured around individual sets of measures, with less discussion about the overall structure of the programme as a whole or the allocation of resources between measures. Consultation was most extensive around the agri-environment measures. There has generally been far less disgruntlement in Wales about the drawing up of the plan than has been the case in Scotland. Furthermore, in Wales, a wider range of organisations has responsibility for operating different parts of the programme (including the Welsh Tourist Board and the Welsh Development Agency, for example).

The English Rural Development Programme is geared more towards agri-environment than the others, while spending on Less Favoured Area (LFA) aid is more significant in Scotland and Wales. For example, the allocation of spending on agri-environment measures accounts for around 20 per cent in Scotland, 25 per cent in Northern Ireland, 35 per cent in Wales and 60 per cent in England, while proposed spending on LFA aid comprises 40 per cent, 65 per cent, 40 per cent and 18 per cent respectively.[5]

Overall, the RDPs have different role and profiles in England, Northern Ireland, Scotland and Wales. In England, the Rural Enterprise Scheme (with its bundle of Article 33 measures) has the scope to fund relatively broad rural development projects from CAP funds. The regionalised structure to the programmes has also added some impetus to the process of a regionalised rural policy for England, including the development of new regional institutional structures. In Scotland and Northern Ireland, the programme has become a much narrower beast of agricultural structures policy, in part because it is felt that wider rural development objectives are better delivered through alternative funding programmes than the CAP. It is strongly asserted that the programme in Scotland should be for the benefit of farmers, and environmental groups, in particular, despair of a missed opportunity to build a broader and more integrated approach to rural and agricultural development. In Wales, the RDP sits within a family of Structural Fund programmes and within a strong policy priority to target support at the 'Welsh family farm'. Most public and political attention around the RDP has therefore centred upon a 'stock-taking' exercise to review the Welsh Tir Gofal agri-environment scheme within the plan, particularly to raise participation among the medium-sized family farms.

Once the Member States of the EU had agreed the RDR, the process of drawing up plans and deciding upon financial allocations between measures has been conducted in a highly devolved way in the UK, with only very limited central oversight. As a result, even within the common framework of the RDR, the UK has a fairly diverse set of rural development programmes tailored to local rural contexts, but also shaped by the relative influence of different rural interest groups in each territory. We are now moving from a period of launching and establishing the schemes programmed in the new plans, to one where the scope and financing of the RDR is likely to come under increasing scrutiny under the mid-term review of both the RDR and the wider CAP. As a result, issues in which the UK is the competent negotiator will come to the fore again, and a key question will be the extent to which the scope for differentiating RDPs within the UK will increase or not.

Handling of the Foot and Mouth crisis in the UK

The handling of the outbreak of Foot and Mouth Disease (FMD) serves as a case study of the comparative efficiency of the national executives and illustrates the scope for competition between devolved structures. Fighting FMD depends upon decisive and forthright action at the local and regional levels to combat the disease. Action at these levels must accord with national and European guidelines but these need to be interpreted and acted upon with dispatch and efficiency by people close to the ground. In a sense, therefore, the conduct of the FMD campaign across the UK was something of a test of the ability of devolved structures for effective action. Scotland's outbreak was a much smaller one than England's and if bigger would have overwhelmed Scottish resources. However, as a smaller country with a smaller administrative establishment it could work more effectively and co-operatively across departments and with partners. A more realistic comparison than that between Scotland and England would be that between Scotland and Cumbria. In epidemiological terms the Scottish outbreak was part of the Cumbrian outbreak. However, the last confirmed case in Scotland was on the 30 May and that in Cumbria was the 30 September. The outbreak lasted three months in Scotland but seven months in Cumbria. In Cumbria also the scale was much greater: there were more than five times the number of confirmed cases in Cumbria compared with the whole of Scotland. However, a critical factor in the relatively rapid treatment of the disease in Scotland was the absence of certain tensions that characterised the disease campaign in England.

First, there were political tensions within Westminster, and a party political divide over the conduct of the disease which picked up on the politicisation of rural matters under the first Labour government. It did not help matters that the disease came about either side of Westminster parliamentary elections. In Scotland, in contrast, the ruling coalition between the Lib-Dems and Labour and the fact that the Minister for Rural Affairs is a Liberal Democrat, meant that the issue was much less party politicised.

A second set of tensions in England was inter-departmental ones. A basic divide in Whitehall was between MAFF on the one hand and agencies and organisations representing the countryside, the rural economy and tourism (the then Department of the Environment, Transport and Regions, the Countryside Agency, tourism organisations and the Department for Culture, Media and Sport) on the other. These divides were not at all so apparent within Scotland. This is partly due to the tradition of corporate working within the Scottish Executive. However, it is also partly due to the weakness of the representation of non-farming rural interests, the lack of strong central representation from Scottish tourism interests in rural areas, and the rural affairs remit of the relevant department. The need in the Whitehall system for the Cabinet Office to get so centrally involved to give a greater strategic direction to the campaign did not arise within Scotland. A key factor was keeping the issue fairly apolitical which meant a clear division between the political and the technical in the management of the outbreak, and that facilitated a great deal of behind the scenes technical joint working and co-operation.

A third tension apparent in the English case is that between the central level and the local level. Staff of the Scottish Executive, including the veterinary service, ran the campaign but did so in part by seconding key staff to the regional councils (that is, they operated completely through the regional council structures). There was therefore a clear co-ordination between the contingency plans of the Scottish Executive and the contingency planning at the regional and local level. This aspect was completely absent for several weeks in the English regions. This reflected a degree of over centralisation within MAFF, as well as MAFF's lack of involvement in the regional Government Office structures, and its lack of tradition of working with English local authorities. However, another element was the evident knowledge within the Scottish Executive of the local complexities of Scottish agriculture compared with their counterparts in London. This partly reflects the tradition of the London civil servants to look not towards the regions but towards Brussels whereas the role of Scottish civil servants has been to deliver policy within Scotland.

Differences in departmental structures were also important. The agricultural division within the Scottish Executive incorporates the functions that used to be operated in England by the Farming and Rural Conservation Agency. These functions are much more incorporated into the central agricultural administration. The net effect is that there are much more direct relationships whereby the civil servants responsible for agriculture within Edinburgh are more informed about the regional diversity of Scottish farming. In contrast, London based officials are not as knowledgeable about the complexity of farming in the English regions. MAFF in London had a poor understanding of sheep movements in Cumbria, for example.

A final comparative issue is the relationship between Government and its partners. The Scottish Executive and the NFU in Scotland worked together very closely and there were not the sort of tensions that were seen in London. On the other hand the rural economy and tourism interests were much less evident in the Scottish crisis. Of course, tourism is not so significant in the worst affected area of Dumfries and Galloway than in the rest of Scotland, especially tourism from UK and overseas visitors. Therefore, the local economy was much less affected by the problem of UK or overseas tourists staying away, less so than Cumbria and less than would have been the case if FMD had hit other regions of Scotland.

FMD has also highlighted issues about post-devolution governance in Wales and Northern Ireland. In Northern Ireland, a stronger tradition of devolved administrative discretion (than is the case in the English regions, for example) allowed for a stronger, swifter and more decisive response on the part of the Northern Ireland Executive. The Northern Ireland minister placed an immediate ban on imports the day after the first FMD case was confirmed in England and only four cases were suffered in the Northern Ireland outbreak in all. In Wales, the experience of FMD has led to calls for the National Assembly for Wales to be given an extension of its powers to cover animal health matters.

Conclusions

We have argued that even before devolution, the governance of rural affairs showed different characteristics in England, Scotland, Wales and Northern Ireland. This was not only as a result of different rural geographical conditions, but also a function of the decentralised administrative state in Scotland, Wales and Northern Ireland. The different balance of priorities expressed in the Rural White Papers for England, Scotland and Wales in 1995/96 are a useful benchmark against which any further divergence after devolution can be assessed. Post-devolution, some new initiatives can be identified that suggest increasing scope for discretionary action in the governance of rural affairs in Scotland, Wales and Northern Ireland. The creation of new National Parks and an early ban on hunting with hounds in Scotland are symbolic examples of devolution in practice.

Devolution has led to the establishment of new institutions in the devolved administrations, and these have titles that suggest a broadening of approach from more narrowly sectoral, agricultural departments to more holistic and territorial departments of rural development or rural affairs. However, the relatively greater importance of the farming industries in Scotland, Wales and Northern Ireland compared to England have meant the continued dominance of agriculturally-oriented approaches to rural development. If anything, agricultural sectoralism has become more entrenched in Scotland and Wales since devolution. In any case, the importance of European policy frameworks such as the CAP has been one constraint on the divergence of agricultural policies within the four parts of the UK. However, the need for a single UK negotiating position on CAP issues has also meant the improved co-ordination of discussions on these issues between ministers and officials.

The politicisation of rural and agricultural issues is principally a function of the political geography of representation within the devolved administrations and the fact that opposition parties represent more rural areas. In Scotland, rural issues have become more politically salient because they are an important portfolio for the Liberal Democrats in the coalition government.

The balance of arguments for and against the use of modulation to expand resources for the CAP's second pillar – the Rural Development Regulation – varies across the four parts of the UK. As the arguments for modulation, and for a deepening and accelerating of the approach, gather strength in England, this will produce increasing tensions in policy co-ordination in the coming few years and will test the post-devolutionary arrangements. The approach to the CAP's second pillar also varies in the four parts of the UK, including the contents of the respective rural development programmes and the processes by which they were drawn up. In England, the ERDP is partly regionalised, and is dominated by spending on agri-environment schemes. It has been used to develop a more devolved framework for what might be termed 'integrated rural development'. In Northern Ireland, Scotland and Wales, LFA payments are more significant components, and rural development programmes are treated as more narrowly concerned with agricultural structures policy.

The handling of the FMD outbreak in Scotland seemed to have been characterised by fewer of the difficulties faced in England. While the scale of the outbreak clearly differed, a stronger Scottish tradition of the agricultural administration working more closely with local authorities meant the disease control, and especially the culling, could be carried out more quickly, and with less challenge, than in England. This differential handling of the foot and mouth crisis may also point to the greater scope, post-devolution, for competitive efficiency in public administration. Competition between different territorial units could serve as useful tool in policy learning and in administrative learning between the different parts of the UK.

Devolution has brought into sharper light the rural/agricultural version of the English question: what is English (as distinct from British) agricultural and rural policy? The regional re-organisation of MAFF/DEFRA, and the increasing dialogue between rural and regional development means that the notion of a (regionalised) English rural policy is beginning to emerge.

Endnotes

1   We would like to thank Douglas Greig, Pat Toal, June Milligan, Kevin Morgan, Sarah Thomas and Nicola Thompson for their helpful comments on a draft of this paper. We are also grateful to the participants at an ippr/ESRC Devolution Programme seminar at the University of Birmingham for their comments and suggestions. However, as authors we alone are responsible for the views expressed in the chapter.

2   English Nature was formally a large part of the Nature Conservancy Council for the UK. The Countryside Commission covered England and Wales, and the Rural Development Commission was the Development Commission for the UK.

3   Even prior to FMD, the Government had given a total of £435million of emergency aid additional to CAP payments between 1997 and 2000 (Cabinet Office 2000, p35).

4   SERAD Press release, August 2000, www.scotland.gov.uk/news/2000/08/se2177.asp

5   These proportions are for the early years of the programmes and will change as the modulation money comes on stream (Dwyer and Baldock 2000, p25 & 30). Of course, these different proportions partly reflect the proportions of agricultural land in LFAs in each country. Only approximately 10 per cent of England's farmland is in LFAs, while the designation covers the vast majority of Northern Ireland, Scotland and Wales.

References

Cabinet Office (2000) *Sharing the Nation's Prosperity: Economic, Social and Environmental Conditions in the Countryside* London: Cabinet Office

Department of the Environment and Ministry of Agriculture, Fisheries and Food (1995) *Rural England: A Nation Committed to a Living Countryside* Cm 3016 London: HMSO

Department of the Environment, Transport and the Regions (1998) *Digest of Environmental Statistics* 20 London: The Stationary Office

Dwyer J and Baldock D (2000) *The Rural Development Regulation in Britain: Fulfilling the Promise* London: Wildlife and Countryside Link

Falconer K and Ward N (2000) 'Using modulation to green the CAP: the UK case' *Land Use Policy* 17, 269-77

Lord Chancellor (2000) *Devolution: Memorandum of Understanding and supplementary agreements between the United Kingdom Government, Scottish Ministers, the Cabinet of the National Assembly for Wales and the Northern Ireland Executive Committee* London: Lord Chancellor's Department

Lowe P (1997) *The British Rural White Papers: A comparison and critique, Journal of Environmental Planning and Management* 40(3), 389-400

Lowe P and Ward S (1998) (eds) *British Environmental Policy and Europe: Politics and Policy in Transition* London: Routledge

Lowe P, Buller H and Ward N (2002) 'Setting the next agenda? British and French approaches to the second pillar of the Common Agricultural Policy' *Journal of Rural Studies* 18, 1-17

Ministry of Agriculture, Fisheries and Food (1999) *Reducing Farm Subsidies – Economic Adjustment in Rural Areas* London: MAFF

Morgan K and Mungham G (2000) *Redesigning Democracy: The Making of the Welsh Assembly* Bridgend: Seran

National Assembly for Wales (2001) *Farming for the Future: A New Direction for Farming in Wales* Cardiff: National Assembly for Wales

Policy Commission on the Future of Food and Farming (2002) *Farming and Food: A Sustainable Future* London: Cabinet Office

Scottish Executive (2001) *A Forward Strategy for Scottish Agriculture* Edinburgh: Scottish Executive

Scottish Office (1995) *Rural Scotland: People, Prosperity and Partnership* Cm 3041 Edinburgh: HMSO

Ward N and Lowe P (1999) 'Insecurities in contemporary country life: rural communities and social change' pp154-68 in Vail J, Wheelock J and Hill M (eds) *Insecure Times: Living with Insecurity in Contemporary Society* London: Routledge

Ward N and McNicholas K (1998) 'Objective 5b of the Structural Funds and rural development in Britain' *Regional Studies* 32, 369-74

Welsh Office (1996) *A Working Countryside for Wales* Cm 3180, London: HMSO

Wright S (2002) 'Curry strays into regions row' 29 January *Farmers Weekly Interactive* newspage [www.fwi.co.uk]

9. Subsidiarity without solidarity? The rural challenge in post-devolution Britain

Kevin Morgan

One might quibble with some of the details but this should not detract from the key point – which is that that Neil Ward and Philip Lowe have produced a robust and convincing analysis of 'rural affairs' in post-devolution Britain. Inevitably in a chapter which addresses such a wide array of issues, the authors have had to sacrifice depth for breadth. To try to compensate for this I propose to elaborate on some of the issues which merit further discussion, namely:

- the advent of 'proto-federal' structures to regulate rural affairs

- the reform of the Common Agricultural Policy (CAP), and

- the Curry report on the future of farming and food

In each of these thematic comments I shall draw on recent experience in Wales because this highlights a very different rural agenda to what seems to emerging in England.

Proto-federalism and uneven development

One of their key arguments is that devolution did not create rural differentiation; on the contrary, rural uneven development was an established fact of life long before the advent of democratic devolution in 1999. The real significance of democratic devolution was that it gave *voice* to these differentiated rural systems. Pre-devolution the organisation of differentiated rural interests took the form of a political hierarchy in which MAFF saw itself at the apex of a command and control system. Post-devolution we still have a hierarchy with DEFRA at the top, but this is leavened by proto-federal structures which make it more of a negotiated order than a command and control system.

The monthly meeting of the four rural ministers provides the key forum in which policy differences are resolved, where the UK 'line' is established so to speak, and this proto-federal mechanism simply did not exist pre-devolution. The legal requirement on the UK government to have an agreed line vis-à-vis Brussels inadvertently confers on the devolved administrations a de facto power of veto over Whitehall, a power which paradoxically grows in significance the less it is used. None of the devolved administrations like to exercise this power unilaterally because they are anxious not to damage the goodwill on which so much of the new governance system depends. When this veto power was successfully exercised – most notably when Wales and Northern Ireland withheld their agreement to DEFRA-sponsored reforms of the Beef Special Premium which would have damaged their livestock farmers – it was done with a heavy heart, underlining the great reluctance to use this power of veto.

The new proto-federal structures also embrace direct meetings between the devolved administrations and the European Commission. In addition to the monthly EU Agriculture Council meeting (which the devolved ministers attend), the devolved administrations organise their own bilateral meetings with the Commission, but these tend to be brokered by UKREP, whose officials prepare a 'note' of the proceedings to keep Whitehall in the new multi-level governance loop. Far from resenting the UKREP presence the devolved administrations set a high premium on having good relations with UKREP because the latter can cut them into a wide array of Brussels-London information networks. In other words the devolved bodies see enormous advantages in having a good relationship with UKREP and other central state departments. This suggests that the scenario of a Europe of the Regions – in which regions are portrayed as forging an alliance with Brussels to denude the central state of its powers from above and below – is a singularly inappropriate prism through which to understand the emerging politics of multi-level governance.

If rural policy agendas diverge more openly in the future, as seems likely, one of the potential conflicts could be DEFRA's dual role as an English rural department on the hand and the UK lead department in the EU on the other. At this point the politics of uneven development could threaten the new structures of proto-federalism because the latter depend on goodwill to a greater extent than we realise.

Reforming the CAP: from productivism to sustainability?

The CAP has been written off so many times before that its continued existence is a testament to the awesome power of vested interests in agriculture. However, the vested interests of the productivist coalition – particularly agri-chemical companies, farmers and their political representatives at national and EU levels – have never looked more vulnerable, hence the prospects for reform would seem to be better today than at any time in the history of the CAP. The CAP is under siege not just from the usual suspects – the neo-liberals who equate subsidy with original sin – but more importantly from a loose coalition of forces which espouses a more sustainable form of agriculture and rural development (for example, environment groups, consumer groups and public health groups).

Philip Lowe and Neil Ward have been in the forefront of academic analysis of CAP reform, particularly of the Rural Development Regulation, the so-called 'second pillar' of the CAP, which was designed to put the CAP on a more acceptable footing by allowing member states to support sustainable farming and a living countryside (Falconer and Ward 2000; Lowe *et al* 2002). Although Lowe and Ward's chapter alludes to it, the key problem for the UK with the 1999 reform of the CAP was that it was allocated such a low share of the overall RDR budget (just 3.5 per cent, a sum described as 'scandalous' for a country which represents 12 per cent of EU agricultural land (Policy Commission on the Future of Farming and Food 2002)). As the authors rightly say, however, this allocation was based on historical patterns of spending on agri-environmental measures, which were low due to the low priority accorded to sustainable development by successive Tory governments. This is a stunning example of 'lock-in', where a country's future is shackled to its past.

Along with Germany, Sweden, Denmark and the Netherlands, the UK is pushing for a radical reform of the CAP, but this may have to wait a few years because the broad framework for agriculture has been agreed until 2006. The main change in the interim is likely to be a further shift of resources from the commodity regime (pillar 1) to rural development (pillar 2), further modulation in other words. Up until now modulation has been a discretionary device, indeed it has only been used by the UK, France and Portugal. However, one of the changes which might be introduced as part of the mid-term review of the CAP could be compulsory modulation to shift new resources into the more sustainable activities of pillar 2 of the CAP.

Although pillar 2 subsidies are generally more acceptable than pillar 1 subsidies, the UK Treasury remains nervous about the shift of resources because pillar 2 activity involves domestic match-funding as the authors rightly emphasise. Some Treasury mandarins appear to think that domestic match-funding is tantamount to throwing good money after bad and that 'degressivity' as it is called – the progressive reduction and eventual elimination of direct CAP payments – should be the priority not modulation. This issue lies at the heart of the third and final theme I want to address, the Curry report.

Deconstructing Curry: for Britain, see England?

Ostensibly a report about the future of farming and food in England, the Curry report has much wider implications. As the authors correctly note, the recommendations of the Curry report, particularly the call for higher rates of modulation in the UK, induced a furious response from the farming lobbies of Celtic Britain. Although modulation dominated the headline coverage of the Curry report, it is worth reminding ourselves that the key theme of the report was the highly laudable theme of *reconnection*. Its aim was:

> to reconnect farming with its market and the rest of the food chain; to reconnect the food chain and the countryside; and to reconnect consumers

with what they eat and how it is produced (Policy Commission on the Future of Farming and Food 2002).

The authors are absolutely right to note that this theme is part of a wider trend towards the 're-territorialisation of food production', a trend which is developing from a very low base in Britain because a 'food as fuel' culture has triumphed over a 'food as pleasure' culture, an outcome which owes much to the levelling effect of the supermarkets.

Although the authors stop short of saying so, the Curry vision of a re-localised food chain will never be realised unless supermarkets are obliged to undertake more local sourcing. It is worth noting that the CPRE has challenged supermarkets to set targets for five per cent of all food sales from each store and five per cent of food lines to consist of local foods by 2005 (CPRE 2002). Re-localising the food chain could offer a multiple dividend, in urban and rural areas, by creating local markets for local producers, by reducing food miles and by supplying more nutritious food for schools, which has health and educational benefits. This is an example of how the devolved administrations could become laboratories of development by using creative public procurement in schools and hospitals to promote a sustainability agenda where it matters most: in the prosaic warp and weft of everyday life (Morgan and Morley 2002).

In the absence of radical CAP reform in 2006 the Curry report recommended that the UK government should go for the maximum rate of modulation (20 per cent), adding that 'further progress in this area must hold good in all countries of the UK'. In terms of the politics of devolution this is the most incendiary issue in the Curry report because modulation is more popular in England than it is in Celtic Britain. Conscious of this differential support, and painfully aware of the de facto veto which the devolved administrations enjoy, DEFRA is beginning to champion a more devolved approach to modulation so as to allow England the freedom to go its own way and to reduce the power of the Celtic veto.

Although Ward and Lowe do not address the full implications of the issue, we might say that the consequences of uneven rural development are finally coming to the fore in the sense that the Curry vision is not the Celtic vision. Taking Wales as an example we might say that the rural vision contained in *Farming for the Future* covers all three dimensions of sustainability – economic, environmental and social sustainability – the social dimension being essential to the future of the 'family farm' which is deemed to be vital to the preservation of the Welsh language (National Assembly for Wales 2001). The Curry report, in contrast, is totally silent about the social dimension of sustainability and in this sense it can be read as an outrider for the Treasury vision dressed up in an environmental garb.

The greatest calamity from a Celtic standpoint would be for DEFRA to succeed in devolving responsibility for modulation and for the domestic match-funding requirement to be dropped, as could happen in the event of compulsory modulation across the EU. This would cut Celtic Britain off from the central supply of Treasury match funds; the spectre of *subsidiarity without solidarity*.

While the Curry report tries to establish an intellectual case for pillar 2 subsidies as public goods, one must ask if there is a sustainable future for the 'family farm' in Celtic Britain in the absence of pillar 1 support? Ward and Lowe are right to see modulation as a major test of the devolution settlement, but the Curry report elides as much as it reveals and its silence on the social dimension of sustainability needs to be remedied in the evolving debate about the future of rural Britain.

References

CPRE (2002) *Down Your Way? A CPRE Briefing on Supermarkets and Local Food* CPRE, London

Falconer K and Ward N (2000) 'Using Modulation to Green the CAP' *Land Use Policy* 17, 269-77

Lowe P *et al* (2002) 'Setting the Next Agenda? British and French Approaches to the Second Pillar of the CAP' *Journal of Rural Studies* 18, 1-17

Morgan K and Morley A (2002) *Re-localising the Food Chain: The Role of Creative Public Procurement* Cardiff University: The Regeneration Institute

National Assembly for Wales (2001) *Farming for the Future* Cardiff: National Assembly of Wales

Policy Commission on the Future of Farming and Food (2002) *Farming and Food: A Sustainable Future* London: Cabinet Office

VI:
Conclusions

10. Beyond Barnett? Financing devolution
David Heald and Alasdair McLeod

Although there are now Devolved Administrations outside England, the United Kingdom is still essentially a unitary state, not a federal one. This is a distinction which matters. Moreover, in comparison with other unitary states, there is highly centralised and unified control over public expenditure and taxation, exercised directly by, or on behalf of, the Treasury. Whatever the nominal autonomy of public authorities, whether at different tiers (for example, Devolved Administrations and local authorities) or within central government (departments, executive agencies and Non-Departmental Public Bodies), very little fiscal activity eludes this highly centralised overall control. Any exceptions are usually either accidental or tolerated specifically to promote certain kinds of centrally approved behaviour by public authorities.[1]

A consequence for UK devolution finance is that the expenditure basis is paramount. There is thus no guarantee that tax increases by sub-national governments would necessarily enable higher expenditure. Only the Scottish variable rate of income tax (tartan tax) is excluded from this rule (Treasury 2000a). This centralised context is the one within which the arrangements for UK devolution finance will have to evolve.[2]

The United Kingdom may be thought of as having a public expenditure system characterised by a division between two types of expenditure. The first is expenditure undertaken on a UK basis, either on 'national' programmes, such as Defence (all UK residents and non-resident UK citizens are presumed to benefit), or on 'uniform' programmes, such as Social security (uniform benefit scales lead to geographically differentiated expenditure).[3] The pattern of demography and economic activity means that an inevitable result of uniform UK policy is substantial implicit territorial equalisation in terms of benefits.

The second type of expenditure is undertaken on a country basis,[4] with well-defined and separate systems for Scotland, Wales and Northern Ireland. England is also treated separately, though this is often obscured by the frequent assumption, particularly by London-based commentators, that England and the United Kingdom are geographically coterminous. UK departments, generally based in Whitehall, have had substantial difficulty in managing the fact that they usually act for England, but sometimes act for Great Britain or the United Kingdom. The greater confidence enjoyed by Devolved Administrations compared to that of their territorial office predecessors means that Whitehall departments can no longer take their UK policy leadership for granted, as Keating notes in Chapter 1. Evidence of this has already appeared on student fees and care for the elderly.

On this second type of expenditure, the expenditure systems in the three territories are semi-detached from those applying to England. As explained in the next section, the most important part of the funding of the Devolved Administrations is the Assigned Budget, a system representing a continuation of the pre-devolution system which had been in place for 20 years.

There is no formal system of explicit equalisation among countries, whether for resources or needs, of the kinds familiar in federal countries such as Australia, Canada and Germany. Since England constitutes 84 per cent of the UK population, there is clearly a substantial danger that English policy will drive policy elsewhere. The Barnett system is best viewed, first, as a political accommodation (the Devolved Administrations are largely unconstrained on how they spend existing and additional resources) and, secondly, as a means of containing political conflict (asymmetrical structures and differences in country population make conventional 'federal-provincial' negotiating machinery difficult to envisage). Much of the political attention currently paid to the Barnett formula hinges on the contradictory assertions that it is extravagantly generous to the Devolved Administrations, or that it is imposing destructive financial pressures upon them.

Within each country, there are parallel and complex systems of territorial allocation which distribute the resources that have accrued through the Barnett system. These systems operate autonomously, though in parallel. Differences in structure, policy and financial mechanisms make it extremely difficult to draw comparisons between how a public authority in one country would have fared on the funding allocation system of another.

The lack of transparency is partly a consequence of a general lack of understanding of how the territorial system operates. This obscurity afforded protection for the policy and financial autonomy of the territorial offices which preceded the Devolved Administrations. There is a considerable literature on the reasons why there was limited policy variation pre-devolution, in spite of financial freedoms to switch expenditure (Midwinter *et al* 1991). The Secretaries of States' membership of the UK Cabinet was an obvious constraint.

The discussion in this chapter is almost exclusively about the expenditure side of the public budget. The only systematic data on revenue at a sub-national level are found in *Government Expenditure and Revenues in Scotland* (GERS) (Scottish Executive 2001), published annually over the last decade. The Welsh counterpart (Welsh Office 1996; 1997a) was abandoned by the present Government after two issues, and there has never been a comparable document for Northern Ireland. In Scotland, political debate about GERS frequently revolves around how oil revenues from the UK Continental Shelf should be treated in discussions about Scotland's viability as an independent state. The UK convention is to attribute oil revenues to 'Extra Regio', part of the United Kingdom but not of its constituent regions.

In this chapter it is argued that, under devolution, the expenditure basis will remain; this is the UK tradition and the absence of a proper federation makes a formal revenue-based system difficult to envisage. Realistic reform should aim to increase fiscal accountability at the margin (Bell *et al* 1996, Blow *et al* 1996) by allowing some tax variation within defined limits.

The territorial level

Description of the devolved funding system

There are many complexities to the UK devolved funding system, but the basic outline can be readily explained. The budgets of the Devolved Administrations are determined in three ways: an unconditional block ('Assigned Budget'),[5] covering most of their activities; specific allocations for services operated according to UK or EU policy; and the amounts raised by the Devolved Administrations and their local authorities and public bodies from taxes and charges under their control. Expenditure in the first two categories is financed mainly, but not exclusively, by transfers from the UK government.[6]

Changes to the levels of the Assigned Budgets are determined primarily through the mechanism known as the Barnett formula, established in 1978.[7] This formula operates only on increments, not on the base, allocating to each country a population-based percentage of the increase in comparable expenditure in England. Specific allocations are negotiated bilaterally. The Devolved Administrations have limited control over total budget size, but have extensive discretion over expenditure composition.

Accountability for spending rests with the Devolved Administrations, which are accountable to the devolved Parliament and assemblies. Audit is undertaken by the public official (Auditor General for Scotland, Auditor General for Wales and Comptroller and Auditor General for Northern Ireland) who heads the respective territorial audit offices.

The idea of a formula determining part of territorial expenditure is not new. The Goschen formula (allocating 11/80ths of English expenditure) was used to determine part of Scottish expenditure from 1888 until the 1950s. The Barnett formula was first introduced at the time of the previous devolution (to Scotland and Wales) legislation in 1978. The intention was to set up, in consultation with the devolved Assemblies, a system whereby a formula was settled for each four-year period, giving each devolved Assembly a fixed proportion of English expenditure on comparable services (Cabinet Office 1977). The proportion would have been fixed on the basis of a needs assessment. The Barnett formula seems to have been an interim arrangement, pending the introduction of that system.

In the event, devolution did not proceed at that time, but the Barnett formula remained. It was continued by the incoming Conservative Government, possibly because it eliminated disproportionate argument over settling a small part of overall UK public expenditure totals.

The existence of the formula became public knowledge in 1980 (Committee on Scottish Affairs 1980), although the details of its operation remained opaque until the 'block rules', first produced in 1984,[8] finally reached the public domain on 30 March 1999 (Treasury 1999), just before elections to the devolved Parliament and assemblies.

Applied systematically, the Barnett formula would result, in time, in equal expenditure per capita, on devolved services in aggregate, across the United Kingdom (expenditure indexes converge asymptotically on 100). The expenditures on individual services would not necessarily converge since the Devolved Administrations can decide to give priority to particular services, though that would be at the expense of other services (unless Scotland levied the tartan tax). The speed of convergence depends upon the rate of growth of nominal public expenditure.

However, population relatives change through time, and this brings about different convergence limits for each country. Cuthbert (2001) proves this mathematically; the limiting value becomes a function both of the rate of change of relative population and of the rate of change of nominal expenditure.[9]

A formula, such as Barnett, which distributes equal per capita increments to each country automatically delivers smaller percentage spending increases to those territories with the highest starting values of the index. In consequence, Scotland's expenditure rises faster than Northern Ireland's, but rises slower than England's. Particularly in Northern Ireland and Wales, such comparisons of 'headline' year-on-year increases have brought discomfort to the Devolved Administrations, even in times of 'plenty'.[10]

The Barnett formula has not, in fact, been operated on this 'clean' basis; instead, a number of important factors have combined to qualify the analytical results. First, there have been changes in the public expenditure framework within which the formula has operated. The most important of these is that the formula originally operated in a volume-planning environment, and thus only operated on real terms increments. Even after the advent of cash planning, echoes of volume planning remained in that new baselines for the horizon year (that is to say, the year coming into the Survey for the first time) were constructed with an uplift giving some allowance for inflation (Thain and Wright 1995). This uplift procedure ceased in 1993, though this fact was not made public until 1997 (Treasury 1997b). Second, formula bypass[11] seems to have occurred in the 1980s and early 1990s, but has become less important as the formula has been more strictly applied. The third point is not about the operation of the formula but about demographic change: Scotland's relative population has continued to fall, thereby mitigating the predicted falls in the expenditure index.

There are two popular misconceptions about the Barnett formula. Contrary to some claims, it was never intended to equalise spending per head across the UK. The formula, initially an interim arrangement, operated at first only on real terms changes, thus making convergence extremely gradual. After the change to full cash planning, the territorial Secretaries of State understood that they could call for a successor needs assessment to that published in 1979 (Treasury 1979), should they feel it necessary. The fact that this was never done suggests that they calculated that such a needs assessment would not be in their interests.

Despite recent ministerial statements, there was never a formal allocation based on need; the Barnett formula is a *population-based* mechanism to allocate increments of public expenditure, not a *needs-based* formula as it is sometimes described. Perceptions of differential need played some part in shaping the public expenditure allocations before the 1978 establishment of the Barnett formula. These allocations formed the original baseline on which the system is built. But political bargaining had also been important in determining those allocations (Midwinter *et al* 1991).

There are two principal advantages of such a system to the Devolved Administrations. First, they are not constrained to spend formula consequences according to the pattern set in Whitehall. They enjoy the expenditure-switching discretion previously much valued by territorial Secretaries of State, without some of the political inhibitions on its use. What matters crucially to the Devolved Administrations is how the UK government prioritises, say, Education and Health against Defence and Social security. The UK government's decisions on the composition of 'English comparable expenditure', say, between Education and Health, is of no direct concern. Second, this insulates the Devolved Administrations from the Treasury, which has used techniques such as Public Service Agreements and Cross-Cutting Reviews as instruments for strengthening policy control over Whitehall departments. Those who believe that such centralised control will lead to better policy making will regard this as a disadvantage. Those, like the present authors, who do not share this view will recognise this insulation as one of the crucial advantages of the Barnett arrangements to the Devolved Administrations.

Formula consequences

Although there is now much more detailed information in the public domain about the operation of the Barnett formula (Treasury 2000a), it has hitherto been impossible to replicate from data in the public domain the calculation of formula consequences. This can now be done for Scotland, with regard to the Spending Review (SR) 2000 settlement (Treasury 2000b), using data published by the Scottish Affairs Committee (Scotland Office 2002).

Table 10.1 shows the formula consequences for the years 2001-02, 2002-03 and

2003-04, with the total for 2003-04 being £3,000 million. The first three columns show changes in comparable expenditure in England, with the third column referring to 2003-04. The fourth column shows the weighted comparability percentage for each main programme; the derivation of these weights is detailed in the Funding Policy document (Treasury 2000a). The fifth column shows the Barnett formula proportion, based on population shares, which was then 10.34 per cent of England. Strikingly, 97 per cent of Scotland's formula consequences were derived from changes in six main programmes: Education and employment; Health; three then Department of the Environment, Transport and the Regions (DETR) programmes; and the Home Office.

The formula-driven Assigned Budget is the principal, but not sole, part of the funding available to the Devolved Administrations. Figure 10.1 shows the funding scheme for the Scottish Parliament; there are also parallel diagrams for the National Assembly for Wales and the Northern Ireland Assembly in the July 2000 Funding

Figure 10.1 The funding regime for the Scottish Parliament, 1999-2000 onwards

Assigned budget	Non-assigned budget	
Departmental Expenditure Limit (DEL)		**Annually Managed Expenditure (AME)**
Barnett formula determined	Non-Barnett determined	Main programme spending
Secretary of State's/Advocate General's office		
Education and arts Health and social work Industry, enterprise and training	HLCAs (now renamed LFASS)	CAP
Transport and roads Housing, Scottish Homes external finance Law and order Crown Office	Welfare to Work (now transferred into the Assigned Budget)	Housing support grant
		NHS and teachers' pensions
Domestic agriculture Environmental services Forestry CalMac and HIAL's External Finance Requirements Student loans: implied subsidies and provision for bad debts Capital Receipts Initiative Trust Debt Remuneration Scottish Renewables Obligation Bus Fuel Duty Rebates		Other AME: Certain accrual items such as capital charges and depreciation charges
		Local Authority Self- Financed Expenditure (LASFE)
		Scottish Non-Domestic Rates
		Scottish Variable Rate of Income Tax
Other expenditure outside DEL: Police Loans charges		

Source: HM Treasury (2000a) p27
KEY: CAP = Common Agricultural Policy; HIAL = Highlands & Islands Airports Limited, a public corporation which runs certain small airports; and HLCAs = Hill Livestock Compensation Allowances (now renamed Less Favoured Area Support Schemes).

Table 10.1 Derivation of Spending Review 2000's Change in the Scottish Parliament's Assigned Budget DEL (£ million)

	Changes to comparable expenditure in England			Weighted comparability proportion	Barnett formula proportion	Formula consequences		
	2001-02	2002-03	2003-04	(%)	(%)	2001-02	2002-03	2003-04
Education and employment	1,600	3,770	5,960	93.3	10.34	154.36	363.70	574.97
Health	2,760	7,740	12,310	99.7	10.34	284.53	797.92	1,269.04
DETR – Transport	1,000	2,450	4,100	71.2	10.34	73.62	180.37	301.85
DETR – Housing & other environmental services	260	1,130	1,820	96.5	10.34	25.94	112.75	181.60
DETR – Local Government	650	3,090	5,710	56.4	10.34	37.91	180.20	332.99
Home Office	1,560	2,240	2,580	92.3	9.77	140.68	202.00	232.66
Legal Departments	310	370	390	97.8	9.77	29.62	35.35	37.26
Trade & Industry	1,020	710	650	20.2	10.34	21.30	14.83	13.58
Domestic Agriculture	210	300	330	84.3	10.34	18.30	26.15	28.76
Forestry	10	10	10	100.0	10.34	1.03	1.03	1.03
Culture, Media and Sport	80	130	200	95.3	10.34	7.88	12.81	19.71
Chancellor's Departments	350	550	580	2.1	10.34	0.76	1.19	1.26
Cabinet Office	120	120	190	0.1	10.34	0.01	0.01	0.02
Total formula consequences as per calculations						795.95	1,928.32	2,994.73
Total formula consequences as per Scotland Office (2002)						800.00	1,940.00	3,000.00
Rounding error						4.05	11.68	5.27

Notes:
1. Rounding errors originate in the change to comparable expenditure in England being published to the nearest £10 million.
2. England and Wales population proportions apply to Home Office and to Legal Departments.

Source: Scotland Office (2002)

Policy document (Treasury 2000a p27). There is a common structure to the funding system in all three territories, though there are some differences in the kinds of functional expenditure devolved. For example, Scotland alone has 'Law and order' (though this could be devolved to the Northern Ireland Assembly should the security situation make this possible), and the Northern Ireland Assembly alone has responsibility for the social security system (though this is best seen as an agency arrangement, as there is no policy discretion).

Embedding within the UK Public Expenditure System

The exposition above has highlighted how deeply the Devolved Administrations are embedded into the UK public expenditure system. The 1998 Comprehensive Spending Review saw the introduction of a new public expenditure control system, focusing upon Total Managed Expenditure (TME), itself composed of Departmental Expenditure Limits (DELs) and Annually Managed Expenditure (AME). From 2001-02, government accounting switched from a cash basis to an accruals basis, under the project known as Resource Accounting and Budgeting (RAB) (Treasury 2001b).[12]

When the devolution funding scheme was determined in 1997, it was not known that the Treasury would, in 1998, revamp public expenditure control aggregates and move to a biennial survey. The Assigned Budget is classified as DEL, as are certain other items of expenditure which, for various reasons, are not formula-controlled. An example is Hill Livestock Compensation Allowances (now renamed Less Favoured Area Support Schemes). Until recently, Welfare-to-work (a programme originally financed out of the windfall tax on privatised public utilities) also appeared here, but has now been absorbed into the Assigned Budget. At the time of a Comprehensive Spending Review, namely in 1998, 2000 and 2002, DELs are set three years ahead. Changes to the Assigned Budget are controlled by the Barnett formula, with the costs of running the residual territorial offices top-sliced in the cases of Scotland and Wales.

In contrast, AME is set one year ahead, largely on the grounds that these items are more difficult to control and forecast. AME covers three distinct types of expenditure. The first is for the agency-type functions over which the Devolved Administrations exercise almost no discretion. Expenditure on the Common Agricultural Policy has to be negotiated bilaterally with the Treasury, since this is a demand-led programme. The second type is a temporary one; the non-cash items such as capital charges and depreciation, consequent upon RAB, will be scored as AME until they are integrated into DEL, as from 2003-04. The third type represents the revenue-raising sources under the control of the Devolved Administrations, namely Non-Domestic Rate revenue, Local Authority Self-Financed Expenditure and the proceeds, if any, of the tartan tax in Scotland. Treatment as AME is a practical mechanism for allowing discretion to the Devolved Administrations. However, this discretion is not guaranteed except in the case of the tartan tax.

Although there is greater transparency post-devolution about the *system*, largely thanks to the publication of the hitherto secret 'block rules' (Treasury 1999; 2000a), there is not transparency about the *numbers*.[13] An indication, however, of the predominance of Barnett formula-determined DEL is that, for 1999-2000 plans, this accounted for 79 per cent (Scotland), 87 per cent (Wales) and 84 per cent (Northern Ireland, excluding Social security benefit expenditure).

The Treasury controls, directly or indirectly, all borrowing on programmes controlled by the Devolved Administrations, which themselves can only borrow temporarily for timing reasons. Moreover, the 'consent' counterpart of (borrowing for) capital expenditure by local authorities and public corporations is scored against the Assigned Budget. One of the reasons why the Private Finance Initiative (PFI) (a Treasury programme to bring private finance and management into asset provision in, for example, transport, education and health) has been embraced in Scotland is that it is an approved route to evade borrowing restrictions. This is despite the fact that there remain ideological and Value-For-Money (VFM) doubts. The standard justification offered politically in Scotland for the adoption of the PFI route is one of capital starvation and the non-availability of public funds ('only show in town'); this sits uncomfortably with concerns that the Barnett formula will in future bring convergence.

Contrary to the purposes of various EU programmes of regional support to less prosperous regions, the award of funds from the European Regional Development Fund (ERDF) generally does not bring additional resources to the beneficiary UK country or region. Despite EU pressure, UK governments have consistently argued that there is additionality in aggregate, namely that public expenditure as a whole is higher than could have been afforded in the absence of ERDF receipts. The most politically dramatic event connected with devolution was when Alun Michael, having been parachuted into the Welsh Labour leadership by the Blair Government to stop Rhodri Morgan being elected First Secretary, had to resign in February 2000 because he failed to deliver extra money following the acquisition of Objective 1 status[14] by West Wales and the Valleys (a geographic construction covering 63 per cent of the area and 65 per cent of the population of Wales). Subsequently, Rhodri Morgan became First Secretary, the Treasury allowed funding 'above Barnett', and the minority Labour administration in Wales followed the Scottish precedent and went into coalition with the Liberal Democrats.

The formula bypass, obtained by the National Assembly for Wales to provide cover for Objective 1 ERDF receipts, received media and political attention beyond its importance. It was described as blowing a hole in the Barnett system. This Welsh exceptionalism provoked outrage in the Scottish media, always keen to spot offence, until someone pointed out that an extension of this concession to Scotland (which was losing ERDF funds) would have meant a reduction in the Scottish Parliament's Assigned Budget. Including European Social Fund transfers, Wales received an additional £420 million over the three years of SR 2000; the matching requirements of ERDF had to be met out of either the existing expenditure base or the Barnett formula consequences. Even without the intense politics surrounding EU funding, there was a case for exceptional treatment, as indeed there would have been if, say, Wales had been the only part of the United Kingdom to suffer from BSE or foot and mouth disease.[15]

As the operation of the formula becomes more transparent, with the numbers entering the public domain, cases of formula bypass will attract more attention. If the bypass is favourable to the Devolved Administrations, this will reduce the amount of convergence which takes place. Contemporary examples of bypass include parts of the 'Reinvestment and Reform' package announced for Northern Ireland by the Prime Minister and Chancellor of the Exchequer on 2 May 2002 (Treasury 2002b), and elements of the write-off of Glasgow City Council housing debt as part of the transfer of municipal stock to a housing association.

Comparative expenditure statistics

There are severe limitations to existing territorial and regional analyses of public expenditure (Heald 1994, Heald and Short 2002). Much misunderstanding has been created by looking at the wrong expenditure aggregate (for instance looking for convergence at the level of identifiable expenditure) and by comparing expenditure in an English region with expenditure in the territories, without adjusting for unallocated expenditure in England.

The starting point for identifiable expenditure analysis is Total Managed Expenditure on Services (TMES). From TMES are then deducted those items of public expenditure held to be of general benefit to UK citizens, and thus not identifiable to countries or regions. Territorial analysis into country can then be undertaken on Identifiable TMES. In 1999-2000, Identifiable TMES constituted only 77 per cent of TME, the Treasury's current control aggregate (itself one step removed from General Government Expenditure, the international definition).

In the absence of better and more relevant data, inter-country comparisons fall back on the figures for identifiable public expenditure published annually by the Treasury in *Public Expenditure: Statistical Analyses (PESA)*.[16] Taking data primarily from the 2001 issue (Treasury 2001d), the top half of Table 10.2 shows public expenditure indexes for Scotland, Wales and Northern Ireland, on the base UK = 100. Although these are imperfect proxies for devolved expenditure (against which comparative data for England are not published), the indexes for identifiable expenditure less Social security are interesting. The striking point is that the index, when Social security is excluded, is much higher for Scotland and Northern Ireland, but not for Wales.

There have been longstanding complaints about the poor quality of expenditure data for the English regions (Treasury and Civil Service Committee 1989). One aspect of this has been a large amount of expenditure identified to England but not to individual regions. One of the improvements in *PESA 2001* (Treasury 2001d) was that the analysis of English regions is now integrated into the country analysis, so that the England Total disaggregates fully into regions.[17] The data for 1999-2000 are tabulated in Table 10.2 (overleaf). When interpreting the indexes on individual programmes, attention should be paid to the UK weight, indicating the percentage of total expenditure accounted for by that programme. The entries for Totals in each column are weighted averages. These figures show marked variations in levels and compositions among countries and regions. Certain figures should be interpreted with caution. For example, the figures for 'Housing' in some prosperous regions are clearly affected by the netting off of the proceeds from council house sales. There are grounds for concern about data quality, particularly for programmes which are identifiable but not devolved, and for the within-England analysis. Much greater expenditure disaggregation is a precondition for analytical work on these differences.

There has always been a lack of transparency to the operation of the Barnett formula. A crucial point is that there are no published data for 'comparable English expenditure' on the same definitions and coverage as the Scottish, Welsh and Northern Ireland Assigned Budgets. Because of different functional responsibilities, three separate series of data are needed. The Treasury takes a proprietary view of its public expenditure database and refuses access to this even to the pre-devolution territorial offices and the Devolved Administrations. There has been so much recent change to the definition and measurement of public expenditure aggregates that do-it-yourself calculations are likely to be inaccurate. It will become increasingly difficult for the UK government not to publish counterparts to Table 10.1 (formula consequences), immediately after settlements such as SR 2002. However, what are really required are systematic time series data.

When better data become available, the Devolved Administrations will have to be ready to resist pressures to replicate the changes in English comparable programmes. As the levels of comparable expenditure in England are not published, it is not possible to express the changes by main programme, as shown in Table 10.1, as percentage increases. However, it can be seen that the formula consequences for Education and employment accounted for 19 per cent of increases in the Scottish Assigned Budget DEL in 2003-04, with Health accounting for 42 per cent. Suggestions that, for example, Health in Scotland should therefore take 42 per cent of the formula consequences have to be firmly resisted. Quite apart from denying devolved policy choice, the base positions of programmes are different.

Table 10.2 Indexes of identifiable expenditure per capita, by territory, region and function 1999-2000

1999-2000 data, expressed as £ per capita (cash), relative to UK = 100

	UK weight	Scotland	Wales	N Ireland	England	England weight	North East	North West	Yorkshire & Humberside	East Midlands	West Midlands	South West	Eastern	London	South East
Education	15.4%	126	100	136	96	15.4%	100	101	96	93	101	92	96	108	82
Health and personal social services	24.1%	119	110	111	97	24.3%	102	100	98	88	92	91	92	121	85
Roads and transport	3.1%	130	112	89	96	3.1%	96	97	74	85	89	88	95	122	105
Housing	1.1%	176	145	325	82	1.0%	57	90	71	35	37	35	4	304	25
Other environmental services	3.2%	131	168	106	93	3.1%	117	106	45	90	92	79	76	126	94
Law, order and protective services	7.1%	96	96	206	97	7.1%	104	101	93	90	88	85	75	144	83
Trade, industry, energy and employment	2.6%	149	113	255	90	2.4%	103	94	91	96	90	87	86	94	76
Agriculture, fisheries, food and forestry	1.7%	267	155	283	73	1.3%	75	73	75	73	69	75	73	72	73
Culture, media and sport	2.0%	99	157	60	99	2.1%	143	88	87	81	82	83	75	176	76
Social security	38.7%	108	115	120	98	39.3%	119	112	101	94	99	97	89	97	84
Miscellaneous expenditure	1.0%					1.0%									
Total	**100.0%**	**118**	**113**	**133**	**96**	**100.0%**	**109**	**104**	**95**	**90**	**94**	**92**	**88**	**113**	**84**
Total excluding social security		**125**	**112**	**142**	**95**		**102**	**99**	**91**	**88**	**92**	**88**	**87**	**123**	**84**

Source: Treasury (2001d), Tables 8.6B and 8.12.

Note: An index of miscellaneous expenditure is not calculated since the administration costs of departments other than in the territories are not separated from functional expenditure. Such an index would be misleading.

Possible technical developments

There are no data in the public domain which would enable confident judgements to be made about whether there has been convergence, or, if not, why. Although it is generally thought that the formula was applied with less bypass in the 1990s than in the 1980s, no satisfactory data are available. The 1990s represented a period of low nominal expenditure growth, reflecting both low inflation and low real expenditure growth. Under such circumstances, the mathematics of the formula suggest that there would be limited convergence.

The annual rate of nominal expenditure growth in England obviously has an impact upon convergence. This is explored in Figure 10.2, the horizontal axis of which represents years over which the Barnett formula is strictly applied. No allowance is made in Figure 10.2 for the effect of relative population change, as a result of which indexes converge asymptotically on 100, meaning that they will never precisely reach 100. Practical measures of the rate of convergence are therefore required, and it may be useful to borrow the concept of half-life from nuclear physics. The half-life indicates the number of years it takes for the activity of a radioactive particle to decay to half its original value. If the Barnett formula is strictly applied, with no bypass, with an annual rate of nominal expenditure growth of two per cent, it would take 35.0 years for half

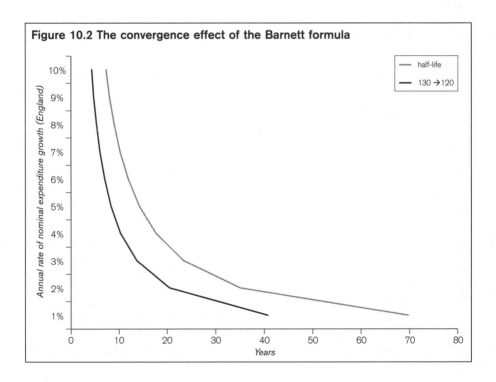

Figure 10.2 The convergence effect of the Barnett formula

the differential (upwards or downwards) from 100 to be eliminated, for example to move from 120 to 110, or from 110 to 105. With a nominal annual expenditure growth rate of eight per cent, this half-life becomes nine years.

It is also possible to consider how many years it takes for the index to fall from one value to another. For the index to fall from 130 to 120 would take 20.5 years at two per cent growth, and 5.3 years at eight per cent growth. Comparable figures can be calculated for any pair of index values, and both the 'half-life' and the '130→120' functions of Figure 10.2 are steep when there are annual rates of nominal expenditure growth above six per cent.

If the annual rate of nominal expenditure growth envisaged by SR 2000 were to be continued throughout the first decade of the 21st century, and the Barnett formula was strictly applied, evidence of convergence with regard to the formula-controlled DEL would soon appear. Nevertheless, were this to happen, devolved expenditure would be at a much higher level in real terms than would have been envisaged when devolution was implemented in 1999.

Such a development would make a needs assessment much more likely. If a needs assessment had been completed for all four countries, the issue would then arise of how the upward or downward adjustments from the actual expenditure indexes to the needs indexes would be effected. It would certainly not be feasible for a sudden drastic reduction to be imposed on any of the Devolved Administrations, as that would destabilise them. It would be possible, though the Treasury might resist, for a Devolved Administration whose expenditure index was below its needs index to receive a sudden increase. The availability of End-Year Flexibility on DEL within the three-year SR system would offset some of the traditional concerns about a sudden budget increase not being well used. Consequently, something looking rather like the Barnett formula, operating on increments, would be quite likely to follow the conduct of a needs assessment.

High rates of growth of nominal expenditure, and stricter application of the Barnett formula (there is less opportunity for formula bypass favourable to the territories), may now bring considerable convergence. This necessitates thought as to how the convergence process should be managed as the expenditure index comes closer to the needs index. Figure 10.3 plots expenditure and needs indexes on the vertical axis (England = 100). The horizontal axis measures cumulative incremental expenditure, which begins at zero and increases along that axis. The horizontal axis can also be thought of in terms of years, provided that the annual rate of growth of nominal expenditure is known.[18] Line B represents the Barnett formula convergence on 100, in the case where there is no relative population change.[19]

There has been concern that rapid nominal expenditure growth would produce excessive convergence, with a Devolved Administration 'crashing through' its needs index as the Barnett formula drives convergence on England = 100. Thus a 'needs-weighted' formula, following the path of B^{nw}, could be adopted: instead of incremental expenditure being allocated on the basis of population, it is allocated on the basis of weighted population (population multiplied by the needs index, possible only after the conduct of a needs assessment). Convergence would then be upon N, the needs index of that Devolved Administration. It would be possible to adopt B^{nw} either immediately (when expenditure is at E_0) or when the expenditure index reaches some threshold value above N. In Figure 10.3, the threshold is represented by T and the horizontal dotted line. The convergence path from Z (the intersection of B with the threshold) is labelled B_z^{nw}.

The adoption of either B^{nw} or B_z^{nw} would be more favourable to the Devolved Administrations than using B, on the assumption that their needs indexes were above 100, and would therefore be more expensive to the Treasury. Regardless of the political importance of devolution, territorial funding remains a minor part of the Treasury's portfolio of activities. An advantage from the Treasury's viewpoint would be that, by avoiding the risk of overshooting the needs index, there would be less risk of excessive strain on the devolved funding system. A possible consequence of excessive strain would be large amounts of *ad hoc* formula bypass. Consequently, the cushioning of convergence, as shown in Figure 10.3, might increase the resilience of the formula system.

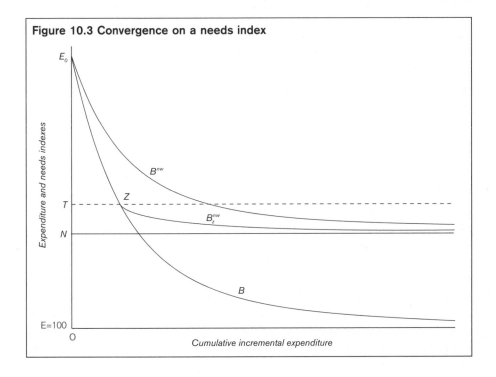

Figure 10.3 Convergence on a needs index

Resource allocation within countries

Whereas there has not been any formal equalisation scheme across the United Kingdom, highly complex systems exist within each of the four countries. Important examples are: National Health Service (NHS) funding allocations; the allocation of Aggregate External Finance to local authorities; and the formula funding of universities and higher education institutions. Even before devolution, developments often took place in each country largely in isolation from developments in the other countries. Post-devolution, these internal allocations have begun to attract more attention, particularly in relation to the NHS. In England, the formula funding of schools and further education colleges has attracted a great deal of attention.

There has been pioneering work in all parts of the United Kingdom on the use of performance indicators, and not solely needs indicators, within such funding formulae (Carr-Hill *et al* 1994, Smith *et al* 2001). Much of the literature is prescriptive about how funding systems should operate. Particularly in the local government sphere, there has been concern about the extent to which such formula mechanisms are used to exert central control rather than simply to fulfil their equalisation role. Peter Smith (1988) noted the potential for gamesmanship in the context of the local government finance distribution system in England. Moreover, Stephen Smith (1999) noted the danger that, after many years of tight central government control over English local authority spending, the regressions run for Standard Spending Assessments now pick up the effect of controls in earlier years, not just variations in local preferences and expenditure needs. This is a powerful argument against bringing the Devolved Administrations within existing English mechanisms for resource allocation, as proposed by Davies (1997). Such penetration 'through the veil' of the Devolved Administration tier to the constituent local authorities and NHS bodies would unleash strong pressures for spending in the territories to conform to the English pattern.

Institutional machinery

UK government has been very top-down, with a hierarchical relationship between central government and local authorities, even before the 1980s saw a removal of functions, the imposition of compulsory competitive tendering, and the diminution and restriction of revenue raising. Even within the territories, with their separate territorial offices, political authority came through the Secretary of State from the Prime Minister and the UK Cabinet. On a constitutional level, devolution does not necessarily change this. The Scottish Parliament was established by Westminster legislation, which any future government can repeal, and the funding basis is only contained in the devolution White Papers (Scottish Office 1997, Welsh Office 1997b) and non-statutory Treasury guidance (Treasury 1999; 2000a). There can be no such thing in the United Kingdom at present as a constitutional assignment of powers.

Nevertheless, the political reality is quite different. Devolution 'all around' fundamentally alters the politics; between them, the three territories elect about one fifth of the UK Parliament.[20] The withdrawal of devolved powers is unlikely to be attempted by a UK government unless it enjoyed significant support for such a policy in that territory. Although the UK government can exercise the power to suspend the Northern Ireland Assembly, it is far less likely that this could be done in the case of Scotland and Wales, where primary legislation would be required. There are now credible alternative political mandates, with Devolved Administrations looking to their own electorates, whose behaviour in UK elections may differ from that in devolved elections. A further complication arises from proportional representation to the devolved bodies, together with coalition government which is a likely consequence. In Scotland and Wales, this has facilitated a revival of the respective Conservative Parties, making UK commitments to roll back devolution highly problematic for a UK Conservative leader.

External to the Devolved Administrations

Various bodies and processes are in place to facilitate close working relationships between the UK government and the Devolved Administrations, such as the Joint Ministerial Committee, the agreement of concordats on various topics, and the role of the Judicial Committee of the Privy Council. What remains unclear is how financial disputes would be resolved, especially given the highly centralised system of public expenditure control and the limited own revenues of the Devolved Administrations.

The aborted devolution plans of the 1970s produced a needs assessment conducted by an interdepartmental committee chaired by the Treasury (1979). This work provided the context within which the Barnett formula was adopted. Although nothing has ever been published, the Treasury has periodically updated its assessments of the relative needs of Scotland, Wales and Northern Ireland. Understandably, the Devolved Administrations do not trust either the Treasury's ownership of public expenditure data or the potential uses to which its private estimates of relative need might be put. Such concerns will have been magnified by the Deputy Prime Minister's promise during the 2001 General Election campaign that there would be 'blood on the carpet' about the Barnett formula (Hetherington 2001). Sensationalised reports about threats to the Barnett formula frequently appear without the source being identified.

Given this context of suspicion and of poor data, only a body independent of the UK Treasury would command consent in any future needs assessment. There is presently a remarkable amount of confusion about even basic facts, stemming in part from an apparent failure to understand the difference between relative and absolute changes. The Barnett formula is regularly portrayed in Scotland, Wales and Northern Ireland as a means of depriving them of equal percentage increases to those in England, whilst in England it is regarded as feather-bedding the territories, particularly Scotland (McLean 2000; 2001). Politicians and the media work themselves up into a lather, sometimes about things which are unimportant or irrelevant. To what extent this is playing political games, and to what extent genuine ignorance, is sometimes difficult to assess.

What the United Kingdom will need is some kind of forum for minimising areas of conflict over factual matters, and a mechanism for resolving disputes about financial questions. Different federations deal with this matter in various ways: for example, the Commonwealth Grants Commission in Australia plays an important role in the operation of fiscal equalisation among the states, and the Supreme Court has regularly been involved in taxation disputes. Machinery, such as a Territorial Exchequer Board to undertake the data collection and statistical analysis, will be required if there is to be a needs assessment, the technical and political difficulties of which should not be underestimated.

Prior to a needs assessment, clear rules for its conduct would have to be established. These might cover, for example, whether there is a universal entitlement to use the NHS and public education, and whether the existence of two languages in Wales, and parallel Catholic and non-denominational secondary school systems in Scotland, is a 'topographical' feature or a matter of policy choice. Similarly, it would have to be established that needs indicators must relate to services actually devolved, rather than to indicators of economic activity such as GDP per head. Controversial issues are likely to include the treatment of tax expenditures and of forecast relative population change.

There is an obvious temptation for all countries and regions to believe that their needs are above average. It would be better to adopt the term 'comparative expenditure needs assessment' in order to emphasise that what is involved is a relative measure. Otherwise, such exercises are plagued by the ingenuity which can be exercised to demonstrate that every country and region has above-average needs. An assessment of this type attempts to judge the amount of expenditure required to provide an equal level of public services, taking account of factors such as differential rates of morbidity, for the same level of 'local' fiscal effort. It does not attempt to assess *absolute* need; that would be impossible since it is dependent on political judgements about desired outcomes. It is not advisable at present to guess, other than in very general terms, what the results of a needs assessment would be. Particularly, the frequent presumption that Wales has fared very badly from the Barnett formula system (MacKay 2001, Morgan 2001) might not be upheld.

Within the Devolved Administrations

Albeit in different ways, all three Devolved Administrations have experienced a politically fraught beginning: there have been three First Ministers in Scotland; two in Wales; and three Assembly suspensions in Northern Ireland. In Scotland in particular, the media have been hostile and impatient.

Pre-devolution, the territorial programmes were the sole responsibility of the respective Secretary of State, to whom in Scotland and Wales the Principal Finance Officer latterly reported directly through the Permanent Secretary. In Northern Ireland, the Department of Finance and Personnel functioned as a mini-Treasury for both Northern Ireland Departments and the Northern Ireland Office. Compared with Whitehall, individual departments were relatively weak in relation to the territorial 'corporate' centre, and junior ministers usually had limited authority. Two changes seem to have been happening post-devolution. First, there is some replication within the Devolved Administrations of the conflict between No 10 Downing Street (Prime Minister) and No 11 (Chancellor of the Exchequer and Treasury), which is often said to be a distinguishing feature of the Labour Government. In the case of the Devolved Administrations, the building up of the 'centre' is combined with some indications that 'Finance' no longer has the status or leverage which it possessed under the Secretary of State system. Second, Finance may now be weaker relative to individual departments, in part because of reduced status but also because of changes in the nature of the political Executive. The nature of the change is particularly marked in Northern Ireland, where Direct Rule ministers with no local political affiliations have been replaced by ministers from four parties, with portfolios allocated by means of the d'Hondt system (Northern Ireland Assembly 1999). Spending ministers do not have the same bonds to the First Minister and Finance Minister which would be customary under Cabinet government. This structural vulnerability of Finance might be offset by the political influence of particular Finance Ministers; for example, Edwina Hart has held the Finance portfolio in the National Assembly for Wales since May 1999.

These developments may not attract great attention when resources are plentiful and the problem is one of unprecedented underspending.[21] The expenditure-based Barnett system imposes hard budget constraints on the Devolved Administrations, with underspendings indicating that they have recently been operating well within those constraints. The growth in real resources may have protected the Devolved Administrations, at least in the short term, from the consequences of poorly costed initiatives (Mitchell and the Scottish Monitoring Team 2001). Such a situation will certainly not continue indefinitely, at which time the diminished status of Finance may prove costly. Some policies are undoubtedly difficult to cost, whether because they break new ground or because there are uncertainties as to what will happen to policy in England (and therefore to formula consequences). If the Devolved

Administrations adopt expensive policy options across a broad range of services, and England subsequently follows, there are obvious implications for the Treasury.

Assessment

This final section concentrates on six points. First, it is essential to recognise where the UK devolved funding system is coming from and not to criticise it on the grounds that it would not have been invented in that form had there been a clean slate. Devolved government in Scotland and Wales is only three years old and the restoration of devolved government in Northern Ireland has suffered 24-hour suspensions for reasons unconnected with the subject matter of this Chapter.

Secondly, the economic theory of fiscal federalism is helpful in constructing an analysis of a particular country in terms which resonate elsewhere. However, prescription ought to proceed with great caution. The mainstream literature on fiscal federalism has a strongly normative orientation, relating to the optimal tiering and spatial design of government. Much of its development predated the influence of public choice theorists, a factor which probably explains the relatively optimistic view of government characteristic of this tradition. Clearly, those who start with a Leviathan model of government are likely to reach different conclusions from those making more benevolent assumptions (Boadway 2000). Moreover, the trade-offs between efficiency, equity and broader political considerations (such as sustaining territorial integrity) will crucially depend on context. In some cases, the units of a devolved or federal structure are themselves open to negotiation; in others, they are historically and culturally determined. Similarly, traditions about the degree of completeness of fiscal equalisation can be deeply embedded, as illustrated by the contrasts between Germany (high) and Spain (low), and between Australia (high) and Canada (low).

There is an urgent need for the United Kingdom to be open to learning from other jurisdictions, though this would be contrary to inclination and history. There is clearly relevant experience in countries such as Canada and Australia (where there is a shared institutional heritage) and Germany and Spain (where EU membership provides common context). As the literature shows, policy transfer and lesson-drawing are not simple matters (Dogan and Pelassy 1990, Rose 1993). However, that difficulty does not justify insularity. Fortunately, such attitudes will be more difficult to sustain in a more integrated world and with devolved institutions in place. However, there are no secret maps detailing instant solutions; each governmental system has to navigate its own course.

Thirdly, one possible line of constitutional development would see Wales and Northern Ireland converge on the Scotland model, at the same time as the Scottish Parliament sought to expand its fiscal powers. By far the greatest uncertainties attach to developments in England, where the Labour Government's commitment in principle to regional government did not produce much action between 1997 and 2001. The White Paper (Cabinet Office/DTLR 2002) was published in May 2002, and this will have to be followed by primary legislation, first to authorise referendums and then to implement regional reforms. This leisurely approach has been indicative of different views within the Government, in relation to, *inter alia*: the interface with local authorities; the electoral system; the possible effect on the Government's centralised approach to public service delivery (perhaps the highest-profile priority of its second term); and the interface with the business-led Regional Development Agencies (the highest-profile English regional measure of its first term). It remains unclear whether the long-term response to devolution in the territories will be a new emphasis on England as a unit, or a focus on at least some regions. In turn, uncertainties about how to deal with England may have ramifications for the Devolved Administrations. The November 2001 Pre-Budget Report (Treasury 2001a, para 6.56) noted:

> the Government has set a long-term regional economic ambition to reduce the gap in performance between the regions. To advance this ambition, the 2002 Spending Review will assess how departments' policies impact on different regions and seek to ensure that spending is fairly distributed and targeted at those areas where it is needed most and will be most effective. This will include an examination of rural priorities to ensure an equitable balance in allocations.

This review has been a within-England exercise, though there must be potential for it to spill over to the devolved funding arrangements. In future, the existence of grants to English regional assemblies, over which expenditure flexibility is conditional upon meeting 'certain specific targets' set by central government, may encourage attempts to conditionalise the Assigned Budgets.[22]

Fourthly, it will always be possible to construct scenarios which test the devolved funding arrangements to destruction (Hazell and Cornes 1999). For example, a UK government, hostile to devolution, could substitute tax expenditures for private healthcare for public expenditure, thereby starving the Devolved Administrations, which would suffer negative formula consequences. In such a case, either the Devolved Administrations would have to follow the UK government's policy, or the United Kingdom might break up. No system for devolved funding in the United Kingdom could possibly cope with such policy divergence, especially if it were intentionally destabilising. Those supporting devolution (Heald *et al* 1998) recognised the strains on the Barnett formula-controlled Assigned Budget which might arise after devolution. The public expenditure situation was expected to be restrictive, with the surge in spending coincident with devolution not being anticipated. A longer-term fear has been that a collapse of public service quality in some parts of inner London might take opinion formers and the middle class further out of public provision. This would reduce the need, and weaken political support, for the increases in expenditure in England which then generate formula consequences for the Assigned Budgets.[23] Intergovernmental conflict over resources has been minimal, probably because of the lubrication of unexpectedly large real expenditure growth. This is one of the factors which have, thus far, falsified Midwinter and McVicar's (1996a; 1996b) predictions of conflict.

Fifthly, whilst there is devolution in the United Kingdom, some mechanism which is recognisably a descendant of Barnett is likely to be in place, even if the name were to be dropped because of adverse connotations. There needs to be much more transparency about the numerical workings of the formula, including the derivation of formula consequences being in the public domain immediately after public expenditure announcements. Moreover, discussion is needed as to how the Barnett formula could be amended after a needs assessment, for which new institutional machinery is essential.

Devolution has undoubtedly raised the profile of territorial funding mechanisms (Edmonds 2001), with territorially based politicians and media all claiming that their country or region is badly treated. A formula with convergence properties would not have been adopted in the late 1970s had there not been an implicit judgement that the territories were then over-funded.[24] The Barnett formula, apparently a transitional arrangement pending the introduction of a more formal system, has proved remarkably durable. As Bell and Christie (2001) observed, it is now orphaned, as 'Nobody's child'. Nevertheless, the formula's notoriety is based on totally contradictory understandings of how it works and interpretations of what is currently happening. Some evidence of convergence would be advantageous in sustaining the formula mechanism.

Unexpectedly, the post-devolution challenge to the Barnett formula system does not relate to the automatic generation of formula consequences but to the expenditure-switching discretion of the Devolved Administrations. The build-up to SR 2002 announcements in July 2002 has been depressingly marked by planted media items from Whitehall departments, typically using 'failure' or 'catastrophe' to bid for greater inputs over the head of the Treasury. The drip-feeding of extra money to the NHS in England, at Pre-Budget and Budget announcements, has begun to erode this discretion. Some of these changes have been in-year allocations of the Reserve, and some have been transfers from DEL to AME within a constant TME. This danger has become more obvious in the aftermath of the 2002 Budget. There was clearly an expectation that the Devolved Administrations would devote the formula consequences of the increases in Health spending in England to their own Health programmes. The Budget Report (Treasury 2002a, para 1.13) provides figures for UK

Health expenditure on that assumption. Indeed, the Scottish Executive appeared to announce the next day that this would be done, though many would dispute whether this will be the most effective way of responding to Scotland's health problems.

Sixthly, the 'official' Treasury has long been suspicious that the territories are over-generously funded, and also too far out of reach. However, the 'ministerial' Treasury has been hesitant about opening up territorial political issues, especially as the achievable public expenditure savings are likely to be limited (Midwinter 1997) because of relative population size and the potential macroeconomic effects on the territorial economies of any sudden downward adjustment. Paradoxically, this makes the Treasury an unlikely ally of the Devolved Administrations, in attempting to build on the Barnett system, rather than attempt anything radical. Above all, the Treasury would resist attempts to breach its highly centralised control of revenue. The approach of the 2003 elections will bring more attention, particularly in Scotland, to the issue of 'fiscal autonomy' (Muscatelli 2001), amidst renewed concerns about divergent regional economic performance. The Treasury is likely to resist the 'Stormont model', by which the Devolved Administrations would pay (what used to be called) the 'Imperial' contribution for non-devolved services. Not least, such an arrangement would give the Devolved Administrations legitimacy in challenging central government expenditure. The impact of the 1999 Budget changes on the tartan tax is a reminder of the vulnerable position of the Devolved Administrations on revenue raising, whatever their precise powers, when control over the definition of tax bases and bands remains with the Treasury.[25] The most promising area for relatively early development is perhaps in local government taxes, which are fully devolved in Scotland and Northern Ireland, and in charging policy.

Endnotes

1   One example is not counting the borrowing of housing associations, putting local authorities in a position whereby the only way that council house renovation can take place is to transfer the stock to a housing association, classified into the private sector and therefore excluded from public sector net borrowing (Hetherington 2002).

2   Issues concerning revenue-raising and tax sharing are discussed in Heald and McLeod (2002). A symposium within the November 2002 issue of *Scottish Affairs* will examine the topic of fiscal autonomy.

3   In practice, some functions are managed on a GB basis, rather than a UK basis. Social security is one of these. However, the Northern Ireland social security system, separated for historical reasons, is almost entirely the same as the GB system.

4   There is much political sensitivity in labelling the component parts of the United Kingdom: for example, 'nation' and 'region' may be seen to carry implications for

the nature of governance. When discussing England, Scotland, Wales and Northern Ireland, the Treasury's current practice of describing these as 'countries' (Treasury 2001d) is followed. Formerly, it used the term 'territories'. In this Chapter, the term 'territories' is applied collectively to Scotland, Wales and Northern Ireland. The internal components of England are described as 'regions'. The analysis of public expenditure by country and region is referred to as 'territorial analysis'.

5   The Assigned Budget is often described as a block grant. Used in this way, the term 'block grant' is not synonymous with transfers from the UK Exchequer.

6   The Assigned Budget is determined irrespective of the means of financing. It includes expenditure funded by borrowing by local authorities or other bodies within the Devolved Administration's sphere of influence, whether or not that borrowing is from the Administration; and it includes some expenditure funded by the EU.

7   The non-statutory Barnett formula provided that increases in public expenditure in Scotland and in Wales for specific services within the territorial blocks would be determined according to the formula consequences of changes in comparable expenditure in England. Initially, Scotland received 10/85ths and Wales 5/85ths of the change in England. A parallel formula allocated 2.75 per cent of the change in comparable expenditure in Great Britain to Northern Ireland. The essential distinction is between base expenditure, whose current levels are carried forward, and incremental expenditure, which is determined by the formula (Heald 1994). As of Autumn 2001, the percentages, all now expressed relative to England and updated annually, were: Scotland 10.23 per cent; Wales 5.89 per cent; and Northern Ireland 3.40 per cent.

8   These were never formally 'signed off' by the Treasury and the territorial offices.

9   Strictly, it is also a function of the lag between actual population change and this being incorporated in the calculations; this effect is not significant.

10   A fuller exposition of these properties of the Barnett formula, including diagrams, can be found in Heald (1996).

11   First, there appears to have been a considerable amount of formula bypass, in the sense that not all incremental expenditure has gone through the formula. Heald (1994) provided several illustrations, later to be confirmed by Treasury (1997a, 1997b) evidence to the Treasury Committee. There has been no quantification of the numerical importance of bypass, though it would appear that this now occurs less frequently than in the 1980s. Most of the identified cases of bypass seem to have benefited, rather than disadvantaged, the territories. When, as on health, the territorial expenditure index is substantially above UK = 100, this is likely to reflect in part a higher per capita employment of nurses. If the Treasury were to underwrite the full cost to each health department of a UK nurses' pay settlement, the territories would receive more than if the total UK cost of the award were to be distributed through the Barnett formula. Second, and much less publicly documented, the Treasury has on at least one occasion implemented an across-the-board percentage reduction in departmental baselines, before applying the formula. Whether by

accident or design, this procedure allows ministers to state that the Barnett formula has been implemented, even though it erodes the protection afforded by the formula to inherited expenditure. Money 'saved' by applying a constant percentage cut to the territorial blocks and to comparable expenditure can then be passed through the Barnett formula, generating formula consequences supplementary to those generated by year-on-year increases in comparable expenditure. Naturally, the arithmetical effect is disadvantageous to the territories because the constant percentage cut generates more 'savings' from their blocks than they subsequently receive back in these 'artificial' formula consequences. There have been no across-the-board reductions to the Assigned Budgets of the Devolved Administrations.

12   Comprehensive explanations of the present system are available in the annual *Public Expenditure: Statistical Analyses* (Treasury 2001d).

13   In consequence, it is not possible from data in the public domain to put precise values in the cells of Figure 10.1.

14   Objective 1 is the classification which brings eligibility for the highest level of ERDF support. On the role of EU funding in Wales, see Blewitt and Bristow (1999).

15   The strength of such a hypothetical case would be affected by judgements as to whether public policy failures had played a part. In practice, the territorial agriculture departments seem to be emerging better from the inquiry processes than the (former) Ministry of Agriculture, Fisheries and Food.

16   The data on identifiable expenditure should always be read with two points in mind. The first is the impact of non-identified expenditure on services such as defence. Debates about the territorial pattern of defence expenditure are a telling reminder that political concerns are as often about inputs (hence employment effects) as about outputs. The second is the impact of tax expenditures (eg on owner-occupied housing). When the focus is upon both expenditure and revenue, these cancel out because regional revenue is correspondingly depressed. However, they do affect the comparability of expenditure.

17   However, the basis of the allocation of the previously unallocated expenditure is not known.

18   Strictly, the annual rate of nominal expenditure growth must be constant, or the average rate up to a specific date must be known.

19   With higher levels of nominal public expenditure growth and thus convergence over shorter time periods, relative population change becomes less important.

20   At present, Scotland, Wales and Northern Ireland account for 130 (20 per cent) of Westminster constituencies, with that percentage likely to fall to 18 per cent.

21   In 2000-01, the first full financial year of devolution, the Northern Ireland Departments underspent by 3.87 per cent against the final DEL, and the Northern Ireland Office underspent by 3.85 per cent. Underspending was greater than in Wales (3.22 per cent), though lower than in Scotland (4.23 per cent) (Treasury 2001c).

22   Strictly, this would require new legislation, as there is no power for the UK government to set conditions on the Assigned Budgets. However, the power of the paymaster is strong, given the dependence of the Devolved Administrations on cash transfers determined by the UK government, and there is clearly scope for administrative and political pressure.

23   The issue of there being no English counterpart to generate formula consequences already arises in the case of water and sewerage, privatised in England and Wales but not in Scotland and Northern Ireland.

24   If they had then been thought under-funded, one would have expected arguments to be made for a step increase in resourcing. Without access to unpublished papers, it is not known when the convergence properties were first understood. Attention was drawn to these by Heald (1980), who also noted that, in periods of expenditure reduction, there would be divergence. The fact that the territorial offices received less under the Barnett formula than they would have done under a flat percentage increase would certainly have been understood from the beginning.

25   The UK Government made major changes to the structure of income tax in the 1999 Budget (by lowering the starting rate but reducing the size of the starting band, while extending the basic rate band). These changes would have had the effect of raising the potential yield of the Scottish tax-varying power to £230 million per percentage point. Accordingly, the tartan tax would now generate more revenue than was initially expected, but the lower starting point makes the power more politically difficult to use.

References

Bell D and Christie A (2001) 'Finance – the Barnett formula: nobody's child?' in A Trench (ed) *The State of the Nations 2001: The Second Year of Devolution in the United Kingdom* Thorverton: Imprint Academic pp135-51

Bell D, Dow S, King D and Massie N (1996) 'Financing Devolution' *Hume Papers on Public Policy* 4.2 Edinburgh: Edinburgh University Press

Blewitt N and Bristow G (1999) *Unravelling the Knot* Cardiff: Institute of Welsh Affairs

Blow L, Hall J and Smith S (1996) *Financing Regional Government in Britain* IFS Commentary 54 London: Institute for Fiscal Studies

Boadway R (2000) 'Recent developments in the economics of federalism', in H Lazar (ed) *Canada: The State of the Federation 1999/2000 – Towards a New Mission Statement for Canadian Fiscal Federalism* Montreal: McGill-Queen's University Press pp41-78

Cabinet Office/DTLR (2002) *Your Region, Your Choice: Revitalising the English Regions* Cm 5511 London: The Stationery Office

Cabinet Office (1977) *Devolution: Financing the Devolved Services* Cmnd 6890, London: HMSO

Carr-Hill R, Hardman G, Martin S, Peacock S, Sheldon T and Smith P (1994) *A Formula for Distributing NHS Revenues Based on Small Area Use of Hospital Beds* Occasional Paper 22, York: Centre for Health Economics, University of York

Committee on Scottish Affairs (1980) *Scottish Aspects of the 1980-84 Public Expenditure White Paper: Minutes of Evidence* HC 689 London: HMSO

Cuthbert J (2001) 'The effect of relative population growth on the Barnett squeeze' *Fraser of Allander Quarterly Economic Commentary* 26 pp34-37

Davies Q (1997) 'Oral Questions 104-108' in Treasury Committee *The Barnett Formula* Second Report of Session 1997-98, HC 341 London: Stationery Office pp15-17

Dogan M and Pelassy D (1990) *How to Compare Nations: Strategies in Comparative Politics* Chatham, New Jersey: Chatham House

Edmonds T (2001) *The Barnett Formula* Research Paper 01/108, London: House of Commons Library

Hazell R and Cornes R (1999) 'Financing devolution: the centre retains control', in Hazell R (ed) *Constitutional Futures: A History of the Next Ten Years* Oxford: Oxford University Press pp196-212

Heald DA (1996) 'Formula-controlled territorial public expenditure in the United Kingdom' *Public Finance/Finances Publiques* 51 pp534-58

Heald DA (1994) 'Territorial public expenditure in the United Kingdom' *Public Administration* 72 pp147-75

Heald DA (1980) *Territorial Equity and Public Finances: Concepts and Confusion Studies in Public Policy* 75 Centre for the Study of Public Policy, Glasgow: University of Strathclyde

Heald DA, Geaughan N and Robb C (1998) 'Financial arrangements for UK devolution' *Regional and Federal Studies* 8 pp23-52

Heald DA and McLeod A (2002) *Revenue Raising and Tax Sharing by Sub-National Governments: the United Kingdom* Conference on Comparative Fiscal Federalism, ESRC Research Programme on Devolution and Constitutional Change 18-19 January, University of Birmingham

Heald DA and Short J (2002) 'The regional dimension of public expenditure in England' *Regional Studies* 36 (forthcoming)

Hetherington P (2002) 'Blow to council housing transfer campaign' *Guardian* 9 April

Hetherington P (2001) 'Scots and Welsh face subsidy axe: funding said to be unfair to English regions' *Guardian* 24 April

MacKay RR (2001) 'Regional taxing and spending: the search for balance' *Regional Studies* 35 pp563-575

McLean I (2001) 'The national question', in Seldon A (ed) *The Blair Effect: The Blair Government 1997-2001* London: Little Brown pp429-447

McLean I (2000) 'Getting and spending: can (or should) the Barnett formula survive?' *New Economy* 7 London: ippr pp76-80

Midwinter A (1997) 'The Barnett formula and Scotland's public expenditure needs' Treasury Committee *The Barnett Formula* Second Report of Session 1997-98 HC 341 London: Stationery Office pp29-32

Midwinter A, Keating M and Mitchell J (1991) *Politics and Public Policy in Scotland* Basingstoke: Macmillan

Midwinter A and McVicar M (1996a) 'The devolution proposals for Scotland: an assessment and critique' *Public Money and Management* 16 pp13-20

Midwinter A and McVicar M (1996b) 'Uncharted waters? Problems of financing Labour's Scottish Parliament' *Public Money and Management* 16 pp1-6

Mitchell J and the Scottish Monitoring Team (2001) 'Scotland: maturing devolution' in Trench A (ed) *The State of the Nations 2001: The Second Year of Devolution in the United Kingdom* Thorverton: Imprint Academic pp45-76

Morgan K (2001) 'The new territorial politics: rivalry and justice in post-devolution Britain' *Regional Studies* 35 pp343-48

Muscatelli A (2001) 'Life after Barnett: future options for fiscal devolution in the UK' *Fraser of Allander Institute Quarterly Economic Commentary* 26 pp33-38

Northern Ireland Assembly (1999) *Allocation of Seats in the Assembly Executive and Chairs and Deputy Chairs of Committees: d'Hondt System* Belfast: mimeo

Rose R (1993) *Lesson-Drawing in Public Policy: A Guide to Learning Across Time and Space* Chatham, New Jersey: Chatham House

Scotland Office (2002) 'Supplementary Memorandum Submitted by the Scotland Office' Scottish Affairs Committee *Minutes of Evidence Taken before the Scottish Affairs Committee, Wednesday 7 November 2001* HC 345 of Session 2001-02 London: Stationery Office pp19-23

Scottish Executive (2001) *Government Expenditure and Revenue in Scotland 1999-2000* SE/2001/294, Edinburgh: Scottish Executive

Scottish Office (1997) *Scotland's Parliament* Cm 3614 Edinburgh: Stationery Office

Smith P (1988) 'The potential gains from creative accounting in English local government' *Environment and Planning C: Government and Policy* 6 pp173-85

Smith P, Rice N and Carr-Hill R (2001) 'Capitation funding in the public sector' *Journal of the Royal Statistical Society Series A* 164 pp217-57

Smith S (1999) *Mechanisms for Budget Transfers to Devolved Government in the UK* Intergovernmental Relations Senior Seminar 2: Finance, Constitution Unit, School of Public Policy, University College London

Thain C and Wright M (1995) *The Treasury and Whitehall: The Planning and Control of Public Expenditure, 1976-1993* Oxford: Clarendon Press

Treasury (2002a) *Budget 2002 – The Strength to Make Long-Term Decisions: Investing in an Enterprising, Fairer Britain – Economic and Fiscal Strategy Report and Financial Statement and Budget Report, April 2002*, HC 592 of Session 2001-02 London: Stationery Office

Treasury (2002b) *New Economic Settlement for Northern Ireland: Barracks and Prisons to be Replaced by Business and Prosperity* Press Release 42/02, 2 May London: HM Treasury

Treasury (2001a) *Building a Stronger, Fairer Britain in an Uncertain World: Pre-Budget Report, November 2001* Cm 5318 London: Stationery Office

Treasury (2001b) *Managing Resources: Full Implementation of Resource Accounting and Budgeting* London: HM Treasury

Treasury (2001c) *Public Expenditure 2000-2001: Provisional Outturn* Cm 5243 London: Stationery Office

Treasury (2001d) *Public Expenditure: Statistical Analyses 2001-02* Cm 5101 London: Stationery Office

Treasury (2000a) *Funding the Scottish Parliament, National Assembly for Wales and Northern Ireland Assembly,* Second edition London: HM Treasury

Treasury (2000b) *Spending Review 2000 – New Public Spending Plans 2001-2004 – Prudent for a Purpose: Building Opportunity and Security for All* Cm 4807 London: Stationery Office

Treasury (1999) *Funding the Scottish Parliament, National Assembly for Wales and Northern Ireland Assembly: A Statement of Funding Policy* London: HM Treasury

Treasury (1997a) 'Memorandum Submitted by HM Treasury' Treasury Committee *The Barnett Formula,* Second Report of Session 1997-98 HC 341 London: Stationery Office

Treasury (1997b) 'Supplementary Memorandum Submitted by HM Treasury on Tuesday 16 December 1997' Treasury Committee *The Barnett Formula,* Second Report of Session 1997-98 HC 341 London: Stationery Office pp36-39

Treasury (1979) *Needs Assessment Study: Report* London: Treasury

Treasury and Civil Service Committee (1989) *The Presentation of Information on Public Expenditure,* Sixth Report of Session 1988-89 HC 217 London: HMSO

Welsh Office (1997a) *Government Expenditure and Revenue – Wales, 1994-95* Cardiff: Welsh Office

Welsh Office (1997b) *A Voice for Wales: The Government's Proposals for a Welsh Assembly* Cm 3718 London: The Stationery Office

Welsh Office (1996) *Government Expenditure and Revenue – Wales, 1993-94* Cardiff: Welsh Office

11. Uniformity and diversity in policy provision: insights from the US, Germany and Canada

Charles Jeffery

Uniformity and diversity

One of the sets of questions this book is designed to address is whether the variation of policy standards around the UK matters after devolution. Policy variation of course happened before devolution. Administrative decentralisation to the territorial offices of UK government allowed significant scope for territorial differentiation in policy outcomes. But devolution opens up territorial policy variation to new forms of scrutiny and accountability both within the devolved institutions and, through devolved elections, at the popular level. And, naturally enough, devolution was introduced precisely to allow further variation as an expression of (what were assumed to be) differentiated territorial preferences. Asymmetry adds further spice to the mix: some parts of the UK have the powers to be more varied than others.

So, how much does post-devolution policy variation matter (as much press comment at the UK centre in London suggests it does)? Or better, at what point does variation in policy outcomes from one part of the UK to the next start to matter? How much variation is desirable, how much legitimate in the context of a shared state structure and tradition, in a *United* Kingdom? Earlier chapters in the book have presented 'takes' on these questions based on emerging evidence for policy variation in particular policy fields in the UK. This chapter approaches the question from a different vantage point.[1] It looks more abstractly at ideas about policy variation drawing on experience in other decentralised systems: the US, Germany and Canada. It does not present a systematic account of how much variation there is in particular policy fields in those countries. Nor does it focus on the political structures which produce policy variation such as the divisions of competence and intergovernmental relations between centre and regions.[2] Rather it explores the normative dimension of policy variation. Norms are collective understandings of what it is or what it is not appropriate to do. The normative question this chapter explores is one which faces all decentralised systems of government:

What is the appropriate balance to strike between territorial social diversity, which implies some amount of variation in standards of policy provision, and the logic of membership of a common state, which implies some amount of uniformity of policy provision?

The chapter begins with some general reflections about this balance between uniformity and diversity, before looking at how that balance can play out – and change – in questions of economic management and social policy. A final section draws out some insights for the UK after devolution.

In a recent book on health policy in federal systems Banting and Corbett (2002a, 18) restated the question posed above as a distinction between two values: a) 'social citizenship, to be achieved through a common set of public services for all citizens across the entire country;' and b) 'respect for regional communities and cultures, to be achieved through decentralised decision-making and significant scope for diversity at the state/provincial level.' How those two values play out depends on a society's collective judgements about 'which community should be paramount in the definition of social benefits: the community of all citizens on the one hand; or regional communities defined by state/provincial boundaries on the other' (Banting and Corbett 2002a 19). Such judgements can vary on at least three dimensions:

- They reflect a sense of what is appropriate and what is not in and for the country (and regions) concerned. Such judgements inevitably vary from one country to the next reflecting different national traditions and political debates.

- These judgements may also vary by policy area. Most people in most places would think unequivocally that central government should be responsible for national defence; most people in most places would think it inappropriate for central government to organise refuse collection. Judgements about other policy fields are typically more contested or ambiguous.

- Judgements may vary in the same country over time. Normative judgements are never fixed, but are subject to processes of re-evaluation through communication and debate as wider circumstances change.

This chapter explores some of the variations by country, by sector and over time in the balances struck between uniformity of national policy standards and territorial variation in standards at the regional level in the US, Germany and Canada.

Laboratories of democracy

A theoretically powerful argument in favour of allowing greater territorial variation is that of regions as 'laboratories of democracy'. There is a tradition of argument in the US that the existence of the states as fifty separate locations for policy-making promotes a 'competition of ideas' which fosters innovation, benchmarks alternative approaches and diffuses good practice. This is an argument which marks out different normative attitudes about the balance there should be between federal uniformity and state-level diversity in policy provision. Those suspicious of federal government (broadly, but not only Republicans) tend support the laboratory idea as one unleashing the creativity and adaptability necessary to compete in a rapidly changing economic environment; others concerned more strongly with social equity (broadly, but not only Democrats) favour minimum levels of nation-wide – that is federally determined – standards, fearing that 'laboratory' federalism in practice equates to a 'race to the bottom' (Peterson 1995, 108-28) with states competitively cutting back policy standards to maintain locational advantages.

The argument for regional 'laboratories of democracy' has not been widely mobilised in European contexts, in part because of the whiff of 'race to the bottom' that adheres to them. In particular, there has been a stronger notion of social equity in European states which has sustained arguments for uniform policy provision. But arguments for a more uniform policy provision now seem to be weakening. A number of European states have embarked on decentralisation processes designed to give voice to distinctive regional communities: Spain, Belgium, Italy, more recently the UK and even France. Strikingly, no member state in the EU 'became more centralised since 1980, while half have decentralised authority to a regional tier of government' (Marks and Hooghe 2001, 18). Even established federal states like Germany have begun to consider a more decentralised, 'competitive' federalism allowing for more diverse regional policy standards. These developments were reflected in the recent European Commission White Paper on Governance, which gives centre stage to the apparent benefits of policy experimentation and policy learning by tiers of government below the level of the member states (Commission of the European Communities 2001). In this light the notion of 'laboratories of democracy' is worth further exploration as an entry point for arguments about where the line should be drawn between uniformity and diversity, between social citizenship and respect for regional communities.

The 'laboratories' metaphor is normally traced back to the US Supreme Court Justice Louis D Brandeis who wrote in a dissenting judgement in 1932:

> Whether [the state's] view is sound nobody knows... The economic and social sciences are largely uncharted seas... Yet the advances in the exact sciences remind us that the seemingly impossible sometimes happens... The discoveries in physical science, the triumphs of invention, attest the value of the process of trial and error. In large measure these advances have been due to experimentation. In those fields, experimentation has, for two centuries been not only free but encouraged. Some people assert that our present plight is due, in part, to the limitations set by courts upon experimentation in the fields of social and economic science... To stay experimentation in things social and economic is a grave responsibility. Denial of the right to experiment may be fraught with serious consequences for the nation. *It is*

one of the happy accidents of the federal system that a single courageous state may, if its citizens choose, serve as a laboratory, and try novel social and economic experiments without risk to the rest of the country.[3] [emphasis added]

Though there is an arcane debate about Brandeis' motives (Greve 2000) and his assumption that natural-scientific premises can be applied to politics and policy (Tarr 2001) interest in the laboratory idea has revived in the US in recent years. This renewed interest has reflected in part the vogue in and since the Reagan era for decentralising policy responsibilities (and the problems, in particular in social policy, that went with them) to the states. It has also reflected what David Osborne (1988) called 'a new breed of governor' in the states who used the enhanced, post-Reagan room for manœuvre to develop new policies for regional economic growth. Michael Greve (2001, 1) sums up the laboratory idea as follows:

Much can be said for the piecemeal diffusion of new policies: when we do not know what we are doing, it is best not to do it everywhere at once. A state-based process facilitates gradualism and, therefore, feedback and institutional learning. Successful state and local experiments...build confidence in innovative policies, and provided testing grounds for social scientists' models and policy recommendations that might have gone unheeded in a centralised policy environment. State-based policy innovation also facilitates adaptation to local needs, circumstances and preferences.

Although Greve is at the hyper-decentralist end of the spectrum in US debate, the issues he raises articulate strongly with European-style debates about the advantages of decentralisation focused on 'the possibility of tailor-made policies', 'service delivery based on greater knowledge of the actors at the local level, with regard for local circumstances', 'flexible, innovative and creative administration', 'learning from diversity' (De Vries 2000, 193, 197). There are further echoes in the UK as some of the earlier chapters in this book have suggested, with devolution allowing (some) scope for new policy innovations which depart from inherited Westminster standards. As Tony Blair put it in the National Assembly for Wales in October 2001, 'devolution...allows the energy and diversity of different parts of our country to breathe and develop', it expresses a 'desire to seize back control over local issues'.[4]

So how much energy, diversity and local control is it appropriate to let loose? The following offers some considerations in the fields of economic, then social policy, drawing on the practice of decentralised government in the US, Germany and Canada. The US, Canada and Germany are all mature federal systems, each drawing on a long state tradition of decentralisation. Despite the novelty and different constitutional character of devolution, comparison with the UK is not inappropriate in terms of policy variation; the Scottish Parliament and Northern Ireland Assembly certainly have an autonomous legislative clout comparable to that of US states, German Länder and Canadian provinces. The National Assembly for Wales, the Greater London Authority and, in due course, the English regions have fewer powers, but nonetheless also have the capacity to bring about different policy outcomes in their territories.

The US, German and Canadian traditions of decentralisation also provide different kinds of benchmark for thinking about the UK. US federalism was conceived as a system in which the federation and the states would have separate spheres of influence, within which each level would act autonomously. That neat separation has been gradually and successively eroded by the imperatives of national integration, in particular the establishment of a US Single Market, the American Civil War, Roosevelt's New Deal and its postwar successor programmes, and by the civil rights movement. A far higher degree of national standardisation of public policy now exists than was intended by the founding fathers. Nonetheless, there is still an 'extraordinary variety of contrasting public policies displayed by the states' (McKay 2001, 59) which is sustained by a national political culture which lionises individualism and diversity, and which has been reinvigorated by post-Reagan trends to decentralisation.

Germany by contrast is unusual as a federal system in that it was re-established after World War II not to reflect distinctive regional preferences, but rather to strengthen checks and balances on political power after the Third Reich. Its guiding constitutional rationale – crafted against the background of extreme social and economic dislocation caused by war and national division – was to attain and maintain a 'uniformity of living conditions', not to promote territorial diversity. To that end the main role of the regions – the *Länder* – is to participate in the formulation of national legislative standards through Germany's territorial second chamber and then to apply those standards on the ground. The *Länder* do possess a range of their own legislative powers, but these have typically been absorbed into joint federal-*Länder* decision-making (as with regional economic policy) or subjected to a voluntary co-ordination of standards across the *Länder* (for example, in education). The dense co-ordination of federation and *Länder* in generating common, nation-wide standards of public policy has aptly been termed 'co-operative' federalism. Only in the last decade or so has there been (as a legacy of the need to digest the former communist East) pressure to reverse the tendency to national policy standardisation and allow greater territorial policy variation.

The Canadian example is different again. Canada's colonial origins as British North America brought together territories with different British and French linguistic, cultural and legal backgrounds. These were cast into a federal union in 1867, to which additional provinces were subsequently added to form a vast transcontinental state. The persistent challenge for Canada has been one of nation-building, and has had two dimensions: first, how to build shared loyalties in a nation stretching from the

Atlantic to the Pacific; and second, how to do so while accommodating the distinct, Francophone society of Quebec alongside an overwhelmingly Anglophone 'rest-of-Canada'. The nation-building project accelerated with and after World War II as a federal government grown by war sought 'to build a more secure and fairer society than the one that Canadians had experienced in the 1930s' (Lazar 1999a, 9). Growing use was made of the federal 'spending power', in the mobilisation of funding flows from the centre, to establish Canada-wide programmes even in areas formally under provincial jurisdiction. Only more recently has this pan-Canadian project has run into difficulties in part caused by the funding cuts of a federal government in fiscal crisis, in part by the series of (failed) attempts at constitutional reform designed to maintain Canadian unity in the face of separatist tendencies in Quebec.

Economic policy laboratories

The revival of interest in the US states as 'laboratories of democracy' has had a primarily economic rationale, that of how to respond to the development of the 'new economy' of technological advance and global competition. The transnational operation and rapid technological shifts of the new economy have placed limits in what the traditional (broadly 'Keynesian') levers of economic management – as wielded at the centre of the state by national governments and parliaments – can do to manage their national economies. As a result the central state has become progressively 'hollowed out', by default or – less often – by design, leaving regions to try to fill the gap and find the right niche for the regional economy amid global economic flows. As Rosabeth Kanter (1995) put it, economic policy decentralisation is about how to 'thrive locally in the global economy', how to build at the regional level 'world class places' for economic location and development.

This rescaling of economic policy-making has broadly come to be known as the 'new regionalism' (see Jeffery and O'Sullivan 1994; Keating 1998), a set of strategies for economic development which operate from the 'bottom up'. This kind of strategy has increasingly replaced the old form of regional economic policy, where the central state designated development areas from the 'top-down' and then handed out cash to business as an incentive for development. Instead the new regionalism is about nurturing and maximising the 'endogenous' potential in resources and know-how that regions possess, and about offering different kinds of locally grown incentive – cultural, environmental, educational – to help tie down footloose global capital in the form of inward investment. Put another way, the new regionalism is about a shift from demand-side to supply-side economic intervention and has to varying degrees come to shape regional economic policy debates in the US, Germany and Canada.

It is precisely this shift that Osborne's new breed of 'laboratory' governor had pursued in the US in the 1980s, 'a decade of enormous innovation at the state level' in which 'governors of both parties were embracing an unprecedented role as economic activists' (Osborne 1988, 1). The policy levers they used are widely diffused as a new regional economic policy orthodoxy: investment and venture capital funds, technological innovation and transfer programmes, skills-focused education and training policies, the concentration of state, business and other regional actors behind regional growth strategies. The use of these levers also diffused rapidly from 'pioneer' states like Massachusetts and Pennsylvania to second tier innovators, including Clinton's Arkansas. Some initiatives have failed, including some of the early pioneers, but most prominently the deregulation of the Californian electricity industry. But failure can be positive in the sense that it has clear lines of accountability in the state concerned, and a clear deterrent effect on others: 'Learning from a failed experiment is the...benefit of the California fiasco and the most potent argument for state experimentation' because its effects were limited to the unfortunate Californians (Greve 2001, 4-5). They are unlikely to repeat the experiment, nor are others likely to want to emulate it.

The wider message of these trends to policy variation is a normative one. They reflect a shift in collective understandings of how it is appropriate to do politics in the US (at least in the field of economic development): 'deep-seated economic and social changes have eroded the social contract – the predominant understandings about core economic and social relationships – that was built up in the post-war era' (Banting, Hoberg and Simeon 1997, 4). Those changes are widely seen to have created a crisis of governance consisting of both democratic and performance deficits, the former focused on questions of representativeness and accountability, the latter on perceptions of policy failure.

Federalism has played a key role in generating the sense of crisis. Unlike for example in Germany, the states are not represented corporately at the centre, but rather through the activities of Representatives and Senators in Congress. While central to American traditions of the 'pork barrel', there is a cost attached to this form of 'intra-state' federalism: 'importing all the localist influences into Congress is to accentuate the burden of overload on the central government and increase the paralysis, immobilism and parochialism in federal decision-making' (Simeon and Willis 1997, 179). The outcomes of this sense of over-big and overloaded federal government have included:

- the decentralist policies of Republican federal administrations under Reagan and the two Bushes, most notably in 'untying' federal programme allocations to the states into block grants;

- meshing with this 'top-down' decentralisation, there has been the new 'bottom-up' activism at the state level noted above;

- these changes have been underpinned by a popular mood of hostility towards politics 'in the Beltway'. Regular surveys on public opinion towards government in the US have tracked a shift of mood away from federal government so that 'by 1999 the federal government was least often chosen as the government most likely to give citizens the most for their money. The federal income tax was chosen most often as the worst tax, and the public expressed the lowest levels of trust and confidence in the federal government compared to state and local governments' (Cole and Kincaid 2000, 199). Unsurprisingly, 'many voters [now] expect state rather than federal authorities to be responsible for a wide range of public policies' as a result (McKay 2001, 76).

Put another way, there has been a normative shift in the uniformity-diversity balance, with an earlier confidence in the capacity and competence of federal government to set policy standards now eroded and replaced by a (re)new(ed) confidence in the states to do so in their own ways for their own citizens.

In some respects the pattern is similar in Germany and Canada. The transition to the 'new' economy is, by definition, a global one, and its implications for traditional instruments of economic intervention apply just as much to Germany and Canada as to the US, and arguably more so as both (the then West) Germany and Canada had embraced Keynesianism much more fully than the US. The challenges of adaptation are rather different though and reflect the logics – and the obstacles – created by past assumptions about what the federal system should deliver for German and Canadian society.

In Germany, post-war confidence in the capacity of federal government to secure economic and social goals and implement the constitutional demand for uniformity of living conditions led in the late 1960s to a series of constitutional changes. These embedded a legal obligation of federation and *Länder* to work together to set nation-wide standards in a range of important policy fields (Jeffery 1999, 133-34). As a result, regional economic policy and major infrastructure projects were – and are – subject to a range of joint decision-making and financing processes. These processes of joint policy-making were entirely consistent with public expectations. By the 1960s West Germany lacked significant territorially expressed social or economic cleavages. A homogeneous population was content with a joint decision-making process that maintained broadly uniform standards of economic welfare across the federal territory (Bulmer 1991, 110). The structures and outputs of the system correlated well with its normative underpinnings. This strong correlation began though to erode in the 1980s for much the same reasons as in the US: centrally co-ordinated policy failed to meet the challenges of economic change, especially as heavy industrial areas in the north metamorphosed into rust-belts. At the same time the success of other areas, especially in the south, in boarding the high-tech bandwagon of the new economy focused attention on widening economic disparities – and on a realisation that maintaining uniform living conditions with widening disparities meant growing cross-subsidisation.

While the system creaked in the 1980s, it entered crisis conditions after German unification. The new *Länder* of eastern Germany were economically decrepit. Yet they were absorbed into an unreformed federalism still driven by the commitment to uniform living conditions. There has emerged as a result an intense debate about the right balance to strike between nation-wide policy co-ordination and autonomous policy-making in the *Länder*. Those *Länder* which benefit from joint policy arrangements in economic and infrastructure policy favour the status quo, and appeal to the norms of solidarity around national standards which underpin it; others feel that the status quo restricts their capacity to innovate and maintain their global competitiveness. The latter group, led by Bavaria, has propagated an alternative normative vision of 'competitive' rather than co-operative federalism.

Put briefly, the vision of a 'competitive' federalism is one where the federal level would withdraw from areas of joint policy-making with the *Länder* (in regional economic development); where a wider range of legislative powers would be returned from the federal level to the *Länder*; and where the obligations of financial solidarity and cross-subsidisation among the *Länder* would be cut back in the cause of greater financial self-reliance. The aim is one of growing policy differentiation; or could be an incipient German version of laboratories of democracy.

This is a radical vision of change, but one which is 'selling' well. A growing number of *Länder* have signed up to it in whole or in part. And a growing number of opinion formers – in the media, in the federal-level political parties, in business, in think tanks on the left and the right – are also picking up on the competition theme and running with it (Jeffery 2002, 185-86). There are also indications that public expectations are changing. Though opinion polls show that Germans in principle favour uniform standards of economic development and public services (Grube 2001, 105-10), their voting behaviour in the *Länder* suggests the opposite tendency. Germans increasingly differentiate their voting behaviour for federal and *Länder* elections (Jeffery and Hough 2001), in the latter tending to vote on distinctive regional issues, often favouring different parties and as a result producing different coalition combinations which no longer match the government-opposition constellations they collectively create at the federal level.

The net effect is to promote – and by implication endorse – a new territorial differentiation of government composition and with it of policy standards. Put another way, as in the US, there has been a normative shift in the uniformity-diversity balance, with an earlier confidence in the capacity and competence of federation and *Länder* through joint decision-making to set nation-wide policy standards now being eroded by an emerging politics of territorial policy variation.

Territorial policy variation is much more self-evident in Canada. Despite the growth of federal intervention after World War II, Canada remains one of the more decentralised federations in which highly distinctive provincial political cultures co-exist – at times in considerable tension – with pan-Canadian loyalties. Political debate as a result is highly territorialised. In addition the economic foundations of the provinces are highly differentiated and fragmented further by long-standing patterns of north-south trade with neighbouring US states (rather than east-west economic integration within Canada). Under these conditions the provinces have always had considerable leeway and reason to put into place economic development policies tailored to particular provincial economic needs, though this has probably led more to tendencies to look inward and protect provincial economic structures rather than to act as laboratories of innovation (Knox 1997). Attempts to create a systematic Canadian regional economic policy in this context have unsurprisingly focused on the aim of national economic integration.

This aim has been reflected since the 1960s in a series of federal government programmes which have used the federal 'spending power' to claim a federal role in a policy field ostensibly outside of federal competence. These programmes have gone through a number of phases. The initial focus, consistent with the interventionist orthodoxies of the era, was on tackling the problem of lagging regions, in particular in the Atlantic provinces, with the aim of evening out regional disparities by raising key economic indicators up to the national average. In the 1970s there was a shift of tack to open up federal funding to all the provinces (though still with a heavier weighting to underdeveloped regions). This shift led over time to fully 93 per cent of Canada's land mass and 50 per cent of the population falling under the scope of federal-provincial development agreements. These agreements were 'remarkably flexible and capable of supporting virtually any imaginable type of government activity' (Savoie 1995, 371 in Skogstad 2000, 62).

The breadth of coverage and flexibility of usage of federal funding reflected a trade-off: the provinces got access to federal funds which they could then deploy for their own purposes; and the federal government enhanced its visibility in all Canadian regions and got credit for its funding (Skogstad 2000, 64). There may be serious question marks about the effectiveness of this kind of all-inclusive approach (Skogstad 2000, 65-67), but that is not really the point. The point is for the provinces to realise their own development priorities at the same time as the federal government is seen to make a visible contribution to national integration. There is a different kind of collective normative judgement at play here than that underpinning state policy laboratories in the US and competitive federalism in Germany. It expresses that there are some elements of pan-Canadianism – even if only provided by the federal purse – which overarch a vast and diverse society. In these circumstances the shift away from old-style interventionism to a 'new regionalist' pursuit of endogenous policy innovation is more or less incidental (though the most recent framework for federal-provincial co-operation in regional policy does focus more explicitly on facilitating business development, the provision of venture capital and so on).

Social policy laboratories?

Greater variation (and less of a federal role) in the management of regional economies seems in the US and increasingly in Germany to be considered broadly appropriate, and certainly more appropriate now than it used to be. And regional policy variation in Canada remains more or less self-evident (even if much of it is federally funded). Whether the same acceptance of diversity can be found in social policy is a moot point. Social policy provision would seem to strike at the heart of the idea of 'social citizenship': 'The issue is whether citizens in similar economic and social situations are treated equally, irrespective of where they live in the country' (Banting and Corbett 2002a, 19). In his study of federalism and policy-making Dietmar Braun (2000, 15) is fairly clear that they should be treated equally:

> Obviously social policy and health policy are areas which need a high degree of standardisation and harmonisation... One can expect that these policies are decided and organised by the central state independently of the territorial distribution of powers.

But contrary to Braun's (unsubstantiated) assumption, the debate about 'laboratory' experimentation in the US has come increasingly to impinge on the social policy questions. This is where the fear of a 'race to the bottom' comes in. Some of the decentralist reforms in the US over the last two decades have widened the discretion states may apply in social policy provision. Some fear that this will lead (or has already led) to cuts in levels of provision in the quest to maintain a competitive advantage vis-à-vis other states. In Canada too there has been a decentralisation process in social policy promoted by fiscal crisis at the federal level and the associated offloading of policy responsibilities; this has posed challenges for the idea of Canadian 'social union'. Even in Germany, where the idea of uniformity of provision and the notion of the 'social state' have a constitutional foundation, ideas on the benefits of a more competitive federalism have spilled over into the social policy arena. The following discussion looks at how the uniformity-diversity balance has played out amid these decentralising trends in the fields of welfare and health policy.

Welfare

The main prompt for fears about a 'race to the bottom' in US welfare policy has been the introduction in 1996 of a federal block grant to the states called 'Temporary Assistance for Needy Families' (TANF) which replaced an earlier cash assistance programme run under tighter federal conditions. TANF funds need not be in the form of cash payments to the disadvantaged and could for example be used to fund charity organisations providing soup kitchens and shelters (Schram and Weissert 1999, 3).

More typically, they are deployed as 'workfare' benefits designed to get citizens off the welfare rolls and into work.

TANF was the heart of the so-called 'devolution revolution' in the US. The 'loosening of the federal tether' was going to turn the states 'into fifty "laboratories of democracy" that can develop superior responses to poverty and welfare' (Schram and Soss 1998, 68). The optimistic view of this was that different political opinions in the states might cause different outcomes with governors taking the opportunity to try out new ideas:

> One can even imagine something like a race to the top breaking out among governors who...seek, even at some cost to the fisc, to astonish the public by moving large numbers of welfare recipients into the productive workforce. (Beer 1998, 13)

Rather more widespread, though, were concerns about a 'race to the bottom' in which 'states will slash benefits if they fear that their generosity relative to other states will result in an influx of indigent persons from neighbouring jurisdictions seeking to capitalise on the state's largesse' (Heaney and Lock 1999, 1). Apparent confirmation for this is given by the radical reduction in welfare rolls in some states that has occurred since TANF was introduced.

The reality, predictably, is that the evidence so far is mixed. At one level it is not clear just how far the block grant approach entirely removes federal regulation; there are still US-wide standards that need to be upheld. But some states are using the new leeway of TANF creatively, through a mix of incentives and penalties, to find new ways of getting people off welfare and into work. Some states have done so punitively by tightening eligibility rules for support. This tougher approach to welfare is explained by some commentators as a classic problem of collective action 'in which competition among separate actors tempts them individually to do what they otherwise prefer not to' (Beer 1998, 12). More specifically, states are said to fear ending up as 'welfare magnets, attracting poor people' (Peterson, 1995, 121). There is little unambiguous evidence for such a magnet effect (Schram, Nitz and Kruger 1998; Schram and Soss 1998). But the issue has an evident emotive appeal in the light of a US tradition of local poor relief and hostility to the poor outsider (as evoked by the so-called 'bum blockades' during the Great Depression in Schram and Soss, 1998, 75; the same issue has played out closer to home in some of the more fanciful visions of a stampede of infirm pensioners moving from England to Scotland to take advantage of the Scottish Executive's policy on long-term care). But the fact that there is little evidence for the idea of the welfare magnet does not mean that it has no policy effect. Schram and Soss (1998, 82-86) come to a paradoxical evaluation of recent welfare reform. On the one hand, there has been no race to the bottom on benefit levels. As welfare rolls have fallen, states have invested strongly in getting the remaining recipients into work. But the 'spectre' – rather than the reality – of what in the UK might be called 'benefit tourism' has led entitlement to welfare to non-residents to be radically cut back.

This is a dysfunctional outcome, combining strong examples of policy innovation for established residents with a narrow protectionism to prevent in-migration, with all its implications for the operation of the US internal market. It can happen because of the growing normative agreement in the US that the role of the centre should be reduced and the scope for more autonomous policy development in the states should be enhanced. There is in the US a relatively weak sense of social citizenship which allows citizens in similar economic and social circumstances to be treated differently depending on where they live (and especially if they decide to live somewhere else). In this sense the US provides a stark contrast to Germany and Canada where, for different reasons, a stronger sense of social citizenship underpins a continued and strong role for the federal government in welfare provision. Both the German and the Canadian experiences do though reveal some issues in common with developments in the US, in particular in the shift from welfare payments to the needy to workfare programmes, and in Canada also a significant decentralisation of policy responsibilities in recent years.

In Germany the social dislocation of unification has inevitably left more people dependent on *Sozialhilfe*, the main instrument of welfare payments to those whose entitlement to unemployment insurance has expired. In 1993 dormant 'workfare' elements in the original 1961 legislation were strengthened, placing a greater emphasis on advice and counselling and in that way preventing the need to claim *Sozialhilfe*. These workfare elements have also been increasingly 'remembered' by the local authorities responsible for dispensing *Sozialhilfe* (Annesley 2002). This has led to considerable differences in how welfare recipients are dealt with on the ground. Significantly, though, *Sozialhilfe* is subject to federal legislation. This means that while there is a growing consensus that cash payments should be supplemented/replaced by enhanced measures to encourage people into work, there is still a federal framework which sets minimum standards that apply to all Germans.

There have, though, been some calls – *pace* 'competitive' federalism – to decentralise responsibilities in the field to the *Länder*. Most notable has been the rhetoric of the Christian Democratic Minister-President of Hesse, Roland Koch, on deploying workfare methods observed in a visit to Wisconsin (the 'Wisconsin Works' programme which obliges all work-able claimants to take up a form of work or training offered by the state and which has seen a reduction of the welfare rolls in that state by 92 per cent over the last ten years) (Koch 2001). Koch's attempts to open up the legal possibility for Hesse to experiment with a Wisconsin-style programme have hitherto foundered on the commitment of the Social Democratic federal government to maintain a common nation-wide framework (Annesley 2002). However, as the discussion below of health policy will reiterate, the willingness to think 'outside of the box' of established commitments to common nation-wide policy standards suggests that inherited norms about the desirability of uniform living conditions are now under growing challenge.

Canada presents a subtly different picture. Most fields of social policy are provincial responsibilities. Yet since World War II the deployment of the federal spending power in building the welfare state has created a high level of common provision. This common provision has underpinned the concept of the social union: 'Major social programs operated across the country as a whole and established a set of social benefits that Canadians held in common, irrespective of the region in which they lived' (Banting 1997, 40). The notion of social union rested on a Canada-wide consensus that the state should play an extensive role in social policy. That consensus is still intact, but social policy provision has become increasingly controversial for two reasons. The first is Quebec (even though the Quebecois think in broadly the same way about social policy as the rest of Canada). Quebec's concern is jurisdiction, and more or less all of its governments since the 1950s have sought to roll back the federal government's role in social policy provision: 'Quebec has long been committed to the goal of a Quebec welfare state' (Banting 1997, 61), and this commitment was one of the key concerns which mired Canada in years of ultimately fruitless constitutional negotiations on the rebalancing of the federal system in the 1980s and 1990s.

The second problem was the fiscal crisis of the Canadian federal authorities. On the election of the first Chrétien government in 1993, there had been twenty successive annual fiscal deficits with the accumulated debt approaching 70 per cent of GDP. The response was a cost-cutting programme which hit heavily on federal transfers to the provinces, in particular in social policy. The effect was in part to import tensions into the federal-provincial relationship, in part to reduce the capacity of the federal government to establish common, pan-Canadian standards. The latter effect did not produce the same kinds of dysfunctional result as in the US, but rather a recasting and renewal of the federal-provincial relationship in social policy. This renewal was in part procedural and was set out in the 1999 agreement to establish 'A Framework to Improve the Social Union for Canadians' (to which all the provinces except Quebec signed up) (Lazar 1999b). This Social Union Framework Agreement (SUFA) was mainly about introducing rules about the use of the federal spending power, in particular to prevent disruptions like the post-1993 cuts, and to establish procedures for securing provincial consent to new programmes based on the federal spending power. Its only real policy substance was to reaffirm of key principles of health policy (see below) and to strengthen the principle that Canadians who move from one province to another should not face a reduction in entitlement to benefits. The latter point is highly significant when compared to the situation in the US. The

SUFA has placed a barrier in the way of any 'race to the bottom' driven by the fear that provinces might become 'welfare magnets' and in that sense strongly reaffirms the idea of a social union for all Canadians in all parts of Canada.

The SUFA's focus on procedure was also indicative of a new commitment to 'collaborative' federalism. Collaborative federalism is in part a recognition that a federal government contributing less money needs to develop new ways of partnership working if it wishes still to achieve pan-Canadian goals. Collaborative federalism also acts – through pragmatic use of opt-out mechanisms and an increased flexibility in the implementation of programmes – as a means of keeping Quebec involved in a 'non-constitutional renewal' of the federal system after the (often acrimonious) failure of the wholesale constitutional change negotiations of the 1980s and early 1990s (Lazar 1997). It is this kind of collaborative-pragmatic approach which has been applied in the field of 'welfare to work' since the federal cutbacks of the first Chretien government. One effect of the cuts was to decentralise active labour market programmes designed to reintegrate the unemployed into paid employment. This decentralisation has taken the form of a set of bilateral federal-provincial agreements. Some of these – including an agreement with Quebec – involve devolution of programme design and administration and (part-)funding through federal transfers. Other agreements involve a fuller federal role through joint design and implementation. At the same time a continued exclusive role for the federal government in unemployment insurance and in maintaining and disseminating nation-wide data on labour market trends ensures a broad pan-Canadian framework. In these ways the recast federal role in social policy generally and welfare in particular is still one which reflects a tradition of 'statecraft', of giving expression and meaning to a common Canadian citizenship despite significant changes in circumstance since the original postwar social union. In this way the federal government can still 'fashion appeals that cut across territorial divides, reinforce the legitimacy of [its] role and strengthen Canadians' sense of attachment to their country' (Banting 1997, 60).

Healthcare

The experience of policy variation in welfare presents a different picture than in economic development. Only in the US is there an acceptance that state-to-state differences in policy standards are appropriate (and even there concerns about the 'race to the bottom' show that the appropriateness of growing policy variation is contested). In Germany common nation-wide standards have been maintained despite calls to loosen the federal policy framework. And in Canada considerable efforts have been made to renew the idea of a pan-Canadian social union in the recast form of a more collaborative federalism less subject to the power of the federal purse. One can expect that this higher level of commitment to norms of social citizenship will also be reflected in healthcare. Banting and Corbett (2002a, 19) cut to the chase with their rhetorical question: 'Does a sick baby in one region have access to the same level of care on similar terms and conditions as a sick baby in another region of the same country?' In their comparison of health policy and federalism in five federal states including the US, Germany and Canada, but also Australia and Belgium (in Banting and Corbett 2002b) they find that 'in none of these federations is health policy purely a local responsibility'. Moreover, despite wide variations in the organisation of health care and the division of labour between federal and regional levels in policy delivery, 'the extent to which federal states have succeeded in establishing interregional evenness in health services is striking' (Banting and Corbett 2002a, 30).

As in welfare the most uneven system is clearly the US (Colby 2002), where public health care provision is limited to 'deserving' populations: the elderly and disabled have access to Medicare, a federal-only programme with uniform application. The welfare poor have access to Medicaid and poor children to the State Child Insurance programme. Both of these are joint federal-state programmes which have standard benefit packages supplemented by (jointly funded) additional services on an opt-in basis. Public provision accounts for around 47 per cent of expenditures on health care, with the rest financed privately through insurance and out-of-pocket payments. The provision of insurance is subject to federal level regulation. In other words, though this policy framework allows a significant level of regional variation, there is also underlying federal regulation providing for a minimum level of uniformity of provision across the US. Banting and Corbett (2002a, 17) read this as indicative of 'a special political sensitivity' attached to health care that 'constrains pressures for decentralisation'. The same sensitivity exists in Germany, where much less variation in standards is evident. Health care there is based on statutory (but privately organised) insurance schemes, as are related policies for unemployment, pensions and long-term care. The insurance funds organise the delivery of care and set contribution rates. The role of the *Länder* is minimal and restricted to public health promotion and hospital capital costs. Even more than in the US it appears that there is no normative basis for wide variation in policy standards; health care still seems fully subject to collective beliefs that uniformity of standards should be maintained.

Perhaps the clearest confirmation of this has come in responses to the Bavarian government's ideas on extending the competitive federalism agenda into the field of social insurance (Stamm 1998, 235-241). The various social insurance funds in effect operate equalisation mechanisms to reduce variation in cost-benefit packages around the country. The effect is that some of the contributions made by individuals in *Länder* with less health care needs/pensioners/unemployed/long term infirm end up paying for care/pensions/benefits in other *Länder*. To this end Bavaria has proposed a regionalisation of contributions and benefits for both health care and unemployment. The aim is to 'make clear the causal relationship between the policies of a *Land* and their impact on its citizens' (Stamm 1998, 240). Perhaps unsurprisingly these ideas have not had a wide resonance. Even those sympathetic to an economic policy agenda of competitive federalism, like the Bavarian political scientist Ursula Münch, have distanced themselves from these Bavarian proposals:

> It is desirable and fundamentally necessary not to weaken, but to strengthen those who are willing and able to make contributions [for the care/benefits of others]. However this aspiration hits its limits in the call in the Basic Law [the German constitution] for a social policy which is consistent with human dignity, which establishes legal rights in place of arbitrary poor relief and which ultimately, with all due respect for the regions, addresses the needs of the common weal. (Münch 1998, 78)

This kind of appeal to a higher moral principle – a common weal identified with maintaining human dignity – is just as clearly evident in Canada. Canadian health care, Medicare, rests on the five principles codified in the 1984 Canada Health Act: universal coverage, no limitation on accessibility through user fees, coverage of all medically necessary services, coverage that is portable outside the home province, and public sector administration. These pan-Canadian principles enshrined in federal legislation give shape to a healthcare system which is organised and run predominantly under provincial jurisdiction. As in other fields of social policy, federal-provincial relations were disrupted by federal funding cuts in the mid-1990s. But the reaffirmation of the five principles and the agreement on procedures for avoiding funding shocks in the SUFA reflected federal-provincial agreement that healthcare should continue to be delivered as a common right of social citizenship. As Prime Minister Chrétien put it in 1997 (and as opinion polls confirm): 'Medicare' – and the federal role in setting the parameters for how the provinces deliver health policy – 'is a cherished legacy that we will never abandon' (Lazar 1997b, 119-120).

Conclusions: the limits of the laboratory

In Germany and in Canada the delivery of healthcare is clearly constrained by a normative consensus on the need to maintain a 'solidarity community' (Germany) or 'social union' (Canada) across the national territory. Though healthcare services there as elsewhere are under considerable material pressure from the costs of technological advance that consensus is holding. Even in the US, where regional policy variation in some fields of social policy is more acceptable, it seems that democratic politics is more intolerant of interregional inequality than in other areas: 'the intense political salience of healthcare seems to constrain the politics of regional diversity' (Banting and Corbett 2002a, 31). In the field of welfare and, indeed, in other fields of social policy (see Lazar

1997b; Münch, 1999) the norms of solidarity and national unity also predominate in Canada and Germany. The collective social judgements there – despite the challenges posed by fiscal crisis and visions of competitive federalism – are that it would be wrong to risk removing from some people minimum levels of social policy provision simply because of where they live. The US experience, driven by disillusionment with the federal government and folk memory about the migrant poor, takes up an outlier position on welfare. As such, its mix of state policy innovation on workfare and race to the bottom on entitlement for outsiders is unlikely to be seen elsewhere as a positive combination. Only in the field of regional economic development policy does there seem to be a more general appetite for policy variation and experimentation. Beyond that point the laboratory, in Germany and Canada at least, meets its limits.

It is these kinds of normative reference point that are also playing out in post-devolution UK. In the various, typically modest ways that the Scottish Parliament, Welsh and Northern Irish Assemblies (and, very modestly, London and the English regions) are implementing new forms of policy variation, they are (re-)negotiating the balance in the UK of uniformity and diversity, of the common claims of social citizenship and the specific preferences of the nations and regions of the UK. As Robert Hazell and Brendon O'Leary (1999, 42) put it in their 'history of the next ten years' of devolution, 'the trick will be to identify and understand what items need to be held in common throughout the kingdom as constants of UK citizenship; and what items can be allowed to vary'. Looking at the US, Germany and Canada suggests that regional economic policy is more likely to 'be allowed to vary' than social policy. Indeed, the anticipated benefits of regional economic policy decentralisation have been at the heart of devolution debates, driving the reforms forward in Wales and the English regions and forming a strong part of the rationale for devolution in Scotland and Northern Ireland.

By contrast, there remain symbolic but deep-seated attachments to notions of 'the welfare state' and the 'National' Health Service which operate on a pan-UK scale. Even though health policy responsibilities have been decentralised in Scotland, Wales and Northern Ireland (unlike social security, which remains a reserved power and subject to UK wide standards) it seems likely that wider public expectations about universality of provision will limit the scope for variation. The reluctance of the devolved administrations to depart from the wider (that is, English) funding standard for health in the 2002 UK budget suggests that regional politicians recognise this normative constraint.

However, the discussion of the US, Germany and Canada also suggest that senses of what is appropriate and what is not may vary over time. What was held to be appropriate before, or at the point of, devolution may not remain so as territorial policy debates, now underpinned by territorial electoral and legislative processes, unfold. Any or all of the developments seen in the US, Germany and Canada could unfold in the UK and lead to reassessments of what it is that is appropriate to do commonly nationwide and what to do differentially in the regions. Certainly, disillusionment with central government (the US), growing concern over the implicit or explicit cross-subsidisation caused by regional economic disparities (Germany), the regional spillover effects of fiscal crisis at the centre (Canada), or a growing restiveness of one of more component units about its place in the wider union (Canada) are all conceivable in the UK. A specifically UK prompt for this kind of reassessment may well also follow devolved or general elections which bring about different party majorities in Westminster as compared to Holyrood or Cardiff Bay.

However, a meaningful debate about 'items in common' and 'items to vary' has barely started. It is doubtful that the norms underlying the current balance of uniformity and diversity in post-devolution UK are widely understood. And that is largely because the UK government, which is in the most obvious position to articulate a sense of what the items in common and items to vary should be, has not done so. Tony Blair's speech to the National Assembly for Wales in October 2001 was probably the fullest attempt by any member of his government to present a vision setting out what the union is for and how it overarches and articulates with devolution's territorial rationales of giving expression to social diversity. But even that was nebulous in vision and gossamer-thin on detail. By default, the tendency is the familiar one of 'muddling through'. It seems unlikely that this is the best way of getting to the heart of what it is that constitutes social citizenship in the UK, and how the constants of social citizenship set limits to devolution's putative laboratories of democracy. It seems unlikelier still that a non-debate is the best way of preparing the ground for future controversies – which will happen, as they do in all decentralised systems – about what Westminster should do UK-wide and what the devolved institutions should do territorially. If such controversies are to be negotiated smoothly, that ground needs to be prepared now.

Endnotes

1   The chapter builds on a report written for the Anglo-German Foundation on 'Fiscal and Economic Decentralisation' available at www.agf.org.uk/pubs/pdfs/FiscalEconomicDecentralisation.pdf

2   In the UK as elsewhere 'region' is not a uniformly acceptable term for the component units of decentralised states. It is though routinely used in comparative analysis as a catch-all term referring to 'states', 'provinces', 'Länder', 'nations' (in the UK sense) and indeed the many other variations that exist in decentralised states world-wide. It is this comparative understanding of the term that is used here.

3   Brandeis L (1932) Supreme Court judgement 285 US 262, 311.

4   Blair T (2001) *Speech to the National Assembly for Wales* 30 October 2001

References

Annesley C (2002) 'Reconfiguring (Women's) Social Citizenship in Germany? The Right to Sozialhilfe, the Responsibility to Work' *German Politics* 11

Banting K (1997) 'The Past Speaks to the Future: Lessons from the Postwar Social Union' in Lazar H (ed) *Non-Constitutional Renewal* Montreal/Kingston: McGill-Queen's University Press

Banting K and Corbett S (2002a) 'Health Policy and Federalism: An Introduction' in Banting K and Corbett S (eds) *Health Policy and Federalism* Montreal/Kingston: McGill-Queen's University Press

Banting K and Corbett S (2002b) *Health Policy and Federalism* Montreal/Kingston: McGill-Queen's University Press

Banting K, Hoberg G and Simeon R (1997) 'Introduction' in Banting K, Hoberg G and Simeon R (eds) *Degrees of Freedom: Canada and the United States in a Changing World* Montreal/Kingston: McGill-Queen's University Press

Beer S (1998) 'Welfare Reform: Revolution or Retrenchment?' *Publius. The Journal of Federalism* 28

Blair T (2001) *Speech to the National Assembly for Wales* 30 October 2001 London: 10 Downing Street

Braun D (2000), 'Territorial Division of Power and Public Policy-Making: An Overview' Braun D (ed) *Public Policy and Federalism* Aldershot: Ashgate.

Bulmer S (1991) 'Efficiency, Democracy and West German Federalism' Jeffery C and Savigear P (eds) *German Federalism Today* Leicester: Leicester University Press

Colby D (2002) 'Federal-State Relations in United States Health Care Policy' Banting K and Corbett S (eds) *Health Policy and Federalism* Montreal and Kingston: McGill-Queen's University Press

Cole R and Kincaid J (2000) 'Public Opinion and American Federalism: Perspectives on Taxes, Spending, and Trust – An ACIR Update' *Publius: The Journal of Federalism* 30

Commission of the European Communities (2001) *European Governance: A White Paper* COM (2001) 428 (final), Brussels

De Vries M (2000) 'The Rise and Fall of Decentralisation: A Comparative Analysis of Arguments and Practices in European Countries' *European Journal of Political Research* 38

Greve M (2001), 'Laboratories of Democracy: Anatomy of a Metaphor' *Federalist Outlook* 6

Grube N (2001) 'Föderalismus in der öffentlichen Meinung der Bundesrepublik Deutschland' *Jahrbuch des Föderalismus* 2001 Baden-Baden: Nomos

Hazell R and O'Leary B (1999) 'A Rolling Programme of Devolution: Slippery Slope or Safeguard of the Union?' Hazell R (ed) *Constitutional Futures. A History of the Next Ten Years* Oxford: Oxford University Press

Heaney M and Lock E (1999) 'Are the US States "Laboratories of Democracy" or Do They "Race to the Bottom"?' manuscript

Hooghe L and Marks G (2001) 'Types of Multi-Level Governance: What, Where, How?' manuscript

Jeffery C (2002), 'German Federalism from Cooperation to Competition', in M. Umbach (ed) *German Federalism Past, Present and Future* Palgrave: Houndmills

Jeffery C (1999) 'Party Politics and Territorial Representation in the Federal Republic of Germany' *West European Politics* 22

Jeffery C and Hough D (2001) 'The Electoral Cycle and Multi-Level Voting in Germany' *German Politics* 10

Jeffery C and O'Sullivan B (1994) *The Role of Socio-Economic Interest Groups vis-à-vis Local and Regional Authorities* report for the Economic and Social Committee of the EU

Kanter R (1995) *World Class: Thriving Locally in the Global Economy* New York: Simon and Schuster.

Keating M (1998) *The New Regionalism in Western Europe* Cheltenham: Edward Elgar

Knox R (1997) 'Economic Integration in Canada through the Agreement on Internal Trade', in Lazar H (ed) *Non-Constitutional Renewal* Montreal and Kingston: McGill-Queen's University Press

Koch R (2001) 'Sozialhilfe – eine zweite Chance, kein Lebensstil' www.roland-koch.de/home_cdu.nsf/$pages/content_sozialhilfe

Lazar H (1999a) 'In Search of a New Mission Statement for Canadian Fiscal Federalism' Lazar H (ed) *Toward a New Mission Statement for Canadian Fiscal Federalism* Montreal and Kingston: McGill-Queen's University Press

Lazar H (1999b) 'The Social Union Framework Agreement and the Future of Fiscal Federalism' Lazar H (ed) *Toward a New Mission Statement for Canadian Fiscal Federalism* Montreal and Kingston: McGill-Queen's University Press

Lazar H (1997a) 'Non-Constitutional Renewal: Toward a New Equilibrium in the Federation' Lazar H (ed) *Non-Constitutional Renewal* Montreal and Kingston: McGill-Queen's University Press

Lazar H (1997b) 'The Federal Role in a New Social Union: Ottawa at a Crossroads' Lazar H (ed) *Non-Constitutional Renewal* Montreal and Kingston: McGill-Queen's University Press

McKay D (2001) *American Politics and Society* Oxford: Blackwells

Münch U (1998) 'Entflechtungsmöglichkeiten im Bereich der Sozialpolitik' Männle U (ed) *Föderalismus zwischen Konsens und Konkurrenz* Baden-Baden: Nomos

Osborne D (1988) *Laboratories of Democracy* Boston: Harvard Business School Press

Peterson P (1995) *The Price of Federalism* Brookings: Washington DC

Savoie D (1995) 'Regional Development: A Policy for all Seasons'   Smith F and Smith

M (ed) *New Trends in Canadian Federalism* Peterborough, Ontario: Broadview Press

Schram S and Soss J (1998), 'Making Something out of Nothing: Welfare Reform and a New Race to the Bottom' *Publius: The Journal of Federalism* 28

Schram S and Weissert C (1999), 'The State of US Federalism 1998-99' *Publius. The Journal of Federalism* 29

Schram S, Nitz L and Krueger G (1998) 'Without Cause or Effect: Reconsidering Welfare Migration as a Policy Problem' *American Journal of Political Science* 42

Simeon R and Willis E (1997) 'Democracy and Performance: Governance in Canada and the United States' Banting K, Hoberg G and Simeon R (eds) *Degrees of Freedom. Canada and the United States in a Changing World* Montreal and Kingston: McGill-Queen's University Press

Skogstad G (2000) 'Canada: Dual and Executive Federalism, Ineffective Problem-Solving' Braun D (ed) *Public Policy and Federalism* Aldershot: Ashgate

Stamm B (1998) 'Wettbewerbsföderalismus in der Sozialversicherung' Männle U (ed) *Föderalismus zwischen Konsens und Konkurrenz* Baden-Baden: Nomos

Tarr G (2001) 'Laboratories of Democracy? Brandeis, Federalism and Scientific Management' *Publius: The Journal of Federalism* 31

12. Divergence and the centre

John Adams and Peter Robinson

Devolution is arguably one of the most radical constitutional changes in the governance of the United Kingdom since the Irish Free State was created in the 1920s, and some claim since the Great Reform Act of 1832 (Bogdanor 2001). It has created new centres of political power and new devolved polities in four different territories within the United Kingdom.

However, devolution should not be seen as simply a change to the constitution. It is both an important component of the revitalisation of democracy within the UK and represents a significant change to the public policy-making process. The Scottish Parliament and the Northern Ireland Legislative Assembly have primary legislative powers in a wide range of policy areas, and the National Assembly for Wales and the Greater London Authority are responsible for public expenditure and the development of policy in key areas. The impact on the evolution of public services across the UK could potentially be very significant indeed.

The purpose of this chapter is not to provide a report card on the successes or failures of the devolved institutions but rather to examine the nature of policy divergence and the pressures for and constraints on differentiated policy-making within the UK. There can be no guarantee that devolution will bring about either a more rational public policy process or better outcomes from public services: it is inevitable that mistakes as well as successes will occur. Therefore it would be complacent to claim that an automatic dividend in terms of improved public services is likely to follow from devolution, any more than an automatic economic dividend in terms of improved prosperity.

This chapter is in three parts. First, there is an examination of divergences in public policy in the four nations of the UK, and where appropriate the 12 nations and regions of the UK. Second, the implications of devolution for the centre of government in Whitehall are discussed. Third, we discuss some of the next possible steps in the devolution process.

Divergence in public policy

The contributors to this publication have provided a unique guide not only to some of the headline divergences in policy, but also the arguments and pressures that lie behind policy changes. This section tries to bring out some of the common themes that have emerged from these chapters.

Divergence is not all of the same character and there seems to be five distinct forms that we might discuss:

- whether different *values* exist in the different nations which might find their expression in policy divergence

- how the *structures* of the administrations are changing, including public bodies within their remit

- how the *process* of decision-making is changing

- what new differences in *policy* are emerging

- if devolution is leading to different *outcomes* in key areas of public policy

This typography is intended only as a guide to understanding, and many specific changes in public policy post-devolution will reflect several of these forms of divergence. The abolition of up-front tuition fees in Scotland is an example. This was a clear change in policy in Scotland, made easier by the unique Scottish education system. It may or may not reflect a distinctive set of 'Scottish' values, but the decision was taken after a widespread consultation exercise, including the Education Committee of the Parliament, which proved an exemplar of the new inclusive form of decision-making that devolution has deliberately attempted to foster.

Values

Some advocates claimed that devolution would enable Scotland and Wales to pursue a more 'left-wing' policy agenda than appeared to be acceptable to voters in England (Osmond 1998; Paterson 1994). Such a claim is predicated on the assumption that the people of Scotland and Wales in some sense have a more 'progressive' set of values than those in England, with a more collectivist approach to the provision of services and a stronger commitment to an equitable distribution of income.

Scotland and Wales certainly have a tradition of supporting the Labour Party, and famously in 1997 both countries failed to return a single Conservative MP. Wales also failed to elect a Conservative in the 2001 General Election and in fact has never returned a majority of Conservative MPs to Westminster, staunchly supporting first the Liberal and then the Labour parties. In Scotland there was a majority of Conservative and old-style Liberal-Unionist MPs as recently as 1955, but since that date Labour has been in the majority.

However, support for a political party is more then simply a sign of where one sits on a left–right axis. Professor Alice Brown of Edinburgh University and her colleagues argue that:

> the distinctiveness of Scottish voting is not really a social conflict with England but a political one. Scottish voters dislike the Conservative Party, which until 1997 the majority of the people in the south of England chose to further much the same social and economic goals as the Scots entrust to the parties of the left and centre. (Brown, McCrone and Paterson 1998, 165)

While at first sight it may appear strange to claim that Scotland and South East England shared quite the same social and economic goals during the time of Margaret Thatcher, in truth both would have wished to see improved living standards and better public services. Trust in particular politicians might have differed, and the means of achieving these objectives might not be the same; but the idea of a conflict between radically different values in England on the one hand, and in Scotland and Wales on the other is probably much exaggerated.

In the 1997 Election Survey the Centre for Research into Elections and Social Trends (CREST)[1] included a set of items which between them have been shown to form a scale that measures the degree to which respondents adopt a left-wing or right-wing view on major economic issues[2]. The scale ranges from 1, which represents the most left-wing position to 5, which represents the most right wing. A similar scale exists to measure the degree to which respondents adopt a libertarian or authoritarian view, where 1 represents the most libertarian and 5 the most authoritarian[3].

In the left-right scale both Scotland and Wales returned a score of 2.4, and England returned a score of 2.6. In the libertarian-authoritarian scale England returned a score of 3.15, Wales 3.16 and Scotland 3.08.[4] Unfortunately there are no comparable indicators available for Northern Ireland. Nor are there indicators available on a left-right scale in relation to social policy issues where, as Jeffery in Chapter 11 notes, there may be less tolerance of divergence than for economic issues. It would seem that both Scotland and Wales are slightly more 'left-wing' than England in relation to economic issues, and that Scotland is slightly more 'libertarian' than England and Wales. However, in all cases these differences are quite small and we might conclude that there appears to be a broadly similar set of values at work in Scotland and Wales as in England.

Much of the evidence advanced purporting to demonstrate a more left-wing agenda in Scotland and Wales fails to fully support that proposition. The introduction of free personal long-term care in Scotland was very much the personal commitment of the former First Minister Henry McLeish MSP (who at times had to force it through in the face of opposition from members of his own Executive). Similarly, much of the hesitation of the devolved institutions to experiment with the use of different forms of Public Private Partnerships (PPPs) could be taken as a sign of 'conservatism' and an unwillingness to drop unhelpful ideological baggage in order to explore different models for public service delivery. This is one point emphasised by Woods on health policy in Chapter 2. Ward and Lowe in Chapter 8 suggest that the territories have also shown less enthusiasm for developing a more imaginative approach to rural issues, perhaps because the farming lobby has been better able to influence effectively the new devolved institutions.

A further point worth noting is that despite these broadly similar values across the UK, national identity has been politicised in Scotland to a degree that it has not been in England or Wales (Curtice and Seyd 2001). There is little or no relationship between national identity and voting intention in England; but in Scotland those who feel Scottish are more likely to support the SNP and to a lesser extent Labour, while those who feel British still give significant support to the Conservatives.

While there may not be radically different values in the different nations of the United Kingdom, devolution and devolved polities means that the process by which these values are reflected in public policy are likely to differ. Although people in the different parts of the UK might aspire to similar outcomes from their public services, the means by which those outcomes are secured might also begin to differ more markedly.

Structures

As many of the contributors to this publication have emphasised, devolution did not simply begin with the establishment of the Scottish Parliament and the assemblies in Wales and Northern Ireland. Each of the three territories had experienced significant administrative devolution, and indeed Northern Ireland had a long experience of elected government at Stormont (a unique institution which opened in 1921, was prorogued in 1972 and abolished in 1973).

The distinct administrative structures in these three territories formed the bedrock of the executives of the devolved institutions. As Rees argues in Chapter 7, this led to the development of 'assumptive worlds', which meant that:

> the ways in which the roles and powers were understood within the respective devolved institutions differed significantly and this became self-reproducing. Moreover, the ways in which substantive policy issues came to be conceived and conceptualised also reflected what became conventional ways of thinking. (p97)

These 'assumptive worlds' have persisted from the pre-devolution era, and have laid a policy pathway into the post-devolution polity – influencing the direction of policy. Therefore, as Rees argues, the restructuring of the learning and skills sector in Wales has followed the course determined in the pre-devolution Welsh Office. Similarly, as

Gillespie and Benneworth argue in Chapter 4, the direction of economic development policy in Scotland and Wales altered little as a result of devolution. Even with limited policy autonomy, the pre-devolution structures appear to have laid the pathway for future developments in public policy.

The creation of devolved institutions politicised these structures, most obviously in the distribution of different portfolios for the different Ministers. This was especially true in Northern Ireland. The politics of the peace process and the need for balance in a power-sharing executive required the Cabinet to consist of ten departmental ministers, and departments had to be restructured to achieve this. In addition to the First Minister and Deputy First Minister, the Executive Committee is made up of three members from the Social Democratic and Labour Party, three from the Ulster Unionist Party, two from the Democratic Unionist Party and two from Sinn Fein.

The allocation of political portfolios and changes to the formal departmental structures have been held up by some in the devolved administrations as an important example of divergence. In truth this is probably much exaggerated. Whatever the make-up of formal Ministerial responsibility, behind the scenes the same internal civil service structure has been maintained, and the officials continue in their particular divisions covering their specialist areas. It is unclear, for example, in the Scottish Department of Enterprise, Transport and Lifelong Learning whether even the enterprise and lifelong learning sections really 'join-up' in any meaningful sense. Furthermore, the nomenclature is often misleading. As Ward and Lowe point out in Chapter 8, the change in name of the Scottish 'Agriculture, Environment and Fisheries Department' to 'Environment and Rural Development' has not yet resulted in a significantly different approach to policy.

More importantly, the devolved administrations have made changes to the structure of public bodies in their territory: health providing a good example. The Welsh Assembly Government is abolishing health authorities, and introducing new structures which will make NHS Wales boundaries coterminous with local authority boundaries. The intention is to allow for a greater emphasis on public health and health outcomes. As Woods emphasises in Chapter 2 structural reform in the health services has followed different paths in both Scotland and England, in the latter case with less regard to regional and local boundaries, while the structures in Northern Ireland have always been very different in bringing together both health and social services.

These structural reforms will require time to bed down, so it is obviously too early to judge their effectiveness in improving the efficiency of the health system, never mind health outcomes, in the different territories. Nevertheless, as time goes by we might expect such structural differences to begin to impact on the provision of front-line health care services, their relationship with other public services, and maybe eventually health outcomes. This is especially the case if one recognises that the divergences in formal structure in part reflect more profound divergences in approach to health policy. In England, the Labour government is taking further forward the development of an 'internal market' model for health care. In the territories there is much less enthusiasm for this model, which is reflected in the structural changes outlined here and may in turn reflect some differences in values, if not in relation to outcomes, then certainly in relation to the means to achieve those outcomes.

Changes to the decision-making process

Inclusivity was one of the key principles that lay behind the devolution proposals. Many saw devolution as the key to developing a new kind of politics, a more co-operational, consensual style of governance in stark contrast to the confrontational style of Westminster and perhaps more akin to the way politics is conducted in other small Northern European nations (Welsh Office 1997; Scottish Office 1997).

It is important to distinguish between the impact of this new form of politics on the executive and on the legislature. The devolution proposals contained various structural innovations to try and ensure that the legislatures (the Parliament and the assemblies) formally adopted this more inclusive approach. They were elected under a system of proportional representation; civic forums (in Wales statutory partnerships) were created to provide an institutional locus for representatives of civic society; and the committees of the Parliament and the assemblies were given more power and influence under devolution than their counterparts at Westminster. Such innovations appear on the surface to have been successful: for example there is a greater role for backbenchers via the Committee system in the devolved institutions than at Westminster.

It is perhaps easier for a new legislature to be inclusive than for an executive that in part is built on the foundations of previous administrative structures. Nevertheless, the administrations have made serious attempts to open the decision-making process and consult widely on their plans and strategies. In Chapter 1 Keating makes the point that many interest groups in the devolved territories are struggling to make 'the transition from lobbyist to participant in a policy process' but that this is a challenge their counterparts aiming for influence at Westminster can only envy.

Some interest groups are making the transition better than others. The voluntary sector is widely believed to be one of the more effective interest groups, with much influence across a wide range of policy areas. In contrast, business representatives are seen to be less successful in engaging effectively with the new structures, perhaps retaining too much of a focus on the corridors of Whitehall. Interestingly, local government is seen to be one of the most powerful stakeholders in Wales, but not in Scotland.

The devolved administrations are seen to be somewhat less successful at engaging with citizens directly, as opposed to stakeholder groups. Significantly, in the Mayor's administration in London the Stakeholder Team, which is responsible for liaison with civic society and business organisations, is believed to be much more influential than the Consultation Team, which is responsible for dealing directly with the public. There have been some successes, however. In Wales the Regional Committees, which have no powers or budgets, have attracted significant audiences particularly in North Wales.

The fact that each of the devolved administrations are in coalition is by its very nature more inclusive than Westminster, as it forces different parties to work together. Nevertheless, it should be remembered that, as Ron Davies has pointed out, a coalition government is designed to produce a majority, with the consequent risk of majoritarian government (Davies 2000). While political parties are fully prepared to deal with representatives of business, trades unions or civic society they balk at co-operation with rival political parties, unless forced into coalition government. The four-party coalition in Northern Ireland is a unique result of the peace process, not a conscious desire to reach out across the party divide.

Progressives should welcome inclusivity as a objective in itself: diverse voices and sources of influence are vital for a vibrant political culture. However, many on the left have also claimed that an inclusive approach to policy making results in better decisions being taken. It is asserted that public scrutiny of the actions of government, both politicians and officials, means that any analysis, policy decisions and administrative action by the executive are strengthened through scrutiny; and the worst ideas do not proceed.

In the devolved arena an inclusive approach has been adopted, which has strengthened the decision-making process. It should be remembered, however, that the inclusive approach adopted under devolution was not entirely altruistic. As Keating said, each of the devolved administrations, but especially Wales and Northern Ireland, has been very concerned at the dearth of policy-making capacity in their respective territories. Rhodri Morgan admitted this point:

> I don't think we [in Wales] have the wealth of think tanks, Universities and professional associations, organised interest groups and corporate lobby bodies and political consultancies of London. (Morgan 2000)

The devolved administrations therefore felt obliged to open the circles of decision-making in order to bolster their policy-making capacity. Whether by choice or circumstance, such an approach has successfully enhanced the quality of public policy in the devolved territories. For example, following the decision on free personal long-term care in Scotland, the Welsh Assembly Government had to respond. In developing their 'Older Person's Strategy' the administration heavily involved the Committees and civic society and held numerous public meetings. Through this process a rational debate on the future of long-term care was held, where it was accepted that the policy of free personal long-term care could not be afforded but that certain improvements could be made. This stands in contrast to the ad hoc decision in Scotland by former First Minister Henry McLeish on this issue.

Inclusivity was one of the key principles that drove the devolution process. However, as the devolution settlement matures and the administrations grow in confidence it will be an interesting test as to whether they will continue to rely on civic society and keep the decision-making process open and inclusive.

Changes to policy

Understandably, changes to actual policies in Scotland, Wales, Northern Ireland and London have been the most high-profile form of divergence we have witnessed under devolution. The litany is familiar: free long-term care and the abolition of up-front tuition fees in Scotland, the abolition of school league tables in Wales and the proposed introduction of congestion charging in London.

Such reforms would generally be welcomed by those with a left-of-centre viewpoint, and one commentator has said that 'the Scottish Parliament had begun to craft a far more progressive agenda than anything seen at Westminster with respect to personal care for the elderly, student tuition fees and freedom of information for example.' (Morgan 2002)

However, the situation on the ground is more nuanced. It is true that many of the reforms undertaken by the devolved administrations are generally regarded as progressive. One example would be the stronger freedom of information legislation in Scotland, which provides for stricter time limits for authorities, a narrower ministerial veto, and contents based exemptions that require authorities to show that disclosure would 'substantially prejudice' specified interests (as opposed to the less demanding 'prejudice' test in the Westminster legislation). A second example would be the abolition of Section 2A in Scotland, which applied to local authorities and prevented 'the promotion of homosexuality as a pretend family relationship'. Its counterpart in England and Wales, Section 28, remains on the statute book, as attempts to abolish it fell due to opposition in the House of Lords.

However, the situation is more complex when we turn to consider reforms that lie within the traditional policy areas seen to have political priority such as health and education. Policy changes in these fields will more often have significant funding implications, and if new policies demand extra resources there will necessarily be implications for other public services given the fixed 'block grant' that funds each of the territories' services (and in the Scottish context an unwillingness to use the limited tax-varying powers available). Thus, politics in the devolved arena is most often a question of juggling priorities, a fact of which decision-makers are acutely aware.

For example, the decision to implement free personnel long-term care for the elderly was clearly seen by the former First Minister Henry McLeish as a decision to put 'older people at the very top of the Executive's priorities' (McLeish 2001). The opportunity cost of this decision seems to have fallen on two other areas: in the roads budget; and in other parts of the health budget (in terms, for example, of a lower priority to the development of cancer care services). This was not a universally popular decision within Scotland, and indeed it was a combination of Conservative, Liberal Democrat and Scottish National Party MSPs which forced the hand of the Executive, against the opposition of many in the Labour Party in Scotland. Opponents felt that this was not the most effective and progressive use of resources from within the block grant, that it was too universalist a policy which did not sufficiently target resources at the poorest in society. The ippr has recommended free personal long-term care throughout the UK, but argued that this should be funded by changes to the taxation system and not from within the budget of the Department of Health (Brooks, Regan and Robinson 2002). Such tax options are not, of course, available to the devolved territories.

Another common theme of divergence of public policy under devolution is the essentially reactive nature of decisions. Far from them being 'laboratories of ideas' much of the policy experimentation within the UK has been conducted in Whitehall and viewed with antipathy by the devolved institutions. As Reynolds argues in Chapter 6, the distinctive new Welsh education policy could be seen to flow from a rejection of English policies such as league tables and testing, or from the reintroduction of older policies like student grants. It does not necessarily reflect a set of new and imaginative policies. The point is also true of the hesitancy of the devolved administrations to embrace PPPs with the same enthusiasm as Whitehall, and even the decision to introduce free personal long-term care in Scotland follows the recommendation of a Royal Commission set up by the Department of Health in Whitehall (Royal Commission 1999).

A further theme of divergence in policy arises from the fact that both Scotland and Wales have coalition governments. This is a pressure for divergence in two ways. First and perhaps inevitably, the Liberal Democrats have a somewhat different set of values to the Labour Party and a different set of policies. They share power in Scotland and Wales, and would be expected to use their position to promote their values and policies within the coalition administrations.

Secondly, coalition government also provides 'cover' for Labour politicians in Scotland and Wales. Whitehall does exert considerable pressure on the devolved administrations not to diverge in their policies. This is motivated less from a concern for Scotland and Wales than a worry about non-governmental organisations and trade unions using decisions in the devolved territories to exert pressure for changes in policy in England (see the section on Inter-Governmental Relations below). In these discussions, Labour Ministers and advisers in Scotland and Wales do find it easier to pass the buck and blame their coalition partners for divergence, thereby maintaining good relations with their party colleagues in London.

Health spending dominates the budgets of the devolved territories and as different policies are pursued in the different territories it is this policy area which is likely to test the acceptable boundaries of divergence within the United Kingdom most severely. In the 2002 Budget the UK Government announced a significant increase in funding for the health service in England, which will mean significant increases in the budgets of the devolved administrations. While it is for the devolved administrations to allocate this money, in practice most if not all the extra funding will go into health. However, this need not mean the health service *per se*.

The reforms to the structures of the health services in the different territories may have an impact upon how the extra resources are spent. The result may be that the devolved administrations forge a different type of health system than that in England. While each territory might wish to see the same health outcomes achieved, the structures set in place to achieve these outcomes have already diverged. Will budget allocations now begin to diverge as well, as policy makers in different parts of the UK give different weight to different services and choose not to allocate all the extra funding to front-line health services? Or will popular pressures for convergence in the delivery of front-line services limit the capacity of the devolved governments to pursue different health policies?

Outcomes

Before we discuss the impact of devolution on policy outcomes, it is imperative to remember that nearly fifty years of control from Whitehall in the post-war welfare state had not ensured high and equal standards for all parts of the United Kingdom. While the economic divide between north and south, which has grown over the last decade, is particularly well known there is also a north-south divide in other policy areas, most notably health outcomes. Other areas have more complicated set of 'regional' differences: measured educational attainment is higher in Scotland and southern England than in the north of England; and while both north and south may have housing problems, they are very different in nature.

In Scotland at least, the Referendum survey showed that support for devolution was strongly related to people's expectations that it would improve the quality of their lives in terms of policy outcomes, and not just simply as a means of improving democracy. It was seen as a means to improving outcomes in education, health, employment and housing rather than just an end in itself (Surridge and McCrone 1999).

Evidence does show that the high expectations of the Scottish Parliament have fallen back somewhat since the time of the 1997 Referendum (Curtice 2001) but the available evidence does seem to show that people do credit the Scottish Parliament with some achievements, albeit only modest ones.

Table 12.1 Achievements of Scottish devolution

% saying that from what they have seen or heard, the Scottish Parliament has achieved:

	Feb 00	Sept 00	Feb 01
A lot	5	11	25
A little	64	56	56
Nothing at all	27	29	14

Source: ICM for The Scotsman[5]

However, expectations of the devolved institutions, and of politicians and government in general, are perhaps too high. A different policy-making process and different policies may have only a modest impact on outcomes, a point Rees makes strongly in Chapter 7. Final outcomes, such as greater social inclusion or lower rates of morbidity, are affected by a range of complicated factors over which public policy may have modest purchase. This is not to say that politics or public policy does not matter, but that we should be realistic in our expectations.

It is clearly too early to judge the success of the devolved administrations in improving outcomes for their citizens. However, the different structures and policies now being pursued within the United Kingdom do mean increased divergence, despite some strong pressures for convergence. However, the unanswered question remains: if these divergences lead to different outcomes how can these be reconciled with the broadly similar values we appear to share in the United Kingdom?

The new centre

In the post-devolution world the territorial reach of Whitehall Departments varies by policy area. There is a complicated mix of reserved, devolved and concurrent powers that vary between Scotland, Wales, Northern Ireland and London. Therefore, the responsibility of Whitehall Departments runs to a number of different geographical areas: the UK; Great Britain; England, Wales and Northern Ireland; England and Wales; England; and the 8 English regions outside London.

However, a nation state with devolved polities is still a nation state (albeit in the case of the UK, one consisting of four stateless nations). Westminster and Whitehall do retain a responsibility for all parts of the United Kingdom, and such 'quasi-federal' responsibilities must be exercised in a way that is compatible with the devolution settlement. Far from 'hollowing out' Whitehall, devolution means that it must develop important new roles. In this section we shall examine the two most important of these: ensuring smooth inter-governmental relations and the need to ensure territorial justice.

Inter-governmental relations

At a time when the Treasury has been providing a sustained period of increased funding for public services, it is crucial that Whitehall and the devolved administrations work together to try to meet the expectations of the UK public for service improvements. If citizens feel that those services fail to deliver, there could be a major political backlash that might damage both the devolution process and the case for the public services.

Therefore, one of the key responsibilities of the 'centre' must be to promote smooth inter-governmental relations. This is not just necessary to ensure that disputes and rows are diffused as far as possible, but also to encourage the different administrations to work together actively to improve the standard of public services throughout the UK. The pre-devolution hierarchical system of government with a rigid demarcation of power has not given way to separate silos where the devolved bodies operate in isolation, both from each other and from Whitehall. Rather we have a complicated mish-mash. For, as Keating notes in Chapter 1, modern government does not operate on the basis of strict and watertight divisions of competences and there is a high degree of functional interdependence between reserved and devolved matters.

For example, while most energy policy and issues relating to nuclear safety are explicitly reserved powers under the Scotland Act 1998, it is impossible for Whitehall to build a nuclear power station in Scotland without the Scottish Executive granting planning consent. While long-term care is a devolved issue the introduction of free personal care in Scotland saved the Department of Work and Pensions millions of pounds in Attendance Allowance claims (funds which were not then passed back to the Scottish Executive). The designation of assisted areas is reserved to Whitehall but the administration of regional assistance is a matter for the devolved administrations.

Remarkably little attention was given to inter-governmental relations when the Labour Party, the Scottish Constitutional Convention and others drew up the devolution proposals in the run-up to the 1997 General Election. Rather the fear was that there would be disputes over the precise scope of the competence of the devolved institutions, and the possibility of legal action and court cases. As Keating says in chapter 1 there has been remarkably little legal action so far, in contrast to Spain for example.

However, when Labour entered office in 1997 new mechanisms and structures for inter-governmental relations were developed by officials. The idea of a Joint Ministerial

Committee (JMC) emerged late at night in a Government amendment in the House of Lords.[6] This was to be a regular summit meeting between the heads of the various administrations (including the UK Prime Minister). Concordats would also be agreed between each of the devolved administrations and each of the Whitehall departments.

The concordats seem to have been far from influential. Indeed the concordat between the Welsh Assembly Cabinet and the Department for Education and Skills (and its predecessor the Department for Education and Employment) has yet to be concluded with little or no impact upon relations between the two organisations. One senior official involved in health policy in Scotland frankly admitted that he had not read the concordat between the Scottish Executive and the Department of Health. During the tensions over the introduction of free personal long-term care, he had, however, read the concordat with the Department of Work and Pensions but it had failed to provide him with any real guidance as to the contentious issue of the funding implications of the Scottish decision to introduce free personal care.

It would be wrong, however, to dismiss the concordats as meaningless. They provided a very important function at the start of the devolution process and sent a signal around Whitehall. Merely by encouraging Departments to agree these concordats, lines of communication with the devolved administrations were kept open. Officials in Whitehall could easily have felt uncomfortable in dealing with an institution with different political masters and might have 'raised the drawbridge' to use the phrase of one Whitehall official. In fact, while by no means perfect, the degree of cordiality in the relations between Whitehall and devolved officials has been remarkable.

While inevitably officials in the devolved territories spend less time working with Whitehall, the networks established by individual civil servants prior to devolution still exist and Great Britain still has a single unified civil service. Furthermore, relations can be forged and information can be shared outside the official mechanisms. The administrations of Scotland and Wales are made up of politicians from UK-wide parties, and the parties have a unique role in bringing together politicians from the different elected bodies. Many non-governmental organisations – pressure groups, business groups and trade unions – operate at a UK level and have strong dissemination networks. Furthermore, conferences and seminars in specialist policy areas mean that officials can come together on a UK basis to discuss their particular interests.

In short, the structures for inter-governmental relations are strong and institutions are in place to allow for dialogue between representatives of the different territories. However, far too often the opportunity does not appear to be taken. Whitehall officials too often simply forget the devolution dimension to public policy and proceed as if devolution had never happened.

For example one of the Public Service Agreement targets in 2000 was for the DTI and DETR to 'improve the economic performance of all regions measured by the trend in growth of each region's GDP per capita' (HM Treasury 2000b). In this context, the term 'region' applies to all 12 of the UK's nations and regions, but no mention was made of the contribution devolved administrations could have made to meeting this target.

Conversely, there is a tendency in Scotland, Wales and Northern Ireland to focus on their own affairs and miss the implications of decisions and policy developments in Whitehall. For example, the Scottish Executive could have better appreciated the way in which Attendance Allowance, paid by the Department of Work and Pensions in Whitehall, was going to interact with their policy of free personal long-term care.

Further structural reform might do little to improve the standard of inter-governmental relations in this new era of multi-level governance, but we desperately need a change in attitude to recognise this interdependence.

It must also be remembered that devolution was introduced at a time when levels of public expenditure have been growing at a sustained pace, and tensions have also been eased by the fact that the Labour Party has been in power in Westminster, in Wales and in Scotland (although only as the larger party in a coalition government in the latter two instances). Should a Conservative government be elected at Westminster, or should a nationalist party enter government in Scotland and Wales, relations will inevitably be strained, especially if controversial further constitutional change is promoted.

As Jeffery shows in Chapter 11, other countries have much greater experience of dealing with different political parties elected to different tiers of government. Furthermore, over the years central government has had much experience of dealing with administrations from different political parties in local government, and latterly with the Greater London Authority. The vast majority of the work of government will carry on as normal should there be changes to the political make-up of any of the administrations, as we in the UK pride ourselves on our pragmatism. However, the party political dimension will magnify the inevitable tensions of multi-level governance. Such a situation will not put the devolution settlement under threat, but it will cause tensions in the business of government.

Policy transference

One other point worth noting is that there is the beginning of policy transference between the different administrations. Advocates of devolution claimed that moving from a 'one-size-fits-all' approach to public policy would allow for greater innovation, creating 'policy laboratories' in the devolved territories. As Jeffery notes in Chapter 11, one frequently discussed scenario has been a 'race to the bottom', as might occur when the freedom for innovation is used to cut welfare entitlements and/or taxes to improve a region's competitive status or to guard against an influx of individuals to those regions with higher welfare entitlements. There is no evidence that such a situation has occurred in the UK to date, as most policy innovations in the devolved institutions have aimed to improve social entitlements. Again the background of a generous flow of public spending from the UK Treasury has facilitated this. Moreover, all the governments in the UK have shared a philosophy that the State and the key public services have an important role to play in fostering economic prosperity as well as social justice.

The benefit of 'policy laboratories' is that any successes or failures that result from such experimentation could be valuable for the other territories in their attempts to improve their public services. Any successes would be noted and introduced elsewhere, driving up standards throughout the UK. This is the 'virtuous circle' of devolution, where divergence in one territory leads to a convergence around a new and higher standard.

Such an outcome might also help combat worries about a 'two-tier system', as the inequalities that result from policy divergence prove to be merely a temporary aberration in the general drive towards higher standards all round. There is, however, the risk of 'boutique politics' as Keating suggests in chapter 1, where policies are pursued to promote the territory at the UK level rather than to improve the lives of the people, that is for spin rather than for substance.

While it was argued above that the devolved institutions have not proved to be the innovative 'policy laboratories' many hoped for prior to devolution, there is still clear divergence with Whitehall in many areas. Despite the strong degree of inter-governmental co-operation in the UK, policy transference will never be easy because of the asymmetry of the devolution settlement and the metropolitan nature of the UK media. Nevertheless, there are some examples of quite straightforward and direct policy transference: most notably the concept of a Children's Commissioner, which originated in Wales and has been taken up in Scotland and Northern Ireland.

However, policy transference need not have such obvious and direct consequences: new policies in one territory may not be exactly followed in other territories but may enter the public debate and have an impact upon decisions taken. This type of *policy learning* is also bedding down within the UK.

For example, the decision by the Scottish Executive on free personal long-term care has not been followed in any other part of the UK. Although all territories have expressed sympathy with the decision, they have claimed that resources could not be spared for such an expensive policy. However, in Wales certain cheaper and less extensive moves have been taken to improve the standard of long-term care for the elderly. Furthermore, the decision in Scotland has often been flagged up in the public debate within England, particularly by pressure groups, politicians, trade unions and indeed ippr (Brooks, Regan and Robinson 2002). Nevertheless, it looks extremely unlikely that Whitehall will follow Scotland's lead.

Similarly the decision by the Scottish Executive to abolish up-front tuition fees has helped lead to new student grants being introduced in Wales and to a review of the current situation in England by the Department for Education and Skills. However, this is highly unlikely to lead to a solution in England that mirrors that in Scotland.

Territorial justice: a role for the centre?

There has been a traditional unease amongst some on the left of British politics with the notion of devolution, as the process does highlight the historic tensions between liberty and equality, or between subsidiarity and solidarity. Bevan famously said 'there is no Welsh problem' (Bevan 1944) and thirty years later the future Labour leader Neil Kinnock led the charge against the Welsh devolution proposals in similar terms (Kinnock 1975). However, the rise of territorial politics from 1960 onwards was accompanied (possibly fuelled) by a growing lack of confidence in the ability of Whitehall to deal with territorial inequalities within the United Kingdom. The 1997-1998 devolution referendums institutionalised this territorial dimension of UK politics.

In discussing how to achieve its aim of greater social justice in the UK, the Labour government in Whitehall has not always had a consistent line on the territorial dimension to this objective. Although a plethora of Area-Based Initiatives have been launched, it has also sometimes been claimed that it is people who matter, not places; and even the North-South economic divide has been dismissed as a simplistic notion which ignores disparities within regions (Cabinet Office 1999). Such an approach is illogical in principle, as disparities in individual income and intra-regional disparities do not preclude the importance of inter-regional disparities in prosperity. However, in a post-devolution UK such an approach is impractical as well as illogical.

Those who believe in the unity of the UK and who do not wish to see the stateless nations secede must articulate a role for the centre in tempering inter-regional disparities and achieving social and economic justice *between* the various nations and regions of the UK. Clearly this must be achieved in a way compatible with the principles of devolution. This is what Kevin Morgan eloquently described as:

> the biggest challenge in post-devolution Britain: how to strike a judicious balance between subsidiarity and solidarity or more specifically how to secure the holy grail of a devolved polity, namely equality-in-diversity. (Morgan 2002)

Both subsidiarity and solidarity are values that progressives ought to support, and it must be recognised that these values may occasionally conflict. However as a nation, we need to be better articulate the 'quasi-federal' role which the UK Government must develop in order to promote the concept of territorial justice. No-one in any part of the UK would be satisfied with a situation where disparities in GDP per head or in health outcomes across the territories and regions were growing. Such a situation would be unsustainable politically. However, simply 'passing the buck' to the devolved administrations to address the existing disparities, without articulating the role of the UK government, would seem to be only half a solution at best.

While it should be a responsibility of the centre to play its role in tackling inequalities across the nations and regions of the UK, that role cannot be undertaken without Whitehall having a clearer concept of its territorial functions. Individual Whitehall Departments must start to better understand when they operate on an English basis, when they are performing UK-wide functions and when they are performing a quasi-federal responsibility.

For an indication of the extent of these roles we can turn to *A Statement of Funding Policy*, published by the Treasury as part of the devolution process (HM Treasury 2000a). This sets out some of the arrangements which apply in deciding the budgets for the devolved institutions, and details the extent to which each relevant Whitehall departmental programme is comparable with the services carried out by each devolved administration (the so-called comparability percentage). This is solely an indicator of spending on different programmes, but stands as a useful guide to how devolved are the responsibilities of different Whitehall departments.

The way in which spending is devolved is outlined in Table 12.2, while Table 12.3 goes on to classify Whitehall Departments into rough territorial groupings, in part using this information on spending patterns. We can classify three Whitehall Departments as 'mostly English' in the sense that they exercise only very modest reserved powers on behalf of the UK: Health, Education and Skills and the Office of the Deputy Prime Minister (which has responsibility for the former local government, planning and housing functions of the DETR). There are five 'hybrid' Departments that have their counterparts in one or more of the devolved territories, but that do exercise some significant reserved powers. There are four 'mostly UK' Departments that carry out mostly reserved functions, but also exercise some specifically 'English' functions too. Finally we have three Departments that deal with international issues.

Is this mix of functions across the Whitehall Departments indicative of good old-fashioned British pragmatism at work or is it just an unclear mess? The fact that Alan Milburn was in 2002 still often referring to himself and being referred to in the media as the 'British' rather than the 'English' health secretary might suggest the latter.

The UK government needs to understand better that there is a significant difference between managing smooth inter-governmental relations and making the hard decisions necessary to promote territorial justice. In doing so it also needs to better recognise, to

Table 12.2 Comparability percentages for 2000 Spending Review

	Scotland	Wales	N Ireland
Forestry	100.0	100.0	100.0
Health	99.7	99.7	99.7
Education and Employment	93.3	82.0	99.7
Culture, Media and Sport	95.3	87.5	100.0
DETR – Local Govt	56.4	99.9	41.6
DETR – Housing & Environment	96.5	94.9	99.4
DETR – Transport	71.2	67.1	89.3
Home Office	92.3	0.6	2.6
Domestic Agriculture	84.3	84.3	85.5
Trade and Industry	20.2	19.5	25.7
Legal Departments	97.8	0.0	1.6
Chancellor's Departments	2.1	2.1	6.2
Cabinet Office	0.1	0.1	19.5
Intervention Board	0.0	0.0	100.0
Social Security	0.0	0.0	100.0

Notes

The Treasury defines comparability as 'The extent to which services delivered by Departments of the United Kingdom Government correspond to the services within the assigned budgets of the devolved administrations.'

Compared to the Scottish Parliament and Northern Ireland Assembly, the Welsh Assembly has limited control over the non-domestic rating system. This means that it falls within the assigned budget in Wales, but not in Scotland or Northern Ireland. This technicality should not obscure the fact that Scotland and Northern Ireland have autonomy over local government, and the comparability figure in Wales of 99.9% should be taken as indicative for all three territories.

The administration of Social Security is the responsibility of the Northern Ireland Executive, but they currently accept the policy decisions made in Whitehall.

Source: A Statement of Funding Policy, HM Treasury 2000

use Bogdonor's disconcerting phrase, that 'finance is the spinal cord of devolution'. It is crucial to most of the public policy decisions that the devolved institutions must take, and it is the one issue that could threaten divisive territorial rivalry.

There is a distinction to be made between divergence and inequality. Inequality breeds resentment, and if a nation state has a high degree of territorial inequality one would expect it to be a less cohesive nation. On the other hand, if all parts of a nation state are given similar resources in relation to identified needs but then choose to pursue different priorities, one should not regard this as inequitable nor expect resentment in neighbouring regions. Such resentment has been expressed recently in the North East of England over the 'Berwick Question': why the resources available for public authorities in Scotland seem to be higher than for those authorities just over the border in England. While the policy autonomy of Scotland has not been called

Table 12.3 Classification of Whitehall Departments

Mostly English	Hybrid	Mostly UK	International Departments
Health	Home Office	HM Treasury	Defence
Education and Skills	Legal Departments	Work and Pensions	Foreign Office
Office of the Deputy Prime Minister	Environment, Food and Rural Affairs	Cabinet Office	International Development
		Trade and Industry	
	Transport		
	Culture, Media and Sport		

Notes

A 'mostly English' department has only very modest reserved powers

A 'hybrid' department exercises functions on behalf of England (or England and Wales or England, Wales and Northern Ireland) that are carried out on a devolved basis in one or more of the territories, with Departments explicitly covering these functions in Edinburgh, Cardiff and/or Belfast, but it also exercises significant reserved powers on behalf of the UK

A 'mostly UK' department carries out mostly reserved functions but with some English functions too

into question, the 'Barnett formula' has become perhaps the major political issue in the North East of England.

Devolution was an overdue reform to the governance of the United Kingdom. It created new centres of political power and brought a welcome diversity of voices to the UK body politic. Our conclusion that the centre must articulate better its quasi-federal role in no way impinges upon the responsibilities of the devolved institutions, and the promotion of territorial justice must be done in a manner compatible with both the principle and practice of devolution. It does not mean that the centre can override or micro-manage the decisions of the directly elected devolved administrations, but it does mean that it should take a strategic approach to addressing those inequalities in outcomes that could undermine the union.

The concept of territorial justice includes different aspects of both social and economic justice. Jeffery suggests in Chapter 11 that differences in social policy within a nation state can be less politically acceptable than in economic policy. In the United Kingdom, however, many broad social policy responsibilities, such as health or education, are almost completely devolved to Scotland, Wales and Northern Ireland. As Keating notes in Chapter 1 this represents a very high degree of autonomy by international standards. There is an interesting contrast here with the US, where the Federal role in health policy remains strong. In the US it is 'welfare' policy that has increasingly been passed back to the individual states, while social security in Britain remains one of the most important reserved functions. Clearly the history of public policy differs on the two sides of the Atlantic, but there are also quite divergent views as to which areas of public policy it is appropriate to encourage 'laboratories of democracy'.

The extent and manner of devolution in the UK does not, however, mean the centre no longer has a role in ensuring territorial justice in relation to social policy outcomes, but it does emphasise that the tools at its disposal are in some cases now quite limited. There is also real irony that it is in those policy areas where the desire for solidarity appears to be strongest, most notably health, that the scope for the centre to help deal with inequalities in outcomes appears to be weakest.

The poor standard of the health of the people of Scotland is highlighted in Woods in Chapter 2. Such inequalities in health outcomes between the populations of, for example, Glasgow and Surrey, cannot be seen as acceptable in a modern Western European democracy. It is to be hoped that the Scottish Executive will be able to tackle these inequalities, and it is perfectly possible that the freedom brought by devolution may help achieve such an outcome. But it is also possible that it will not, especially when for some factors that might be related to health — like poverty or income inequality – most of the key policy instruments remain in the hands of 'mostly UK' Whitehall Departments. It is precisely this 'joined-upness' in the causes of different forms of inequality that requires some 'joined-upness' in policy making at the 'quasi-federal' UK level.

Territorial justice in practice

No one in Westminster or Whitehall talks about territorial justice in any formal sense. However, it is often implicit in their actions. It certainly embraces the current responsibility of HM Treasury to allocate public expenditure between the various territories of the United Kingdom. This is perhaps the responsibility that it is most important to carry out judiciously to maintain balance between equity and diversity and to ensure that the UK does not fall into divisive territorial rivalries.

Any concept of territorial justice also includes ensuring, as far as is possible, that all parts of the nation state share in growing economic prosperity. This embraces the on-going debate over the 'North-South divide' and Labour's 'New Regional Policy' (see for example Regional Studies Association 2001; and Balls and Healy 2000). HM Treasury and the DTI have stated that one of the aims of Labour's 'New Regional Policy' is to improve the economic performance of the regions in order to achieve 'the Government's long-term ambition of reducing the persistent gap between regions by increasing the growth rate of the worst performing regions.' (HM Treasury and DTI 2001) This then is the closest the UK government has come to admitting a responsibility for ensuring territorial justice across the UK.

This responsibility would include preventing damaging, zero-sum, inter-regional competition to ensure it does not undermine national priorities, as highlighted by Gillespie and Benneworth in Chapter 4 in relation to economic development. Potentially fruitless inter-regional competition is not limited to the case of attracting inward investment, although this example most obviously illustrates the problem.

These examples relating to the issue of territorial justice in the field of economic policy are matched by a more recent example of the centre acting in one of the key areas of social policy that has been almost totally devolved to Scotland, Wales and Northern Ireland. Many observers queried why the Wanless review of health spending in the UK was sponsored by the Treasury rather than the Department of Health (Wanless 2002). Some assumed this was solely due to the political strength of the current Chancellor, but there was also an obvious institutional reason. Whitehall's Department of Health could not conduct the review because it is essentially the *English* Department of Health, and funding issues across the UK's territories could only be taken forward by the Treasury. The Treasury commissioned Wanless and subsequently invited the participation of the devolved administrations, but the idea of the four constituent parts of the UK jointly commissioning this work was obviously not considered.

This then is one of the most interesting consequences of devolution. The role of the Treasury has been significantly strengthened. It not only represents the single most significant constraint on the ability of the devolved administrations to develop distinctive policies by determining their overall budgets. With some of the Whitehall Departments now effectively *English* Departments, much more of the responsibility for developing UK-wide policies falls by default to the Treasury as one of the few UK Departments dealing with the whole sweep of domestic public policy and not simply with international issues. Of course its role in this respect does also reflect the intellectual appetite and political authority of the current Chancellor, but there are also institutional reasons why the Treasury has effectively developed this 'quasi-federal' role.

It should be emphasised that the Treasury has become the locus for regional economic policy in the post-devolution UK in part precisely because of the relative failure of the Department for Trade and Industry to develop that role for itself. This is part of the wider failure of that Department to conceptualise its mix of UK and other more 'English' functions, post-devolution. The DTI carried out an internal review of its structures in 2001, but with little or no reference to the impact of devolution. The Department of Work and Pensions might be a more logical place to co-ordinate important elements of social policy in the UK post-devolution, but that Department too appears to have handed that role by default to the Treasury.

The Cabinet Office, while the obvious institution to carry out the important role of managing inter-governmental relations, might be less well placed to address these issues of economic and social justice between the different territories: it might only be able to manage the conversations. The confusing plethora of bodies that now reside in the Cabinet Office seem to rule it out as the place where the strategy for UK economic and social policy can be developed (again, handing that role by default to the Treasury). Moreover, some of the units that have existed in the Cabinet Office also have only an English remit, most notably the Social Exclusion Unit (another reason why it has been the Treasury that has driven forward the UK government's social policy agenda).

As argued above, some parts of Whitehall will need to think through the implications of the concept of territorial justice in relation to the policy areas on which devolution has impacted. At the moment only the Treasury appears to be in a position to do this. We were wary in coming to such a conclusion because too heavy a concentration of power within one Whitehall Department cannot be healthy and many feel that the Treasury is already too powerful. However, confusion in the Cabinet Office, lack of independent initiative at the Department for Work and Pensions, and an inability to focus at the DTI, has left the Treasury holding all the cards.

Conclusion: next steps in the devolution process

It has traditionally been claimed, with much justification, that the United Kingdom is one of the most centralised of developed nations. London has been the seat of Parliament and Government, the City of London is one of the world's leading financial markets and the vast majority of the UK media is based in London. The economic performance of the greater South East of England is far superior to that of the other regions of the UK.

However, the 1997 General Election represented a fundamental step away from this portrait of an over-centralised polity. It was the party of the periphery – Labour – that formed the administration in London and one of its first priorities was the creation of a Scottish Parliament and the National Assembly for Wales. New sites of political power were created, forming a fundamental break with the traditional London-centric approach to UK governance.

This publication has tried to examine how public policy is evolving across the United Kingdom, how different policies are diverging, and what pressures have been leading to this divergence. We have not tried to fashion a 'league table' of political institutions, judging the success of the devolved institutions based on whether we agree with their policies or not. Rather we have tried to examine the nature of divergence within the UK and to ask whether divergence matters.

The effects of divergence so far have been remarkably benign. While one may question the merits of particular decisions by devolved institutions, they are generally supported in the territory and cannot be said to have threatened the solidarity of the United Kingdom. Rather, the advent of devolved institutions and devolved polities means a greater preponderance of voices in British public policy and a welcome opportunity to learn from each other.

However, as has been widely recognised, devolution is a process and not an event. How is the process of devolution in the UK likely to move forward? Unsurprisingly it is the two strongest institutions which are least likely to change: the Scottish Parliament and the Northern Ireland Legislative Assembly. Naturally politics in Northern Ireland is anything but settled, but this is due to the peace process rather than any constitutional or institutional difficulties. In Scotland, apart from funding issues, the settlement seems secure. It is England which will see the next step in the devolution process.

At the start of the second term of the Labour Government at Westminster the constitutional issue which was perhaps most pressing was the 'English Question': how was England to be governed following the devolution of power to Scotland, Wales and Northern Ireland. While it is likely that asymmetry will be an inevitable feature of UK governance, it is also likely that an adequate and lasting 'devolution settlement' requires an answer to this so-called English Question. As Marquand and Tomaney (2000) have argued, '[i]t is logically impossible to devolve power to part of a hitherto unitary state without impacting upon the governance of the remaining parts.'

The Government's response, outlined in the publication of the White Paper *Your Region, Your Choice: Revitalising the English Regions*, is likely to be the most significant constitutional event of 2002 (Cabinet Office/DTLR 2002). Regional assemblies with powers over economic growth, planning, culture and housing could be created in some of England's regions by the middle of the current decade, if the relevant electorate vote in favour. The Government has also decided that the creation of any regional assembly will also have to be accompanied by a local government reorganisation in each region to create unitary authorities, a process that could be both lengthy and contentious.

The proposals for English regional assemblies echo the experience of Scotland and Wales, albeit in some respects rather faint echoes. However, there is one feature of the proposals which stands out as an innovation in the devolution process. The assemblies will be required to agree a small number of targets with central government along the lines of the existing local Public Service Agreements for English local authorities. Thus their priorities for public policy will have to be negotiated with the centre. They will not have 'sovereignty' over the setting of those priorities as in the devolved territories.

Economic development will be the single most important function of an elected regional assembly. The Regional Development Agencies established in Labour's first term will become directly accountable to the assemblies and we can expect to see greater divergence in this policy area. However, this in itself will not answer the questions raised here about the role of the centre in promoting territorial justice across the UK. With the best will in the world, a North East Assembly and One North East, its development agency, will still have only a limited capacity to improve the economic performance of the region. If regional disparities in economic prosperity continue to grow what then?

There is less appetite for regional devolution in the South East and Eastern regions, but along with London they form the economic 'winner's circle' in the greater South East of England. The sustainable management of development across this increasingly congested 'super-region' may or may not require some form of institutional innovation, but is unclear whether Whitehall is even aware that it may need to address these issues.

Ensuring that economic prosperity does not continue to be concentrated in the greater South East while the peripheral regions of the UK struggle is surely one of the most important 'quasi-federal' issues that Whitehall will have to address. Will the DTI continue to leave this to HM Treasury or will it rise to the challenge itself? The DTI already has a quasi-federal role and a complicated mix of territorial functions for different geographical areas: UK-wide; Britain; England, Wales and Northern Ireland; England and Wales; England; and England outside London. The advent of a second directly-elected Assembly within England ought to be the spur for the DTI to sort out its different roles.

The confused nature of the allocation of Ministerial portfolios at the DTI may be symbolic of a wider confusion within the Department. At the time of writing Alan Johnson MP was Minister of State for the Regions and Employment Relations, mixing English and UK-wide functions. Even more surprisingly a Scottish MP, Nigel Griffiths, was Parliamentary Under-Secretary of State for Small Business, which at the DTI is actually largely an English policy responsibility. Perhaps the separation of 'English' and 'UK' ministerial responsibilities might help the Department address the wider issues of its role post-devolution.

Within the DTI one could have 'UK' ministers with responsibility for competition and trade policy, consumer protection and employment relations, science and energy and for sectoral industrial policy and regional policy across the UK as whole. A separate minister or two could handle 'English' functions relating to business support and the English RDAs. The other 'mostly UK' and 'hybrid' Whitehall Departments could also usefully think through their internal structures and ministerial portfolios in this way. It should be emphasised that the reason for doing this is not 'administrative tidiness' but to prompt Departments to think through their responsibilities for exercising policies across and on behalf of the UK in order to foster social and economic justice across the country as a whole.

Another of the issues which helps create support for an Assembly in the North East is the perceived unfairness of the 'Barnett formula', or more accurately the historically more generous public spending settlement for Scotland that Barnett is seen to have entrenched. Despite the talk of a 'Barnett squeeze' in Scotland there is as yet little evidence of convergence in public spending across the territories of the UK (Adams 2002a). The data is, however, backward looking and Heald and McLeod in Chapter 10 make the point that in the context of generous increases in aggregate public spending the way the 'Barnett formula' works should bring about some convergence over the medium term.

What is clear is that there is currently no appetite for re-opening the fiscal settlement surrounding devolution in Scotland. In the context of generous increases in public spending, Scotland has no need to use its existing tax-varying powers and no incentive to press for greater fiscal autonomy. In Wales and in Northern Ireland, where GDP per head is significantly lower than the UK average, there is more concern that the 'Barnett squeeze' might lead sooner rather than later to a situation where public spending does not match the objective needs of these nations. Heald and McLeod outline in Chapter 10 the case for the devolved territories thinking now about the institutional arrangements that might be put in place to ensure that any new 'needs' assessment and any reformed 'Barnett formula' would remain fair. Fairness in this regard means a system that would enable all parts of the UK to have the resources to deliver public services in relation to their 'needs', though the latter is inevitably hard to define. When the force of this argument will begin to be heard across all the devolved territories is unclear, but we can expect a North East Assembly to make the issue one of its first and top priorities.

There is, however, the prospect of some change to the fiscal arrangements with regard to capital spending. Northern Ireland is eventually promised a 'prudential' system for capital spending which will allow it to undertake borrowing to help remedy its acknowledged deficiencies in infrastructure investment, so long as it can service that borrowing from its revenue base. This is bound up with the contentious issue of raising more revenue from property taxation, but it will open up options for the Northern Ireland Executive (and incidentally should help create a level playing field in relation to the Private Finance Initiative). Such a prudential system for capital spending is also signalled for those directly elected English regional assemblies that are created. It is very hard to see why such arrangements should not also be extended to the devolved Scottish and Welsh governments. Indeed given the controversy surrounding the Private Finance Initiative in those nations, this would seem imperative.

If allowing regions of England to vote on the creation of assemblies is the next step in the devolution process, the step after that is the need to reform the devolution settlement in Wales. It cannot be said that the current system is yet a major block on the Welsh Assembly Government pursuing its priorities, but in the medium term it may have this effect.

The pressures for change are both practical and political. The Welsh Assembly Government seems to have embarked upon a political strategy designed to achieve primary legislative powers for the National Assembly, although the success of this strategy is by no means assured.

The Partnership Agreement in October 2000, which codified the coalition between the Labour and Liberal Democratic parties, committed the administration to create 'an independent commission into the powers and electoral arrangements of the National Assembly' (National Assembly for Wales 2000). A former Labour Party Cabinet Minister, Lord Richard of Ammanford, has now been appointed Chair of the Commission and it is due to report some time after the Welsh General Election of 2003.

The terms of reference, at the time of writing, have yet to be finalised, but it can be expected that the Commission will consider both the breadth and depth of the powers of the Assembly. It will have to consider whether powers over such policy areas as the railways or the police should be devolved. More fundamentally, we can anticipate that it will detail the case for the Assembly to have legislative powers.

The practical pressure to reform the Welsh settlement comes from a growing consensus that the dividing lines between Whitehall and Wales are unclear. A submission by the Law Society to the separate, but connected, Operational Review of the Assembly (chaired by the Presiding Officer) highlighted the problem:

> It is becoming increasingly difficult for lawyers, voluntary agencies and campaigning organisations advising the public, to gain a clear picture of the National Assembly's powers. As well as the body of powers contained in the Transfer of Functions Orders, there are now the effects of two legislative sessions at Westminster, in which a number of different approaches have been taken to drafting Bills that confer powers on the National Assembly. The result is a rapidly expanding and incoherent mass of statutory powers with no overarching logic to the basis of their devolution to the National Assembly (Law Society 2001).

In the future the National Assembly for Wales may or may not be granted primary legislative powers, but Whitehall ought seriously enter the debate about reforming the current settlement. The halfway house of 'executive devolution' makes significant but needless demands upon both Whitehall and Westminster. Whatever the depth of the powers of the Welsh Assembly, it is in the interests of all sides to foster a cleaner division of powers.

The suggestions outlined here for taking forward the devolution settlement in the UK may appear to be quite modest. However, this itself is a recognition that the process of devolution has so far worked very effectively and the reforms suggested here for the medium term are designed to make it more effective, both for the constituent parts of the UK and for the UK as a whole.

British politics and governance still has a southern-centric axis but at last the diversity and plurality of the UK is better recognised. Over time we can expect to see new centres of political power in the English regions and further divergence in important areas of public policy. Given this, the question of how to secure 'equality-in-diversity' will continue to need addressing by the UK government, by the devolved administrations and by all those who wish to maintain the unity of the UK.

Endnotes

1   CREST is a Research Centre funded by the Economic and Social Research Council

2   The questions are as follows:

Ordinary working people get their fair share of the nation's wealth.

There is one law for the rich and one for the poor.

There is no need for strong trade unions to protect employees' working conditions and wages.

Private enterprise is the best way to solve the country's economic problems.

Major public services and industries ought to be in state ownership.

It is the government's responsibility to provide a job for everyone who wants one.

3   The questions are as follows:

Young people today don't have enough respect for traditional British values.

Censorship of films and magazines is necessary to uphold moral standards.

People should be allowed to organise public meetings to protest against the government.

Homosexual relations are always wrong.

People in Britain should be more tolerant of those who lead unconventional lives.

Political parties which wish to overthrow democracy should be allowed to stand general elections.

4   Thanks to Katarina Thomson and John Curtice of the National Centre for Social Research for their help with this section.

5   www.icmresearch.co.uk/reviews/polls-archive.htm

6   HL Deb, 28 July 1998, col 1487

References

Adams J (2002) 1970s stop-gap measure still makes us better off 20 May 2002 Cardiff: *Western Mail*

Balls E and Healy J (2000) *Towards a New Regional Policy: Delivering growth and full employment* The Smith Institute: London

Bevan A (1944) *Hansard* 10 October, col 2312

Bogdanor V (2001) *Devolution in the United Kingdom* Oxford: Oxford University Press

Brooks R, Regan S and Robinson P (2002) *A New Contract for Retirement* London: ippr

Brown A, McCrone D and Paterson L (1998) *Politics and Society in Scotland* London: Macmillan 2nd Edition

Cabinet Office (1999) *Sharing the Nation's Prosperity: variation in economic and social conditions across the UK* December 1999 London: Cabinet Office

Cabinet Office and DTLR (2002) *Your Region, Your Choice: Revitalising the English Regions* Cm 5511 London: The Stationery Office

Campaign for the English Regions (2002) *Democratic Regions: The Campaign for the English Regions' proposals for inclusion in the Government's forthcoming White Paper* Newcastle: Campaign for the English Regions

Curtice J (2001) 'Hopes Dashed and Fears Assuaged?' in Trench A (ed) *The State of the Nations 2001* Constitution Unit Exeter: Imprint Academic

Curtice J and Seyd B (2001) 'Is devolution strengthening or weakening the UK' in Park A, Curtice J, Thomson K, Jarvis L, Bromley C (eds) *British Social Attitudes The 18th Report: Public Policy, Social Ties* London: SAGE

Davies R (2000) *In Search of Attitude* Caerphilly: Office of Ron Davies AM

Hazell R (2001) *Constitutional Futures* Oxford: Oxford University Press

HM Treasury (2000a) *Funding the Scottish Parliament, National Assembly for Wales and Northern Ireland Assembly: A Statement of Funding Policy* 2nd Edition London: HM Treasury

HM Treasury (2000b) *2000 Spending Review: Public Service Agreements July 2000* Cm4808 London: The Stationery Office

HM Treasury and DTI (2001) *Productivity in the UK: 3 – The Regional Dimension* London: HM Treasury

Keating M (1998) *The New Regionalism in Western Europe — Territorial Restructuring and Political Change* Cheltenham: Edward Elgar

Kinnock N (1975) *Hansard* 3 February, col 1031

Law Society of England and Wales (2001) *Submission to the Review of Procedure of the National Assembly for Wales* May 2001

Lord Chancellor's Department (2001) *The House of Lords: Completing the Reform* London: The Stationery Office

Lord Chancellor's Department (2000) *Memorandum of Understanding and supplementary agreements between the United Kingdom Government, Scottish Ministers, the Cabinet of the National Assembly for Wales and the Northern Ireland Executive Committee* Cm 4806 London: The Stationery Office

Marquand D and Tomaney J (2000) *Democratising England* London: Regional Policy Forum

McLeish H (2001) *Free Personal Care within seven months* 24 September 2001 Edinburgh: Scottish Executive Press Release, SE4033

Morgan K (forthcoming) *The English Question: Regional Perspectives on a Fractured Nation* Seaford: Regional Studies Association

Morgan R (2000) *Address to the Institute of Welsh Politics, Aberystwyth, 13 November 2000* Cardiff: Welsh Assembly Government

National Assembly for Wales (2001a) *Plan for Wales 2001* October Cardiff: National Assembly for Wales

National Assembly for Wales (2001b) *Improving Health in Wales – A Plan for the NHS* Cardiff: National Assembly for Wales

National Assembly for Wales (2000) *Putting Wales First: A Partnership for the People of Wales: The First Partnership Agreement of the National Assembly for Wales* www.wales.gov.uk/organicabinet/content/putting.html

Northern Ireland Executive (2001) *Programme for Government* December Belfast: Northern Ireland Executive

Osmond J (1998) *New Politics in Wales* London: Charter88

Park A, Curtice J, Thomson K, Jarvis L, Bromley C (2001) *British Social Attitudes The 18th Report: Public Policy, Social Ties* London: SAGE

Paterson L (1994) *The Autonomy of Modern Scotland* Edinburgh: Edinburgh University Press

Performance and Innovation Unit (2000) *Reaching Out: the role of central government at regional and local level* London: The Stationery Office

Regional Studies Association (2001) *Labour's New Regional Policy: An Assessment* Seaford: Regional Studies Association

Royal Commission on Long-Term Care (1999) *With Respect to Old Age:*

Long-term Care – Rights and Responsibilities London: The Stationery Office

Runnymede Trust (2001) *The Future of Multi-Ethnic Britain – The Parekh Report* London: Profile Books

Russell Barter W (2000) *Regional Government in England: A preliminary Review of Literature and Research Findings* London: DETR

Sandford M and McQuail P (2001) *Unexplored Territory: Three Models for Regional Government in England* London: The Constitution Unit

Scottish Executive (2001) *Working Together for Scotland* Edinburgh: Scottish Executive

Scottish Office (1997) *Scotland's Parliament* Cm 3658 London: The Stationery Office

Surridge P and McCrone D (1999) 'The 1997 Scottish referendum vote' Taylor B and Thomsom K (eds) *Scotland and Wales: Nations Again?* Cardiff: University of Wales Press

Taylor B and Thompson K (1999) *Scotland and Wales: Nations Again?* Cardiff: University of Wales Press

Tindale S (ed) (1996) *The State and the Nations – The Politics of Devolution* London: ippr

Trench A (ed) (2001) *The State of the Nations 2001* Constitution Unit Exeter: Imprint Academic

Wanless D (2002) *Securing Our Future Health: Taking a long-term view* London: HM Treasury

Wanless D (2001) *Securing Our Future Health: Interim Report* London: The Stationery Office

Welsh Office (1997) *A Voice for Wales: The Government's Proposals for a Welsh Assembly* White Paper Cm 3718 London: The Stationery Office